A History of Islam in Indonesia

The New Edinburgh Islamic Surveys
Series Editor: Carole Hillenbrand

A History of Islam in Indonesia

Unity in diversity

Carool Kersten

EDINBURGH
University Press

Edinburgh University Press is one of the leading university presses in the UK. We publish academic books and journals in our selected subject areas across the humanities and social sciences, combining cutting-edge scholarship with high editorial and production values to produce academic works of lasting importance. For more information visit our website: edinburghuniversitypress.com

Edinburgh University Press Ltd
The Tun – Holyrood Road
12 (2f) Jackson's Entry
Edinburgh EH8 8PJ

Typeset in 11/13pt Monotype Baskerville by
Servis Filmsetting Ltd, Stockport, Cheshire,
Printed and bound in the United States of America

A CIP record for this book is available from the British Library

ISBN 978 0 7486 8183 9 (hardback)
ISBN 978 0 7486 8184 6 (paperback)
ISBN 978 0 7486 8185 3 (webready PDF)
ISBN 978 0 7486 8187 7 (epub)

Contents

Acknowledgements   vi
A note on translation and transliteration   vii
Glossary   viii

Introduction   1
1   The arrival of Islam   7
2   Network Islam   25
3   Islam as resistance   55
4   Islam and nation-building   92
5   An Indonesian Islam?   131
Conclusion   170

Notes   172
Bibliography   180
Index   192

Acknowledgements

The first word of appreciation has to go to Professor Carole Hillenbrand, the long-serving editor of *The New Edinburgh Islamic Surveys* at Edinburgh University Press. A few years ago, she invited me to contribute an overview of the history of Islam in Indonesia to this prestigious series. This book is a condensation of more than fifteen years of study and research into the history of Southeast Asia and in particular the role played by Islam. The people who have helped me in furthering my knowledge on these subjects are too numerous to mention individually. However, in terms of facilitating the completion of this project, I need to single out my Head of Department, Professor Paul Joyce, and the Dean of the Faculty of Arts and Humanities at King's College London, Professor Russell Goulbourne. Without their generous agreement to grant me research leave during the academic year 2015–16, I would have never made the deadline. Finally, I want to express my gratitude to the editors at Edinburgh University Press for their assistance, efficiency and patience in bringing this book to press.

Carool Kersten
London, February 2016

A note on translation and transliteration

This book adheres to the spelling conventions for the Indonesian language introduced in 1972. Many Indonesians have continued to write their personal names
in the old spelling. However, in some instances, I have opted for the current
variant, changing Hasjim Asjʿari to Hasyim Asyʿari, and writing Sukarno and
Suharto, rather than Soekarno and Soeharto. The spelling of names is further
complicated by the parallel use of Indonesian and Javanese. For example,
Hamengkubuwono in Javanese is Hamengkubuwana in Indonesian. In the literature, some scholars have adhered to the Indonesian, others to the Javanese
versions. For Javanese names, I have opted for retaining the original spelling.
Another challenge is that Indonesian has its own system of transliterating Arabic
terms, which deviates from authoritative alternatives used in academic sources
written in European languages. When relying on sources related to Indonesia,
I have respected the Indonesian conventions, in other instances I have used a
simplified version of the transcription used in the *International Journal of Middle
East Studies* (*IJMES*); dispensing with diacritics for long vowels and consonants
with no (near) equivalents in European languages. Those with relevant linguistic qualifications will be able to establish the original Arabic anyway, while
other readers need not be burdened with a possibly distracting idiosyncratic
typography.

Glossary

Abangan	literally 'red ones'. Refers to nominal Muslims (Javanese)
Adat	customary law
Adipati	Javanese title for a ruler
Agama	religion
Ahl al-Sunna wa'l-Jamaᶜah	'People of the Tradition and the Community'
Alam	world
Aliran/Aliranisasi	ideological pillar/pillarisation in Indonesian society
Asas tunggal	sole foundation
Babad	Javanese chronicle
Bangsa	nation; people
Batiniyya	esotericism (see also *kebatinan*)
Bendahara	Minangkabau dignitary
Benteng	fortress
Bhinneka Tunggal Ika	'Unity in Diversity'. Motto of the Republic of Indonesia
Bidᶜa(h)	unlawful religious renewal
Bomoh	shaman, spirit doctor (see also *dukun, pawang*)
Bupati	Javanese title for a regent or governor
Candi	Hindu temple
Chedi	Buddhist temple; pagoda
Churafat (khurafat)	religious practices that are considered heretical; superstitions
Dar al-Islam	'abode of Islam'. Islamic legal science uses it to refer to the lands under Islamic governance where Islamic law is administered. Historiographers have used it to refer to the lands under the control of the great caliphates
Daᶜwa(h) (dakwah)	religious propagation
Dukun	shaman, spirit doctor (see also *bomoh, pawang*)
Dwifungsi	dual function; the dual role of Indonesia's military in society
Dwitunggal (duatunggal)	power-sharing arrangement between first president and vice-president of independent Indonesia

Eid al-Adha	'Feast of the Sacrifice', held after the end of pilgrimage to Mecca (*hajj*)
Eid al-Fitr	feast at the end of the month of fasting (*Ramadan*)
Fatwa	authoritative religious opinion, issued by a *mufti*
Fiqh	Islamic science of jurisprudence
Garebeg Mulud	Javanese ceremony commemorating Prophet's birthday
Garwa ampeyan	unofficial wife; concubine (Javanese)
Ghazwul fikri	intellectual invasion
Guru	teacher
Hajj	pilgrimage to Mecca
Halaqa(h)	teaching circle; group of students studying with a particular scholar
Hijra(h)	migration (of the Prophet Muhammad from Mecca to Medina in 622 CE)
Hikayat	Malay chronicle
Hulubalang	warrior, war chief (Aceh, Minangkabau)
Ibadat	acts of worship
Ijaza	authorisation to teach certain texts or subjects of Islamic learning
Ijma'	consensus of the scholars
Ijtihad	independent reasoning
Ilm	knowledge, science
Ilmu (ngelmu)	mystical knowledge
Iman	faith
Insan kamil	'perfect man'; Sufi notion of human perfection
Jaksa kepala	highest native government official (Minangkabau area)
Jawi	Malay written in Arabised script. Also used to refer to the Malay-Muslim culture of Southeast Asia and as a collective term for the Muslims from that region
Jihad	'holy war'
Jimat	amulet
Kafir/kapir (pl. *kuffar*)	unbeliever. In conflict situations often applied as a blanket category to non-Muslims
Kalam	Islamic (discursive) theology
Kaum muda	'new people/generation'. Islamic reformists
Kaum tua	'old people/generation'. Traditionalist Muslims
Kebatinan	spiritual practice. In the context of Indonesian religious categorisation it is subsumed under Islam, and yet not part of the officially recognised religious traditions

Kemajuan	progress
Kepala negeri/laras	district head
Kepercayaan	'belief', but not acknowledged like one of the officially recognised religious traditions
Khalifa	literally 'successor'; caliph. Title for the successors of Muhammad as ruler of the Muslim community
Khatib	mosque official who delivers the Friday sermon (*khutba*)
Kraton	palace
Kris	dagger
Kyai	Javanese honorific for a teacher at a *pesantren* or Islamic school
Lingam	phallic symbol
Luban jawi	benzoin or benjamin. A frankincense-like resin secreted by a tree (*Styrax benzoin*)
Madrasa(h)	Islamic school. In the Indonesian context usually referring to a reformist-modernist Islamic school
Madhhab (mazhab)	Islamic school of law or thought
Malim	religious functionary in the Minangkabau area
Ma{^{c}}rifat (ma'ripat)	gnosis
Martabat tujuh	'seven stages' (of being), identified in the doctrine of the 'Unity of Being' (see also *wahdat al-wujud*)
Masjid	mosque
Mawlid (Mulud) al-Nabi	Prophet Muhammad's birthday
Menara	minaret
Mu{^{c}}amalat	term used in Islamic to designate secular interactions, to be differentiated from *ibadat*
Mufti	jurisconsult, Islamic religious functionary who can issue *fatwa*s or religious opinions
Muhaqqiq	'man of realisation'; a Sufi who has mastered high levels of insight
Mujaddid	religious renewer
Nasir al-dunya wa'l-din	'Helper of the World and the Faith'. Honorific for Muslim ruler
Negeri (negara)	state; country
Nisba	adjective indicating a person's place of origin, tribal affiliation or ancestry
Noesa Hindia (Nusa Hindia)	nineteenth-century designation for Indonesia
Nusantara	maritime Southeast Asia; nowadays the term is confined to Indonesia
Organisasi massa	mass organisation
Pangeran	Javanese title, equivalent to prince or sultan

Pawang	shaman, spirit doctor (see also *bomoh, dukun*)
Pengajian	curriculum of an Islamic school
Penghulu (panghulu)	title for traditional chieftain
P(e)rang sabil	religious warfare, 'holy war'
Perang sabil	*jihad*, often interpreted as 'holy war'
Perang suci	'purifying' or holy war'
Pesantren	Islamic school (Javanese term; see also *pondok, surau*)
Pondok	Islamic (boarding school), technically only referring to the accommodation part, but also used as the Malay equivalent of *pesantren*
Pradikan (perdikan)	residents of pious villages in specially designated tax-exempted areas
Primbon	divination almanac; treatise (Javanese literary genre)
Priyayi	Javanese aristocracy
Pusaka	heirloom endowed with supernatural powers
Putihan (orang putih)	'white ones'; term used to refer to observant and pious Muslims (see also *santri*)
Qadi (kadi)	judge
Qiyas	reasoning by analogy
Raja	Malay ruler
Rantau	Minangkabau practice whereby adolescent or young adult males leave their villages to travel and seek economic fortune, or learning
Ratu adil	mythic figure of the 'Just King'
Rumi	Latin script
Salaf salih	'pious ancestors'; first three generations of the Muslim community
Santri	observant and pious Muslim (see also *putihan*)
Satria lelono	wandering knight
Sayyid	Islamic honorific for descendants of the Prophet Muhammad through his daughter Fatima and son-in-law Ali
Sejarah	history or chronicle
Sekolah	school
Shah	Persian word for ruler or emperor
Shahadah	Islamic creed
Sha^cir (Syair)	poem; poetry
Shari^ca(h)	Islamic law
Silsila(h)	line of transmission; intellectual genealogy
Sultan	'He who wields power'. A Muslim ruler or potentate

Suluk	particular Javanese religious practice, incorporating elements of various traditions; also the name of a literary genre describing these practices
Surambi	religious court (Javanese)
Surau	Islamic (boarding) school, specifically used on Sumatra (see also *pesantren, pondok*)
Tafsir	Qur'an commentary
Tajdid	religious renewal
Takhayyul	religious practices that are considered heretical
Tanah air	earth; land; territory
Taqlid (buta)	(blind) imitation
Tarīqā (pl. *turuq*) (*tarekat*)	Sufi order or brotherhood
Tasawwuf (*tasauf*)	Sufism
Tawassul	intercession
Tawhid (*tauhid*)	unity and oneness of God
Tuak	alcoholic beverage
Ulama (*ʿulamāʾ*)	Islamic religious scholars. In Indonesian, this plural (of *ʿalim*) is also used as singular
Uleebelang	Acehnese spelling of *hulubalang*
Ulil amri	religious leaders who have to provide the community with guidance
Umma(h)	community of believers (the Muslims)
Undang	legal code; law
Wahdat al-shuhud	'unity of witnessing'; alternative Sufi doctrine, off-setting the (heretical) 'Unity of Being'
Wahdat al-wujud	'Unity of Being', a (controversial) philosophical Sufi doctrine
Wali Songo	'Nine Saints'; (half-)legendary figures credited with introducing Islam to Java
Watan	homeland; fatherland
Wayang	(shadow) puppet theatre
Zawiya	lodge of itinerant Muslim students or scholars
Zill Allah fi'l-ard	'God's Shadow on Earth', a honorific for the caliph, sometimes extended to other Muslim rulers

In loving memory of
my father

Lee Kersten
(1938–2016)

Introduction

Indonesia is the largest and most populous Muslim nation state in the world; a fact that is often forgotten because it was never part of the great caliphates that are historically associated with the *Dar al-islam* or 'abode of Islam'. Also because of its great distance from the so-called Islamic heartlands, it is still often assumed that Islam in Indonesia is just a thin veneer over earlier religious deposits from elsewhere in Asia. Consequently, both scholars of Islam and Southeast Asianists overlook or underestimate the importance of this religion for the formation of Southeast Asian cultures.

Writing a history of Islam in Indonesia presents researchers with the additional challenge that before the late 1800s, it could even be argued until 1945, Indonesia did not even exist. At first glance that seems a preposterous statement. It is obviously nonsense to deny that in terms of topography there is such a thing that can be referred to as 'Indonesia'; it can be easily identified on any map of the world, where it dominates the equatorial zone between the Indian Ocean and South China Sea. Use of the word 'Indonesia' can be traced to James Logan (1819–69), a British lawyer based in the Malay trading port of Penang, while the earliest indigenous use goes back to Indonesian Communist activists and expatriate Indonesian nationalists living in the Netherlands in the 1920s. A related term with greater currency in the early 1900s was *Noesa Hindia*. *Noesa/nusa* is an Old Javanese word, which is persistently – but mistakenly – associated with the Greek word for island: *nèsos*. The word also forms part of an alternative designation for Indonesia, *Nusantara*, which has been translated as Malay-Indonesian archipelago or – more accurately – maritime or insular Southeast Asia. This topographical entity encompasses not just present-day Indonesia and the neighbouring Federation of Malaysia, but also the Sultanate of Brunei, as well as the southern provinces of Thailand and the Philippines. Strategically positioned on the sea routes connecting the Indian and Pacific Oceans, throughout its history, this waterworld has been home to numerous indigenous states and even a few empires, while being simultaneously exposed to the cultural, economic and political influences of other Asian civilisations. Later on it was also subjected to invasions and occupation by European colonisers. Compared against these lengthy historical processes, border demarcation of what are presently internationally recognised states is a very recent phenomenon that did not get properly under way until the 1870s and – in some instances – has remained unresolved until very recently. All this underscores the importance of not losing sight of the fact that Indonesia is best regarded as a political construct based on historical contingencies. To my mind, awareness of such ambiguities also offers the right perspective for appreciating the place of Islam in this part of the world.

For most of its history, the area now covered by the Republic of Indonesia fitted uncomfortably within the concept of the nation-state based on the Treaty of Westphalia, which has governed statehood and international relations in Europe since 1648. That same political order was subsequently introduced – or imposed rather – everywhere else in the world. In that sense Indonesia is a figment of the colonial mind. As a geo-political entity the Republic can be considered as the administrative successor of the Netherlands East Indies, because the country's postcolonial leaders could not or would not think beyond this conceptualisation of statehood. People inhabiting the peripheries of this vast expanse, such as the Acehnese, Moluccans, Timorese and the Papuas of Irian Jaya, often feel like they do not quite belong, or even consider themselves as being subjected to continuing colonisation by Java. In fact, many of the country's political issues – including the question of the public function of religion – also relate to the contested territorial integrity of Indonesia.

All the above considerations illustrate the caveats and disclaimers needed when talking about 'Islam in Indonesia' – let alone when contemplating whether it is possible to speak of an 'Indonesian Islam'. The challenge of finding such a common denominator is actually reflected in the country's national motto: *Bhinneka Tunggal Ika* – a Javanese expression that can be translated as 'Unity in Diversity'. The slogan was adopted in recognition of the daunting task ahead for the young independent republic: forging a feeling of belonging and instilling a sense of solidarity among tens of millions of people spread across 18,000 islands, consisting of a wide variety of ethnicities, speaking a multitude of languages and representing all major religions in the world, as well as an array of indigenous beliefs. 'Unity in Diversity' is also applicable to Islam itself. On the one hand, Indonesia's Muslims are part of the *umma*; the community of believers worldwide. However, in terms of ethno-linguistic affiliation, cultural and historical experience, they are also different from their co-religionists elsewhere.

Also I must point out an imbalance in this book: in terms of the volume and level of detail, the coverage of Indonesia's centuries-long Islamisation process is skewed in favour of developments that have taken place during the last 200 years. Unfortunate as this may be for a work that seeks to offer an overall survey of the presence and evolution of Islam in Indonesia, this historiographical injustice is the result of a dearth of written materials and data concerning earlier periods. Sources for writing a history of Islam in Indonesia become more abundant and detailed as we get closer to the present day. Consequently, also in this book, the chapters on the recent past are the most voluminous.

The earliest modern academic scholarship on Indonesia, including its religions, is in Dutch. Coinciding with the expansion of the Netherlands' territorial control in Southeast Asia, most of this literature is written from the perspective of the 'deck of the ship, the ramparts of the fortress, and the high gallery of the trading house' – as the historian van Leur famously noted in one of the earliest critiques of the Eurocentric focus of colonial history-writing (1967: 261). Many of the early Dutch writings dealing with the place of Islam in Indonesia were produced by the Orientalist and government adviser Christiaan Snouck Hurgronje (1857–1936), and by his disciples at the University of Leiden and in Batavia (Jakarta). Often this research was initiated in response to local resistance to Dutch colonisation by Indonesians rallying – in one way or another – under the banner of Islam. In that sense, this early scholarship forms a Dutch equivalent to the *littérature de surveillance* written by the French about Islam in their North African colonies (Bruinessen 1998a: 192). It also demonstrates that the current securitisation of the study of Islam and the Muslim world is not without its historical precedents. A further – and sometimes older – source of information about religious developments in the Indies is the writings of Dutch missionaries; obviously, their interpretations were often refracted through the lens of their Christian theologies.

One dimension of the Indonesian Islamisation process that has been markedly improved thanks to the work of a rare breed of scholars who feel equally at home in Southeast Asian, Arabic and Islamic studies is the mapping of the connections between Muslim Southeast Asia and West Asia (a designation that seems more appropriate than 'Middle East', when looking westward from the eastern periphery of the Indian Ocean). Too often the unquestioned identification of the Arab world as the heartland of the Muslim world is left unproblematised. While the historical origins of the Islamic tradition lie indeed in the Arabian Peninsula, its further development is a product of intensive intercultural exchange, while in terms of demography, the vast majority of the world's Muslims live east of Hormuz. An important place in this networking was occupied by traders and scholars from a region in South Arabia known as the Hadhramaut. Research on the Hadhrami diaspora of the Indian Ocean basin has greatly contributed to our understanding of the role of such 'cultural brokers' in the Islamisation of Indonesia.

A positive development in the study of Islam in Indonesia is the growing involvement of Indonesian scholars from Muslim backgrounds; especially in (re) writing the history of the country's continuing Islamisation from late colonial times onward. Aside from rightfully claiming ownership of their own past, contributions by Indonesians can also offer instructive counter-narratives and correctives of the particular focus in past Dutch scholarship on Islam in Indonesia, because – one way or another – even the most erudite and empathetic studies were connected to the colonial project. The resulting differences in interpretation, or in the significance and importance attached to specific phenomena, trends and even particular events, as well as the accentuation of certain aspects rather than others, are valuable contributions to our knowledge. All of this is leading to a more nuanced understanding of Islamisation in Indonesia, and a greater appreciation for the complexity of this process as exhibited in its variegated and multifaceted aspects.

Another challenge for the earlier periods of Indonesia's Islamisation is the absence of data on the religious experiences of the common people. At least until the late nineteenth and early twentieth centuries, sources focussed primarily on rulers and scholars. Consequently, a fair amount is known about political and intellectual developments but very little about the lives of ordinary Muslims. Glimpses of this are provided by more recent ethnographic research, allowing tentative and carefully formulated projections into the past, although much of such extrapolation remains speculative. Very valuable in this regard is the work done by social scientists, scholars of religion and linguists who combine fieldwork with the study of texts. Although this was again pioneered by Snouck Hurgronje during his time among the Indonesian Muslim communities in the Hijaz (1884–5) and later in Aceh (1891–2, 1898–1901), I am thinking in particular about the work of a generation of anthropologists who commenced their research a century later.

Aside from the question of demarcation or the paucity of sources for certain periods and aspects of the Islamisation of Indonesia, writing a history of Islam in a country that only came into being so relatively recent also requires decisions on how to organise a story that has to cover not only a time period extending over eight centuries but also a vast geographical space. I have opted for a chronological account, while arranging the narrative around certain aspects of the Islamisation process that seemed to me characteristic of different periods. This comes with the immediate caveat that the dominant features of successive episodes do not constitute a neat sequential order, with distinct temporal markers of clear beginnings and endings. The Islamisation of Indonesia is a multilayered process of overlapping developments. Fitting a history of more than 700 years and encompassing a geographical expanse the size of Indonesia into a brief single volume can only be impressionist at best. I have attempted to find a compromise between the anecdotal and the identification of broader patterns and long-term trends. For this survey I am indebted to the research and writings of historians, linguists and literary experts, scholars of religion, social scientists and other area specialists who have made seminal contributions to the study of Islam in Indonesia during specific periods in time or in specific parts of the country.

When explaining the arrival of Islam in maritime Southeast Asia and the introduction of the youngest of the world religions to its indigenous population, the questions to deal with concern determining when this took place; from where it came; who was involved in bringing Islam to Indonesia; and why it was accepted at that point in time. Together with a brief sketch of the setting and ambience, these questions are addressed in the opening chapter. This is followed in the second chapter with an overview of the dynamics informing the further Islamisation process, discussing such issues as Islamic state formation, the emergence of a Southeast Asian Islamicate civilisation, as well as other cultural and intellectual developments. When putting these factors together, the image of a 'network Islam' emerges. After attaining a foothold and becoming firmly embedded in its regional settings, Islam in Indonesia was also used as a rallying point in resisting the onslaught of new, more invasive and violent, external influences in the form of European imperialism. Chapter 3 presents the Padri Wars in the Minangkabau region of central Sumatra, the Java War involving the remnants of the Mataram Empire, and the protracted armed conflict in Aceh as nineteenth-century instances of Islam as resistance to Dutch colonialism, and a prelude to the confrontation with modernity. This encounter is further elaborated in Chapter 4, featuring the decisive impact of technological advances. These include the introduction of the steamship and opening of the Suez Canal on the growing role of the pilgrimage to Mecca in putting Indonesian Muslims in touch with developments elsewhere; the importance of the printing press in the dissemination of Islamic learning and news from across the Muslim world; and new forms of institutionalising Islam, like the formation of Islamic mass organisations and political parties and their role in emancipating Indonesia's Muslim population and working towards independence during the early decades of the twentieth century. This takes the story to the proclamation of the *Republik Indonesia* and the final chapter's discussion of the role of Islam in what is now the largest majority Muslim country in the world.

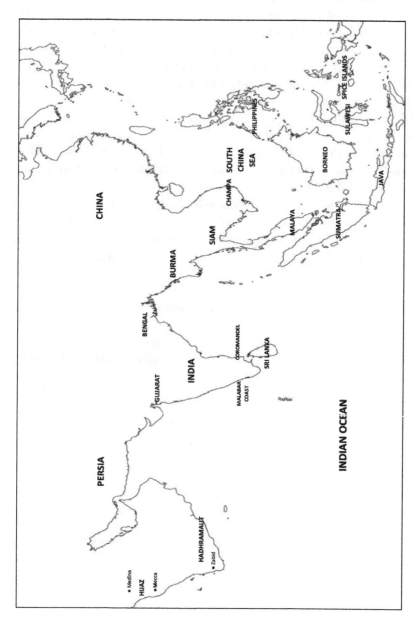

Map 1 The Indian Ocean Zone

CHAPTER 1

The arrival of Islam

Encounter with a world

Before engaging with events surrounding the arrival of Islam, it is advisable to heed a call issuing from the French school of historiography known as the *Annales* School to contextualise historical phenomena into their geographical setting and situate the relevant chronology on a timeline that includes what its historians call 'the *longue durée*'. This *Annales* School approach privileges structural influences, long-range temporal trends, such as – in this instance – the process of Islamisation, and what they call 'mentalities', over singular historical incidents (Burke 1991).

As noted in the Introduction, the politico-geographical area that is now known as Indonesia forms part of a wider region, locally known as *Nusantara*, which outsiders have called by different names including 'Lands below the Winds', 'Further India' and 'The East Indies'.[1] It covers an island world that stretches for thousands of miles across an area along both sides of the equator between the Indian and Pacific Oceans. In terms of its geology, this is a tectonically turbulent area; a link in the 'ring of fire' that surrounds the entire Pacific. This maritime world also forms part of another, relatively novel, topographical unit referred to as Southeast Asia.[2] This consists of a mainland portion, encompassing present-day Burma, Thailand, Cambodia and Vietnam; and the Malay-Indonesian archipelago that is of more immediate relevance to the present study. It extends into the southern provinces of Thailand and the Philippines, because these areas cannot be divorced from an account of the introduction of Islam in Southeast Asia and the early religious and cultural developments affecting Indonesia's Muslims.

As for the region's ecological setting, the key words are water and forest. In an area where large portions of the land are covered by impenetrable jungles, waterways – both maritime and riparian – become the main routes of communication and shipping the prime mode of transport. However, aside from these shared features, there is also a difference between continental and maritime Southeast Asia. Unlike the mainland, much of the archipelago – with the exception of Java – is not suited to intensive rice cultivation. Lacking the kind of economic surplus the latter generates, this explains the absence of empires, such as those of Pagan, Ayutthaya and the Khmer, based in the plains and river deltas of lower Burma, Thailand and Cambodia respectively. The only approximation was the trading empire of Srivijaya centred on an entrepôt near present-day Palembang in southern Sumatra (Wolters 1967). Because it is trade and seafaring on which the inhabitants of maritime Southeast Asia have historically depended for their livelihoods, reliable seasonal winds and associated nautical skills also enabled them to wander beyond their regional confines. In fact, research has demonstrated that people descending from the ethno-linguistic group known as Austronesians are found as far east as the South Pacific and as far west as Madagascar.[3] This westbound expansion points at the enduring importance of maritime Southeast Asia's global positioning on the eastern edge of the Indian Ocean, which has functioned as a contact zone of crucial commercial, cultural and political importance for the inhabitants of its shores.

This basic sketch makes discernible the contours of the structural significance that the *Annales* School historians attach to the impact of the natural environment on humans in terms of the emergence of culture and their development as historicised beings. This also applies to politics and religion, which are of course central in the present account. Chronologically situated between the earlier mentioned Austronesian cultural diffusion and the introduction of Indonesians to Islam, is the historical phenomenon of the Indianisation of Southeast Asia.[4] The mechanics and outcome of this acculturation process hold some instructive lessons and important clues for understanding and appreciating the later Islamisation of Indonesia. Following the path-breaking work of nineteenth- and early twentieth-century archaeologists and philologists, historian Oliver Wolters has developed new insights and alternative interpretations that significantly revise the earlier standard accounts. Central to his narrative are an appreciation for the agency of the peoples of Southeast Asia; the conceptualisation of the Indian Ocean as a 'neutral zone'; and his elaboration of the 'mandala' as a model for indigenous Southeast Asian statehood (Wolters 1982).[5]

There are a number of factors that support an interactive acculturation of Indian influences in Southeast Asia, rather than the assumption that this is a one-directional process: from the 'higher' or more 'advanced' civilisation of India to the 'primitive' peoples inhabiting Southeast Asia. First of all, there are the earlier mentioned nautical inclinations of the Austronesian islanders. Secondly, in India's rigid caste system there is little opportunity for merchants plying the Indian Ocean trade routes to become involved in the diffusion of religion and related cultural expressions. For the same reasons, and notwithstanding the subsequent presence of Brahmins at royal courts throughout Southeast Asia, tradition also prevented – or at least discouraged – members of this priestly caste to leave the subcontinent. Buddhism is not affected by such inhibitions and was also in its country of origin more readily associated with urban commerce than the isolated life at the court. Perhaps it is no coincidence therefore that a trading empire such as Srivijaya distinguished itself as a patron of Buddhism rather than hosting the elaborate synthesis at royal metropoles elsewhere in Southeast Asia involving Hindu elements. This support was not confined to Srivijaya's own geographical sphere of influence, but extended as far as the monastic university of Nalanda in Bihar (Laffan 2009: 22). All things considered, this makes an acculturation process in which Southeast Asians were involved as active participants rather than passive recipients all the more credible.

Wolters defines the Indian Ocean as a 'neutral water', rather than a terminus like the Mediterranean. What he means by that is that the vast expanse of the Indian Ocean basin is too large to be controlled by a single political entity, and that the power centres along the surrounding shores must display a degree of tolerance and hospitality to outsiders, because for traders there is always somewhere else to go. Also the above-mentioned ecological environment of Southeast Asia imposed a degree of flexibility on political systems. Forests interspersed with waterways made expansion through the sustained occupation of territory very difficult, thus forcing those in power to adopt the alternative strategy of bringing groups of people under their control instead. Indigenous 'states' were therefore organised in accordance with the model of a 'mandala' – whereby direct and effective power is only exercised in the immediate vicinity of the capital, from where it radiates with diminishing efficacy towards the peripheries. Suzerainty rather than sovereignty is maintained through a system of tributary vassals, which becomes less coercive the further one travels from the centre. In contrast to the cultural-religious influence exercised by India, in the context of Southeast Asian politics it was usually the Chinese emperor who stood at the apex of this hierarchy.

Southeast Asia and the Muslim world

Already before Islam began making inroads among the indigenous populations of Southeast Asia, there were contacts with the heartlands of the historical *Dar al-Islam*, with Persian navigators en route to China playing a pioneering role (Laffan 2009: 53). In fact, it may be safely assumed that relations predate the emergence of Islam. In his research on Southeast Asian toponyms, Michael Laffan traces the different names used in early Muslim sources for localities and regions in that part of the world (Laffan 2009). His findings are not only useful evidence for early contacts, they are also instructive for the uncertainties surrounding the exact topographical identification of early Southeast Asian entities, such as Srivijaya. With that, his work also points at the continuing challenge involved in determining the arrival of Islam in Southeast Asia.

While scholars agree that Srivijaya's centre of gravity lay in the area of present-day Palembang in southern Sumatra, less clear is the exact nature of its relation with Java and the Buddhist Sailendra dynasty, who are credited with building the Borobudur. The existence of such a connection is indicated by the use of the name 'Yava' for what is assumed to be Srivijaya. By examining the toponyms used by Muslim scholars in subsequent historical and geographical compendia, Laffan has tried to build a conjectural but not implausible case that changes in the Arabic nomenclature related to Srivijaya at present-day Palembang (*Zabaj*) reflect the shift of its centre of gravity first to Jambi/Melayu (*Qamar*) in the eleventh century, and its eventual substitution as the main emporium in maritime Southeast Asia by Malacca, around 1300, when large parts of Sumatra were conquered by the Java-based dynasties of Singasari (1222–92) and Majapahit (1292–1527). This coincides with the use of *Jāwa*, an Arabised cognate of 'Yava'. It is indicative of an awareness among the geographers in the Arabic-speaking parts of the Muslim world of Java's ascendancy in the regional balance of powers – an island that until then had not featured in Arab and Persian itineraries on their way to the terminus of China. It appears then that, aside from the Malacca Straits between Sumatra and the Malay Peninsula, West Asian Muslims now also began using the Sunda Straits between Sumatra and Java to get to the South China Sea. Since then, *Jāwa*, and its adjective *Jawi*, have functioned as collective or generic terms in the Arabic vocabulary for things Southeast Asian. This also includes Muslims associated with that part of the world.

The Indian Ocean as an 'Arabic-speaking Mediterranean'?
This evocative designation can be a bit misleading and therefore needs some qualification. First of all, unlike the Mediterranean, located between Southern Europe, North Africa and the Levant, the Indian Ocean is not a terminus. As argued by Wolters and subsequently demonstrated in the research by French historians influenced by the *Annales* School, that role is reserved for the South China Sea.[6] Also, the Indian Ocean is characterised by linguistic diversity. Aside from Persian and Swahili, various Indian languages had great currency too, while within Southeast Asia Malay functioned as the lingua franca. However, when exploring the provenance and interlocutors, the purpose and qualified validity of this somewhat provocative characterisation will become clear.

The beginnings of the Islamisation process

When discussing the introduction of Islam in Indonesia, four questions need to be addressed: they relate to the time frame (when); provenance (from where); agency (by whom); and motivation for Islam's arrival and acceptance at the time it did (why). Assessing the answers to these questions is a challenge. First of all because they are closely interrelated, so that changes in the findings in regards to one question will also influence the answers to the others. Secondly, because of the paucity of early sources, researchers have been forced into formulating rather conjectural theses, which are then explored using different scholarly methodologies, ranging from historical-philological studies to the ambitious holism of the *Annales* School and speculative theorising informed by a sociological focus. Geographically, two islands are of particular interest when it comes to the early Islamisation of maritime Southeast Asia: first of all, Sumatra – and more specifically the area known as Aceh; an independent-minded entity that became staunchly Islamic, and which still forms a region with special autonomous administrative status within the Republic of Indonesia. The other one is Java, where a section of its northern coast referred to as the Pasisir, and the adjacent part of east Java are especially important. In both instances this is no coincidence, because these areas are located on the busy trade routes connecting the Indian Ocean to the South China Sea.

When?

The interrelation between the various questions regarding the Islamisation of Indonesia is evinced when trying to determine the time frame during which the inhabitants of the Southeast Asian island world began embracing Islam, because the answer has immediate repercussions for the 'why?' question. The previous section showed that Arabs and Persians were already in touch with the rest of Asia before they had become Muslims themselves. However, tangible indications of a presence of indigenous Muslims in Southeast Asia do not predate the late thirteenth century. If this was indeed the moment Islam began to be accepted, this raises the question: why then? And what would explain the 'gap' between that point in time and the emergence of Islam in the seventh century, not to mention the indications that there was a very early and widespread presence of Muslims in China? The evidence for a presence of indigenous Muslims in Southeast Asia is both textual and material, consisting of travel accounts by outsiders and tombstones, complemented by local records in the form of royal chronicles – although the latter have not survived in versions that are contemporaneous with the events they describe.

In his travelogue, the Venetian trader Marco Polo (1254–1324) notes that at the time of his visit in 1292, the inhabitants of the northern Sumatran port city of Perlak (in today's Peureulak Regency in Aceh) had recently converted to Islam. Also important is that, sailing with a mixed Sino-Muslim crew, Polo refers to the island as *Java Minora*; indicative of Sumatra political subservience to Java proper. Half a century later, in his account of Asian riches, such as *luban jawi* or benzoin, Ibn Battuta of Tangiers (1303–68/9) reports of the piety and strict adherence to the Shafic i school of law on the part of Sultan al-Malik al-Zahir, the ruler of the Sultanate of Samudra-Pasai (identified with present-day Lhokseumawe), located in the northeastern tip of Sumatra (Laffan 2009: 35–8).[7] Of a slightly later date are the descriptions in the *Suma Oriental* written by the Portuguese Apothecary Tomé Pires (1465?–1524/40).[8] His records of Muslims in the Malay Peninsula and on Java coincide with d'Albuquerque's conquest of Malacca in 1511 and the growing importance of Muslim-controlled entrepôts along Java's north coast (Ricklefs 2006: 17–20).

The plausibility of these accounts can be tentatively corroborated by the presence of tombstones on Sumatra, Java and elsewhere in Southeast Asia. A tombstone bearing the name of Sultan al-Malik al-Salih who died in 1297 CE was found in Pasai.[9] As shown by the research of Elizabeth Lambourn into the material Muslim cultures around the India Ocean, such discoveries form part of a developing tradition, in which the tombstones of the first Muslim rulers were later replaced by more ornate ones, while by the fifteenth century also rich commoners from Pasai to Gresik in east Java could afford to import such precious headstones from Gujarat (Lambourn 2003, 2004). These artefacts also evince the use of Arabic names, styles and titles for royalty – as *rajas* become *sultans* – and with that the first hints of the Arabisation of the Malay language, in terms of both vocabulary and script – a variant that since then is referred to as *jawi*.[10] The Javanese picture is slightly more confusing. There, the earliest gravestones found in Trawulan (Trowulan) and Troloyo (Tralaya) date back to 1368/9 and 1376/7 respectively – with the graves at the first location also displaying the Shiva *lingam* (Hindu phallic symbol). According to Ricklefs, this demonstrates that Javanese courtiers of the period saw no contradiction in being Javanese and Muslim at the same time. However, the *Deśawarnana* (also known as *Nagarakrtagama*), a Javanese epic poem attributed to the Buddhist author Prapañca (d. 1365), makes no mention of Muslims at all. Ricklefs inter- prets this absence as an indication that being Muslim was still regarded as a contested identity (Ricklefs 2006: 12–15). A similar perception lies at the basis of Azyumardi Azra and Anthony Johns's suggestion that the early phase of the Southeast Asian Islamisation process is best conceived in terms of a sliding scale moving from adhesion to conversion (Azra 1992: 21ff.; Johns 1995: 170). In this they follow Nehemia Levtzion rather than earlier scholar of religion Arthur Nock, who saw these two religious phenomena as separate and mutually exclu- sive categories.[11] Instead, the introduction of Islam was a lengthy process of gradual adoption and adaptation to local circumstances, featuring the integra- tion of existing indigenous religious features, such as the accommodation of a central functionary known as *pawang*. Also known as *bomoh* or *dukun*, the *pawang* is a kind of 'spirit doctor', whose equivalent is also found elsewhere in Southeast Asia where other religious traditions prevail.[12]

Then there are the chronicles of the Southeast Asian 'states' affected by this new process of religious adhesion and conversion, although with the caveat that they survive only in copied manuscripts of later dates. While these chronicles are called *babad* in Javanese, the Malays often use the evidently Arabic-derived term *hikayat*.[13] Thus the *Hikayat Raja-Raja Pasai* of 1350 seems to confirm Ibn Battuta's reports, whereas Malacca's *Sejarah Melayu* (c. 1500) puts the conversion of its alleged founder, a refugee prince from Srivijaya called Parameswara, in the year 1414, after which he continued to rule as Muhammad Iskandar Shah. Further north on the Peninsula, in what is now the southern Thai province of

Patani, the ruler embraced Islam in 1457. In the beginning of the sixteenth century, the port cities of the Pasisir had managed to wrest themselves free from Majapahit suzerainty and the first local ruler to become a Muslim was Pangaran Tranggana of Demak, who then assumed the name Ahmad Abd al-Arifin. By this time, Southeast Asia's most powerful emporium, Malacca, had fallen to the Portuguese and its place as the region's leading Muslim trading post cum 'state' was now shared by Patani, on the eastern side of the Malay Peninsula and looking out over the Gulf of Siam, and in the west by Aceh – the northern Sumatran region protruding far into the Indian Ocean.

Another Islamisation narrative that is of interest here is that of west and central Sumatra, home to an ethnic group known as the Minangkabau. This area stretches from Sumatra's west coast opposite the islands of Nias and Siberut, across the highlands in the interior which are cut off from the coast by a mountain range called the Bukit Barisan, extending into the alluvial plains of what is now the Riau province. This part of central Sumatra is connected to the Straits of Malacca via the Siak, Kampar and Indragiri rivers. Although of a later date than Aceh or the Malay Peninsula, the story of the introduction of the Minangkabau to Islam is not only illustrative of the varying modalities of the Islamisation process in Southeast Asia, especially where it concerns peoples living in the interior and on higher elevations.[14] Singling out this relatively minor group in the totality of Indonesia's demography for special attention also bears relevance to the later development of Islam as a tool of resistance and to the role played by Minangkabau Muslims in late colonial and independent Indonesia – occupying a place of political, intellectual and religious prominence that is disproportionate to their percentage of the country's total population, which will be discussed in other chapters (Hadler 2009: ix, 2–3, 180).[15]

The Minangkabau world (*Darat* or *Alam Minangkabau*) is complex and internally diverse. Its most characteristic exponents – matrilineal kinship and its derivative social structures and cultural expressions – only apply in their full extent to the valley plains of the interior, where a semi-hereditary class of leader figures, known as *penghulus*, stood at the apex of this lineage hierarchy. These features are less discernible among the populations living on higher elevations, in the narrow western coastal strip and in the alluvial plains to the east. These different environments also impact on the economic bases of these respective Minangkabau societies. Intensive wet rice cultivation is limited to valley floors, with areas on higher altitudes focussing on alternative ways of growing rice and the collection and export of jungle produce, including camphor, benzoin (a tree resin not dissimilar to frankincense), cassia (a kind of cinnamon, though of a lesser quality than the variant found on Sri Lanka) and gambir (a wood used as a dye, for chewing betel and for medicinal purposes). Matrilineal kinship, meanwhile, stimulated another feature of Minangkabau society: the practice of *rantau* (also found in Aceh) whereby adolescent or young adult men leave their village to seek (economic) fortune elsewhere.

Aside from agricultural surplus, it was the mining of iron and gold that was important to the Minangkabau economy and the resultant social structuring. Historically, the export of this precious commodity also connected the Minangkabau's interior to the outside world, exposing it to outside influences. This gold trade shaped the emergence of a Minangkabau upper class, consisting of a royal lineage and two other dignitaries known as *bendahara* who are regarded as the originators of two competing systems of Minangkabau customary law, known as Bodi Caniago and Kota Piliang respectively. Both the royal family and *bendaharas* profited from the gold trade which was exported via an eastern trade route, establishing a close relation between Minangkabau royalty and the Sultanate of Malacca. This was also one of the ways through which Islam entered into the Minangkabau world. Indications of a gradual Islamisation via this lowland connection are the Arabised names of a sixteenth-century triumvirate of Minangkabau kings, known as the Raja Ibadat (King of Religion), Raja Adat (King of Tradition) and Raja Alam (King of the World) respectively, as well as Dutch references to one of the *bendaharas* as the Raja Alam's 'absolute *wakil*' (representative) almost a century later (Dobbin 1983: 64–5).

Parallel to this connection to the Malay world of the Straits, Islam also entered via the west coast, through the entrepôts run by middlemen 'nominally linked to the Minangkabau royal court' (Dobbin 1983: 71). Cut off from the interior by the Bukit Barisan, this narrow coastal strip lacked a proper economic hinterland. Consequently, even leading ports like Ulakan, which would become 'famous in Minangkabau history as one of the entry points of Islam into the Minangkabau world, presented "a wretched appearance [. . .]"' (Dobbin 1983: 42). Aside from marketing gold, for centuries these ports had been staple places for jungle produce, such as camphor, benzoin and gambir, supplying them to Indian, Chinese and other foreign traders. Another highly profitable commodity, which was added as a commercially grown crop on the coastal plains from the sixteenth century onward, was pepper. This pulled the Minangkabau's west coast and its ports into the orbit of an expanding Aceh, as it took over from Malacca as the region's most powerful political entity of the Malay world. It was this development that opened the way for the introduction of Islam by Muslim missionaries operating under Aceh's patronage, which will be discussed in more detail in the next chapter.

Putting together indigenous texts with the travel accounts of outsiders and the material culture examined by archaeologists, the only certainty we have is that at the very end of the thirteenth century there were Muslims resident in Southeast Asia, while in the course of the fourteenth and fifteenth centuries there are increasingly convincing indications of the adoption of Islam by indigenous populations as well. However, it is not until the sixteenth century that more abundant evidence becomes available.

From where?

As for the provenance of Southeast Asian Islam, the picture is equally diffuse. The Dutch scholar of Islam G. W. J. Drewes has provided a handy inventory of the various origins that have been proposed over time (Drewes 1968). In 1872, fellow Dutchman Pijnappel had suggested that Arabs settled in India in Gujarat and on the Malabar Coast were responsible for introducing Islam to maritime Southeast Asia. Snouck Hurgronje, however, was of the opinion that its point of origin could be found in the south of the subcontinent, although he did not specify which part. Based on Tomé Pires's *Suma Oriental*, the Pakistani scholar S. Q. Fatimi argued that Islam was imported from Bengal, but he also added a second line of conversion coming to Indonesia from China via Champa, located in present-day southern Vietnam and Cambodia. This may be less far-fetched than it seems, because both Javanese and Cham Muslim traditions make mention of such contacts.[16]

Apart from information derived from early travel accounts, the acceptance of India as the point of origin was also informed by Moquette's discovery and description of the Muslim tombstones found in northern Sumatra. According to Moquette, these tombstones were of Gujarati design. However, the dating of these stones to the late thirteenth century is difficult to reconcile with the fact that at that time Islam had only just begun to make inroads in that part of India itself. For that reason, and also based on stylistic considerations, Fatimi maintains that the tombstones must have been brought from Bengal instead. Drewes himself is inclined to accept the plausibility of the Bengali connection, because of its geographical proximity and the known existence of close trade relations with Southeast Asia, but he has also suggested that more research should be done into the possible influence of Tamil Muslims (Drewes 1968: 479).[17] More recently, the Indonesian historian Azyumardi Azra noted that – in 1913 – the British scholar T. W. Arnold (1864–1930) had added the Malabar Coast and Arabia as places from which Islam may have been brought to Southeast Asia (Azra 1992: 31).

In 1861, the Dutch scholars Niemann and de Hollander pointed to Arabia as the place from which conversion was initiated, based on the self-evident fact that Arabia is where Islam itself originated. Following a comparable line of reasoning, Keyzer suggested Egypt, because that is where the Shafi'i school of law, prevailing throughout Muslim South and Southeast Asia, was first established. Drawing on the writings of Marco Polo and Ibn Battuta, historical-philological studies by Azyumardi Azra himself and by others have put these Arabian provenances back on the table. However, these research projects were not so much focussed on determining points of origin as geared towards the question of agency; investigating the interlocutors – that is, foreign and domestic participants – involved in the Islamisation of Southeast Asia.

Who and why? Agency and motives for Islamising Indonesia

The earlier discussion of Indian cultural-religious influences in Southeast Asia showed that the question of who was involved in the Islamisation of Southeast Asia must not be reduced to simply determining who first carried the message of Islam to that part of the world. Even in the context of searching for the beginnings of the Islamisation process, such a one-dimensional approach is simply reductionist. It is much more productive to break down the question into an investigation of 'senders' and 'addressees'. Catering to an interactive process also offers a more sophisticated insight into motivational forces that are at work in religious conversion processes and will thus contribute to resolving the 'why?' question – which is inseparably connected with that of agency.

Proponents of both West Asia and South Asia as the points of origin of Southeast Asia's Islamisation based their case on the long-standing trade relations between these regions. In his *Indonesian Trade and Society* (1967), the economic historian van Leur also bought into this argument, amplifying the importance of commerce in maritime Southeast Asia's contacts with the outside world. But there are a few problems with that in regards to the modalities of the conversion process. While scholarship has shown that these relations date back to the earliest times of Islam, and were probably even established in the pre-Islamic period, what would then explain the vacuum of nearly half a millennium between the travels of West Asian Muslim merchants from the seventh century onward and the earliest indications of any local Southeast Asian acceptance of Islam on a substantial scale between the thirteenth and sixteenth centuries? In addition, if business was a consideration, why then did Chinese religions fail to make inroads among the indigenous peoples of Southeast Asia? The Chinese have been present in Southeast Asia for much longer and in much larger numbers than Muslim traders from the Indian Ocean basin.

Equally unconvincing is Schrieke's contention that the arrival of Christian Portuguese drove the Malays to Islam, because the Islamisation process had already commenced before any Portuguese had set foot on Asian shores (Schrieke 1957: 232–7).[18] As part of these considerations, Alatas and Azra have sided with Anthony Johns, who was the first to elaborate the thesis that Sufism played an important part in the acceptance of Islam in insular Southeast Asia (Alatas 1985: 170; Azra 1992: 40).

The 'Sufi thesis'

Leaving aside the question of the exact timing and origin of Islam's initial introduction to Southeast Asia, Johns's work was focussed on finding explanations for the apparent acceleration in the spread of Islam between the thirteenth and

fifteenth centuries. In a nun
than forty years of pioneer
come to an increasingly sub
Asia under the rubric of a '{
historical considerations feature prominently. However, ... , g g ce
of the trade route networks criss-crossing the Indian Ocean since time immemorial for the spread of religious traditions, Johns rejected the idea of traders as the chief candidates for the agency of conversion. Instead he looked for other actors travelling along the same trajectories:

> To say simply that Islam came with trade is to beg the question. It is not usual to think of sailors and merchants as bearers of religion. If, however, we think of certain traders belonging to Sufi trade guilds, accompanied by their Shaikhs, there seems a more plausible basis for the spread of Islam. (Johns 1963: 40)

In his studies of the Islamic expansion in the Malay-Indonesian archipelago, Johns has continued to explore, adjust and revise the assumption with which he started in the early 1960s:

> The hypothesis I wish to elaborate then is as follows: the primary impulse behind the development of Islam among the Indonesian peoples is the preaching of the Sufis, and that the Sufis, by virtue of the organization of their orders, and their craft and guild organization were able to gain control of administrative units of the port cities of North-East Java. (Johns 1961: 146–7)

What makes this a plausible hypothesis in Johns's view, is that the increase of the conversion rate in Southeast Asia coincides with the emergence of Sufi orders (tarīqā (s.); turuq (pl.) in Arabic, tarekat in Indonesian) in West and South Asia as the main institutions holding together the fabric of Muslim societies after the collapse of the Abbasid Caliphate, following the sacking of Baghdad by the Mongols in 1258. Apart from this macro-historical development affecting the Muslim world at large and his 'profiling' of likely candidates for Muslim missionaries responsible for the introduction of Islam in Southeast Asia, Johns also emphasised the urban setting of this emerging Islamic culture in Southeast Asia, but adding the caveat that 'the urban history of our region is freakish, disparate and abrupt' (Johns 1975: 37–8).

Martin van Bruinessen has challenged this thesis. While he agrees that the first indications of the Islamisation of indigenous populations in Southeast Asia coincide with the lifetimes of the eponymous founders of the great transnational Sufi orders, he argues that there is simply no tangible evidence of any presence of initiates in these brotherhoods before the late sixteenth century (van Bruinessen 1994b: 3–4).[19] Also he questions whether it is appropriate to conceive of Sufi orders as 'guilds', even if proselytising Sufi teachers travelled along these trade routes. Responding to this criticism in his latest writings on the subject, Johns revised the original hypothesis, augmenting his early focus on Islamic mysticism

– motivated by his self-admitted personal enthusiasm for the spiritual dimensions of Islam – with a greater appreciation of Islam's communal aspects.

The realisation of the significance of these communal aspects provides an opportunity to reassess the economic and political factors that have been brought forward as a motivation for the acceptance of Islam by Southeast Asians. For the *rajas*, or rulers, of trade-based Malay chiefdoms and petty principalities located on the river mouths and estuaries of insular Southeast Asia, Islam offered a way of unifying in the face of the challenges posed by the more powerful wet rice cultivating empires of continental Southeast Asia. The new religion offered the Malay chieftains – often reduced to vassal status within these more powerful political realms – an opportunity to tap into an alternative political alliance: one encompassing the entire Indian Ocean as an ecumenical Islamic zone. This would explain the pattern of rulers accepting the new religion before most of their subjects did. A similar process may have transpired in the Pasisir – the port cities along the northern coast of central Java.

This aspect of Islam as a communal religion is also evident in the centrality of rituals such as prayer, almsgiving and fasting. This significance of the social dimension of Islam also stimulated a greater awareness of the importance of wider religious learning – including Islamic law – throughout the subsequent Islamisation process in Southeast Asia. In addition to mystical, legal and other religious literature, Johns points also to a different kind of texts, 'more Indonesian than specifically Islamic which refer to the coming of Islam' (Johns 1961: 147). These are the Javanese, Malay and Sundanese chronicles mentioned earlier such as the *Babad Tanah Jawi, Hikayat Raja Pasai, Sejarah Banten* and *Sejarah Melayu*. At this stage, Johns is still relying mainly on Fatimi's advocacy of Bengal and China as the places from which Islam reached Southeast Asia. However, in his later rethinking of his hypothesis, together with Farid Alatas and Azyumardi Azra, Johns begins to give more weight to the Arab connection. The Pasai chronicle credits the ruler of Mecca with dispatching missionaries to the court at Samudra in northern Sumatra. Also in the *Sejarah Melayu*, 'six principal references to things Islamic' can be identified, including the Qur'anic Alexander story; the conversion of the ruler of Malacca by a holy man from Jeddah; and the arrival of a Meccan scholar with a book of Islamic teachings (Johns 1975: 40–1).

Sufis, Arabs and the rise of a Malay-Muslim writing culture: two recent discoveries

Van Bruinessen's scepticism regarding Johns's Sufi thesis can be dispelled to a degree by two discoveries that will – to some extent – close the gap between the first rise of the Sufi orders from the thirteenth century onward and evidence for their presence in Indonesia, which until recently was assumed to be not older than the late sixteenth century. They involve the discovery of a Yemeni text mentioning the presence in Southern Arabia of a thirteenth-century scholar by the name of Mas^cud al-Jawi, and archaeological evidence that possibly puts almost a century further back in time the death of one of the founding fathers of a Malay-Muslim literary culture and an indigenous theosophical tradition inspired by Ibn al-^cArabi (1165–1240). Both discoveries invite a corrective and, after further future research, possibly a complete revision of what has been postulated so far in regards to the emergence of the first important Muslim intellectuals of Southeast Asian origin and their involvement in the Islamisation process.

In 1997, Michael Feener came across the name of one Abu Abdullah Mas^cud al-Jawi in a biographical dictionary compiled by Shihab al-Din Ahmad al-Sharji (1410–c. 1487/8). He is mentioned as an established Sufi teacher in the small Red Sea town of Uwaja and colleague of the prominent jurist Isma^cil al-Hadhrami. Al-Sharji himself was a scholar living and working in Zabid, a centre of Islamic learning in Yemen and of central importance in the debates on the legacy of Ibn al-^cArabi's thought in Yemen from the late thirteenth century onward, which have also affected the Islamisation process in Indonesia, and especially in seventeenth-century Aceh.

In a jointly written article, entitled 'Sufi Scents Across the Indian Ocean', Michael Feener and Michael Laffan are able to connect the duo mentioned by al-Sharji to the writings of one of their disciples: ^cAbdallah ibn As^cad al-Yafi^ci (1298–1367) (Feener and Laffan 2005). In terms of biographical facts, al-Yafi^ci chronicles that al-Hadhrami's death coincided with that of the Mamluk Sultan Baybars al-Bunduqari in 1277. This makes also the Muslim scholar al-Jawi a contemporary of the victor over the Crusade of Louis IX in 1250; the sultan then went on to vanquish the Mongols at Ayn Jalut in 1260. This period also coincides roughly with the formative period of the first Sufi orders, as well as the reign of the first identifiable Muslim ruler of Sumatra, the Sultan al-Malik al-Salih of Samudra-Pasai mentioned at the beginning of this chapter. Much of al-Yafi^ci's account involving al-Jawi is cloaked in well-known tropes from the Sufi literature; including dream visitations by past leading mystics, such as Abd al-Qadir al-Jilani (d. 1166), effecting virtual initiation into Sufi orders, as well as allusions to the association of mystical knowledge of the divine with sweet breezes of air, which can ultimately be attributed to a saying of the Prophet Muhammad that 'the breath of the Merciful comes to me from Yemen' – believed to describe his special relationship with the Yemeni mystic Uways al-Qarani (d. 657), although the two never met in person (Feener and Laffan 2005: 196).[20] This latter trope is further enforced through the association of Sufi scents with the role of Southeast Asia, *Jawa*, in the supply of aromatics.

Al-Yafi^ci's writings point at an intricate interplay of factors that also feature in the Islamic networks criss-crossing the Indian Ocean and that are relevant to the accounts of the early phase of the Islamisation process in Southeast Asia.

This includes the role played by the Qadiriyya order and by the Arabs from the Hadhramaut region in southern Arabia – except that the episode in question not only predates by several centuries the sources that have been known so far, but also attributes a much earlier active role to *Jawi* Muslims than has been recognised until now. Feener and Laffan note that stories such as Masᶜud al-Jawi's find support in the rich textual depositories of Cairo's Geniza documents first unlocked by Shelomo Goitein (1900–85).[21] They further surmise that it can form the beginning of a counter-narrative to the overemphasis on the Hadhrami origins of the so-called *Wali Songo*, or 'Nine Saints', credited with introducing Islam to northern Java – on the part of contemporary intellectuals of Yemeni Alawi extraction (Feener and Laffan 2005: 207–8).[22] This latter tendency forms part of a broader thesis proposed by these intellectuals concerning a 'Hadhramaut connection', which argues that 'the Islamisation of various regions of the Indian Ocean cannot be divorced from the presence of the Hadhrami trade diaspora' (Alatas 1997: 29). They present their thesis as a corrective of other studies into the relations between Indonesia and the Hadhramaut, which underscore that large-scale migrations from there did not commence until the eighteenth century (Mandal 1994: 2; Mobini-Kesheh 1999: 21).

Although he does not mention it explicitly, it could be argued that Johns has tacitly recognised the significance of the Hadhrami trade diaspora. As noted above, Johns's thesis also stresses the significance of maritime trade routes across the Indian Ocean zone for the spread of Islam. This also feeds into the resemblances he sees between the situations in the Indian Ocean and the Mediterranean, and which lead him to speak of the Indian Ocean zone as an 'Arabic-speaking Mediterranean' – a concept, he insists, that 'should be taken seriously' because it created the conditions for the development of a Southeast Asian Muslim writing culture and its corollary: 'the variety of ethnic cultures participating in the system' that shaped the Islamisation process in the Malay-Indonesian archipelago (Johns 1975: 38–9).

A Sufi writer named Hamzah Fansuri is generally regarded as the seminal figure for the emergence of a Malay-Muslim writing culture and for introducing the ideas of Ibn al-ᶜArabi into the concomitant indigenous Islamic discourse.[23] In his own writings on the role of Sufi orders in the spread of Islam in Indonesia, van Bruinessen notes that Fansuri was an initiate of the Qadiriyya order, but otherwise frustratingly little is known with any degree of certainty regarding his life, including the most basic details as to when he lived or where he was born (Bruinessen 2000: 362–4). The discovery of an intriguing epitaph in 1999 forms the latest episode in the debates that have been going on about this individual's life story since the 1960s. At that time the Malaysian-Indonesian scholar Syed Naguib al-Attas (1967) and the Dutch Indonesianist Lode van Brakel (1969) disputed Fansuri's birthplace. The biographical data contained in Fansuri's own literary *oeuvre* are deceptively concrete and therefore occasion for some intriguing questions. A reference to Hamzah as 'Jawi' and the name 'Fansuri' establish a connection with northern Sumatra. The latter word comes either from the Malay *pancur* or the Batak *pantsur*, meaning 'source' or 'fountain'. It gained wide currency, including in Chinese as *pin su*, as the place from where to obtain camphor, a secretion taken from a certain species of pine tree indigenous to northern Sumatra and the main reason for Chinese and other foreign traders to visit (Guillot and Kalus 2000: 4; Attas 1967: 43). Even more concrete is the mention of Barus, a locality on Sumatra's west coast opposite the Nias archipelago. But it is the following stanza from one of Hamzah's poems that triggered tantalising questions regarding his actual place of birth:

Hamzah Shahr Nawi terlalu hapus,
Seperti kayu sekalian hangus
Asalnya Laut tiada berharus
Menjadi kapur didalam Barus

Hamzah of Shahr-i Naw is truly effaced.
Like wood, all burnt to cinders;
His origin is the Ocean without currents
He became camphor in Barus (Attas 1967: 44)

This juxtaposition of Barus with Shahr-i Naw – Persian for 'New Town' and also used for the then capital of Siam, Ayutthaya – led al-Attas to posit that, while originating from Barus, Hamzah Fansuri was actually born in Thailand.[24] Van Brakel calls this into question on two grounds. First of all, Shahr-i Naw was a very common Persian appellative and could therefore refer to a variety of localities around the Indian Ocean, including an as yet unidentified place in Aceh. Secondly, reading this stanza together with other passages in which these place names are mentioned, van Brakel wonders why al-Attas decides to interpret these descriptions in such a concrete sense, as they feature in a body of Sufi poetry and are embedded in an idiom consisting of tropes of mystical attainment. This leads van Brakel to the proposition that Hamzah Fansuri is a native of Barus, went into seclusion in the Acehnese jungle near a remote place called Shahr-i Naw, where he achieved a *unio mystica* or mystical realisation – by being burned to cinders and turned into camphor (Brakel 1969: 206–12).

In spite of all their differences of opinion regarding the details as to the place of Hamzah Fansuri's birth or when exactly he died, up until 1999, scholarship was in agreement that his life had overlapped at least partially with the reign of the Acehnese Sultan Alauddin Ri'ayat Shah (1589–1604), possibly even extending into that of his successors Ali Ri'ayat III (1604–7) and Iskandar Muda (1607–36). This assumption was based on alleged allusions to these rulers found in another body of writing that is attributed to Hamzah Fansuri.[25] However, as evinced by the efforts of Vladimir Braginsky, a former professor of Malay literature at SOAS, such readings often involved a fair amount of *hineinterpre-tieren* (Braginsky 1999). All this has been called into question by the discovery by French academics Claude Guillot and Ludvik Kalus – as part of their involvement in a joint French–Indonesian archaeological project in Barus – of a transcription of a funerary stele from the Bab al-Mu͑ala cemetery in Mecca, recording the death on 11 April 1527 of one Shaykh Hamzah bin ͑Abdullah al-Fansuri (Guillot and Kalus 2000). Provided the text has been recorded correctly and can be connected to an authentic find, then – as a bare minimum – it provides evidence of the presence of a Sufi scholar from Sumatra's Barus in Mecca at that time. It also proves the existence of connections between that Sumatran locality and the Middle East, and – very important in the context of what I argue in this chapter – the active participation of the inhabitants of Southeast Asia in these exchanges.

More challenging is the identification of this deceased Shaykh with the Hamzah Fansuri who is regarded as the initiator of a Malay-Muslim writing culture. Using 'circumstantial evidence', Guillot and Kalus make this tentatively plausible by examining Fansuri's work for toponyms and cited authors, and by investigating the *silsilas* – Sufi genealogies of initiation – of his disciples. The most important conclusion of an examination of place names is the absence of any reference to Aceh. This is at least strange if Fansuri had been such a prominent religious and cultural figure in the sultanate, but makes sense if the date of 1527 is correct; at that time Aceh did not yet exist as a leading Southeast Asian Muslim state. Also the latest source reference found in Fansuri's *oeuvre* – to the Persian scholar Nur al-Din Abd al-Rahman Jami, who died in 1492 – is consistent with a death date of 1527. According to Guillot and Kalus, it is also possible to create a greater temporal distance between Fansuri and the individual who is regarded as his most important disciple – Shams al-Din of Pasai, of whom it is known that he died in 1630 – by interposing one or two generations of other students of Fansuri, who are then connected to Shams al-Din as teachers. At the same time, if Hamzah Fansuri did indeed pass away in 1527, that makes him a contemporary or near contemporary of several of the *Wali Songo*, the semi-legendary 'Nine Saints' involved in the Islamisation of Java, who will be discussed in more detailed in the next chapter.

What Guillot and Kalus's findings leave unchallenged is the likelihood of Fansuri's own mixed ethnicity. The fact that he is called a Jawi from Fansur despite the probability of having an Arab father can be explained by the prevailing matrilocality in that part of Sumatra (Braginsky 1999: 167).[26] A similar explanation could apply to the earlier mentioned individual identified by Feener and Laffan, Mas͑ud al-Jawi of Uwaja. Finally, the findings of the French–Indonesian archaeological project demonstrate that Barus was a cosmopolitan place with Persian and Arab, Indian and Javanese expatriates in residence, while locally found tombs evince indigenous Islamic roots that go back to the fourteenth century. All this makes Barus a suitable place for a scholar and Sufi of Hamzah Fansuri's standing without the need for an association with late sixteenth-century Aceh.[27]

Concluding remarks

The two key findings regarding the beginnings of Islamisation in Southeast Asia are that, in comparison with other parts of the *Dar al-Islam* or historical Muslim world, it commenced relatively late and that the religion was initially introduced peacefully – another contrast with the Arab-Islamic conquests of North Africa and the Mediterranean, and West, South and Central Asia.

The discussions in the last few sections of this chapter make clear that there are no grounds for dismissing the 'Sufi thesis' out of hand; the increasing finely tuned elaborations and investigations by Johns conceive of it as part of a much more complex process that also involved other intellectual, social and political factors. Together with other new findings and investigations, such as those of Guillot and his team or Feener and Laffan, they contribute to a more multilayered rereading of the 'Arab connection' as it has been propounded so far.

The most important consequence of this expansion in our knowledge of the Islamisation of Southeast Asia is the realisation that it was not a uniform process. The contact of a region as large and culturally diverse as the Malay-Indonesian archipelago with other parts of the Muslim world was extensive. Therefore, it is not possible to formulate what Johns calls a 'single big-bang theory' (Johns 1980: 164, 1984: 116). He adds that it is 'virtually impossible to over-emphasize the discrete, idiosyncratic and diverse character of the port cities of the region which were the foci of Islamic settlement', and that 'each centre has its own story to tell'. In the absence of a single answer to the questions when and from where Islam was brought to Southeast Asia and by whom, we must look for a 'variety of starting points' and 'numerous modalities for its diffusion' (Johns 1980: 164–5, 1984: 117). The acceptance of Islam by Southeast Asians was therefore not the result of a single act of conversion, but of a long process that is still continuing. In view of this *longue durée* dimension, I have already alluded to the suggestion that the early phases of the Islamisation process in Southeast Asia should not be described by using Nock's terms of adhesion or conversion in a mutually exclusive sense, but rather by seeing that process as a combination of the two.

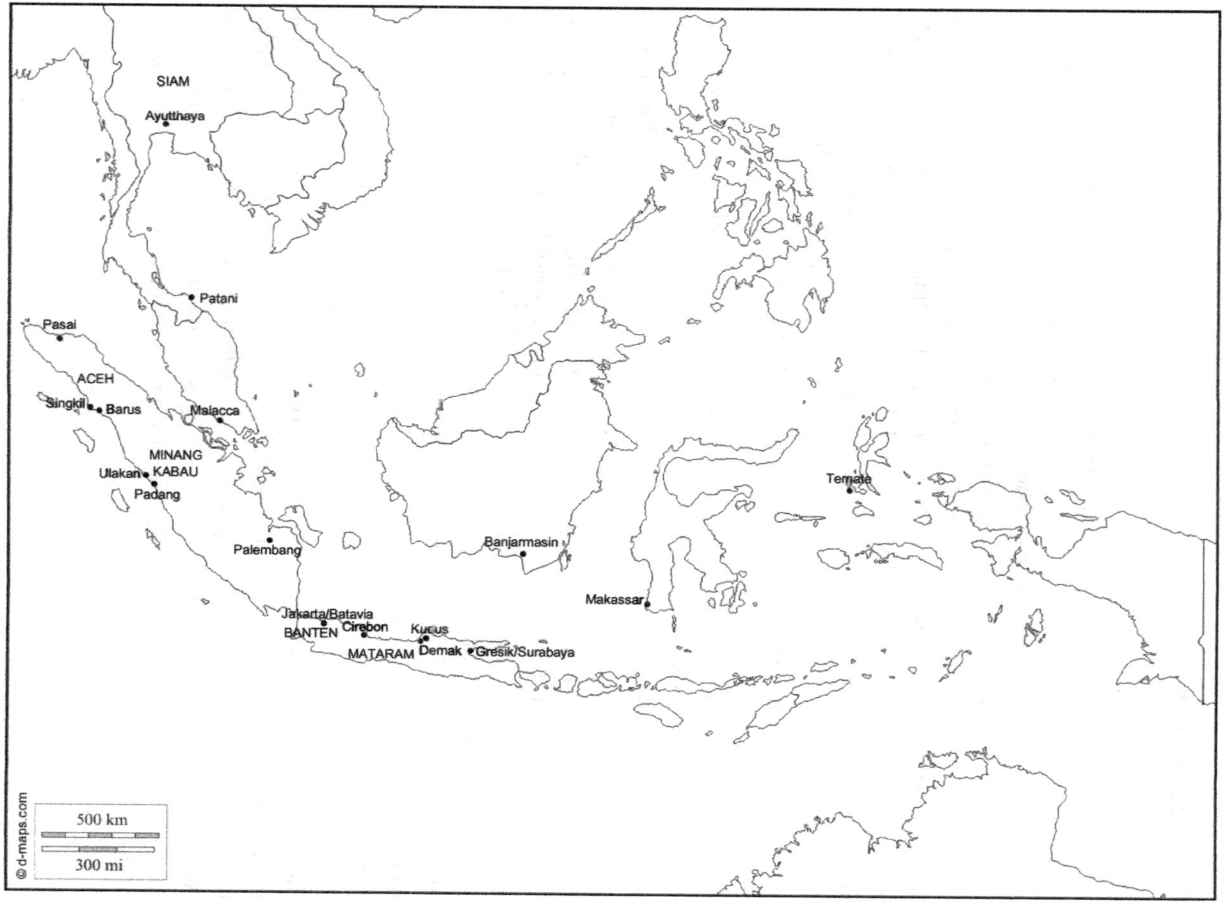

Map 2 Southeast Asia

CHAPTER 2

Network Islam

From the sixteenth century onward, maritime Southeast Asia's integration into the wider Muslim world becomes more discernible. This is mainly thanks to the increased availability of both external and indigenous sources providing evidence that the level of interaction between Indonesia and other areas around the Indian Ocean is growing in intensity, frequency and scale or volume. The effects of these exchanges manifest themselves in the emergence of new, Islamic, concepts of kingship and statehood; the concomitant royal patronage of religious scholarship and learning; and travel by Indonesian Muslims to centres of Islamic learning, further complemented by a more evident presence of Sufi orders in the archipelago. Taking together this set of factors, it seems appropriate to characterise this next stage in Indonesia's Islamisation process as 'Network Islam'. In view of the influence of Azyumardi Azra's mapping of seventeenth- and eighteenth-century networks involving Indonesian and Middle Eastern scholars, it is important to point out that my understanding of 'network' is wider, more intricate and fine-mazed: it extends from relations between Southeast Asian Muslim rulers and the Muslim superpowers of the day down to the micro-level of the agrarian Muslim milieus in rural Indonesia.

Also in this phase, northern Sumatra, and central and east Java remain important. However, other areas deserving attention include the Banten region of west Java and – across the Sunda straits – the Islamised Malay states in southern Sumatra. While Islam also penetrated further east, all the way to the Spice Islands of the Moluccas, but especially into coastal southern Borneo and Celebes (Sulawesi), local intellectual involvement there seems more incidental than structural – at least in comparison with developments on Java and Sumatra. Since Islam often got its first foothold among indigenous rulers, or was spread by Muslim 'middle classes' of foreign extraction seizing power in coastal trade centres, the relation between religion and statehood seems a good starting point for examining this next phase of the Islamisation process.

Islamic state-building

When examining the impact of the Islamisation process on political thinking and statehood in Southeast Asia, definitions of Islamic state formation in terms of the implementation of Islamic law will often fall short of expectations. While some of the early Islamised Malay states seemed to have had judges (*qadi*) and jurisconsults (*mufti*), legal administration often remained in the hands of the old elites, consisting of courtiers and other noblemen. And whereas in some areas, such as Aceh on Sumatra and Banten in west Java, there is anecdotal evidence of the implementation of concrete aspects of Islamic legislation, such as the prohibition of usury and the enforcement of acts of piety and worship (*ibadat*), indigenous legal codes or digests, known as *undang*, or adherence to local customary law (*adat*) seem to have been of greater importance. However, as Milner has pointed out, what Marshall Hodgson characterised as 'shari'a-minded' political thinking 'constituted only one aspect of the Muslim political culture' (Milner 1983: 23).

As Southeast Asian political entities transition from pre-Islamic notions of governance and legitimacy to embryonic Muslim state formation, elements from these indigenous conceptualisations are adapted or translated into this new context. Loyalty is not due to a legal system, a religious community (*umma*), or ethnic group (Malay, Javanese or otherwise), but continues to be conceived in terms of allegiance to the person of ruler. The figure of the leader remains the central political referent in this early phase of Islamising the archipelago's political systems. Royal insignia and rituals continue to play a crucial part in the legitimisation of the monarchical authority, now directed towards the ruler's Islamic credentials. Although the rulers often continue to be called *raja* in Malay or *pangeran* or *adipati* in Javanese, this does not preclude a simultaneous preoccupation with things Islamic on the part of these monarchs, but in these early stages the focus remains on their personal qualities.

Islamic rule in the Malay-speaking parts of Indonesia

Interest in Muslim manifestations or expressions of leadership – in both realistic and idealist terms – can be discerned earlier in the Malay-speaking parts of the Malay-Indonesian archipelago than on Java. This becomes first and immediately evident from the adoption of Arabic – and occasionally Persian – titles and styles; including *sultan* (he who wields power), *shah* (emperor), *khalifa* (caliph, successor), *zill Allah fi'l-alam* (God's Shadow on Earth) or *nasir al-dunya wa'l-din* (Helper of the World and the Faith). However, evidence of these terms comes from chronicles that only survive in versions that postdate the events they describe by centuries.

On a conceptual level, the Islamic influences that have percolated through consist in Persian notions of kingship that had already helped shape the Abbasid Caliphate (750–1258). These were also encapsulated in Islamic versions of a literary genre known as 'mirrors of princes', found in the writings by the Seljuq vizier Nizam al-Mulk (1018–92) or as represented by the *Nasihat al-Muluk*, or 'Advice to Kings', of his intellectual protégé, the Islamic polymath Abu Hamid al-Ghazali (c. 1058–1111). A second important influence is the idea of *insan kamil* or 'perfect man', which found its most articulate expression in a work of Abd al-Karim ibn Ibrahim al-Jili (1366–1428): *Al-insan al-kamil: Maᶜrifa al-awakhir wa'l-awa'il*. It forms part and parcel of a form of theosophy known as *wahdat al-wujud*, or 'Unity of Being' – a very controversial doctrine that is traceable to the Andalusian scholar and Sufi Muhyi al-Din ibn al-ᶜArabi (1165–1240).

Evidence of the latter's influence is detectable at the courts of Malacca and Pasai, but especially in Aceh, possibly since the days of Alauddin Ri'ayat Shah (1589–1604), who was also known as Sayyidi al-Mukammil.[1] The notion of the 'perfect man', as well as the wider theological implications of the 'Unity of Being' doctrine, became central to religious debates among scholars hosted at the courts of two later sultans of Aceh, Iskandar Muda (r. 1607–36) and Iskandar al-Thani (r. 1636–41), which will be addressed in more detail below. This duo also continued the practice of maintaining a functioning Islamic court that had been initiated by their predecessors, with royally appointed judges who dealt with upholding the observance of *ibadat* and the punishment of transgressions, as well as administering Islamic regulations regarding personal and commercial law. Aceh's prestige as a centre of Islamic learning in Southeast Asia was further aided by the sultanate's strategic geographical position; not just vis-à-vis the Malacca Straits, but also by its location at the very top of Indonesia's most western island, Sumatra. Jutting out into the Indian Ocean, Aceh was the ideal point of departure for the crossing of the Indian Ocean by ships carrying hajj pilgrims – earning it the nickname *Serambi Mekkah* – 'Mecca's Veranda'.

Within the Indonesian sphere, the two Iskandars were contemporaries of two other emblematic Muslim rulers in Indonesia, Sultan Agung of Mataram (r. 1613–46) and Sultan Abdul Kadir of Banten (r. 1596–1651). From a wider Asian perspective, their reigns also coincided with the establishment of the Tokugawa Shogunate (1603–1868) in Japan and the collapse of China's Ming Dynasty (1368–1644), as well as the rule of Mughal Emperors Jahangir (r. 1605–27) and Shah Jahan (r. 1627–58). However, despite Iskandar Muda's personal fascination with yet another Mughal Emperor, Akbar (r. 1556–1605), the most important political Muslim player for Aceh was that other 'gunpowder empire': the Ottoman Empire (Lombard 1967: 157–8).[2] Piecing together data derived from local oral traditions and the *Hikayat Aceh*, Denys Lombard and Anthony Reid's research into the Sultanate of Aceh's early history has shown how the *Raja Rum*, the Muslim ruler at Constantinople/Istanbul, spoke to the imagination of Acehnese rulers and their historiographers. However, a further examination of sources, including Ottoman and European records, also demonstrates sustained real-term military and diplomatic relations between the 'Grand Turk' or Sublime Porte and Aceh since the sixteenth century.

These connections began with the dispatch of a contingent of soldiers to Aceh in 1537 by Sulayman the Magnificent (1520–66), as part of the Ottoman expansion into the Indian Ocean basin.[3] They coincided with Aceh's decisive ascendency as the most powerful Malay state along the Malacca Straits. Relations continued with the 1562 Acehnese embassy to Istanbul and the subsequent provision of Ottoman ammunition, engineers and artillery personnel in 1567.[4] These exchanges assisted Aceh in expanding and sustaining its position as the region's main emporium for the trade in pepper and other commodities. In the absence of any precedent in terms of practical and structural political cooperation, the Ottoman–Acehnese relationship continued to be maintained throughout the 1570s and 1580s under the aegis of a rather vague notion of 'Islamic solidarity' (Reid 1969: 407–8).[5] Although the height of these contacts had passed by the time Iskandar Muda came to power, the new sultan's palace guard did resemble the Ottoman Janissary corps, while Aceh's absorption into the Ottoman sphere of influence in the Indian Ocean may have set the stage for the subsequent influx of religious scholars from Egypt, the Hijaz, Yemen and Gujarat to teach in Aceh.

Globally speaking, the time of Iskandar Muda and Iskandar II was also the period of the fastest and largest Dutch expansion overseas, as its East India Company (*Vereenigde Oost Indische Compagnie*, VOC) muscled out the Portuguese from many of its Asian positions. However, constant warfare with Portuguese Malacca and Johore for control over the straits and the principalities on the Malay Peninsula eventually sapped Aceh's energies. For the sixty years following the death of Iskandar II, Aceh was ruled by a succession of four queens, followed by a number of very brief reigns of sultans who found themselves caught in the midst of growing British–Dutch rivalry in Malacca Straits.

Politico-religious symbiosis along Java's northern coast

The early history of Muslim kingship on Java is diffuse, but appears to betray a more complex and multilayered process of Islamisation than that of the Malay world, where a more 'exclusivist' embrace of Islam seems to have taken root. A partial explanation for this is the lingering influence of the Hindu–Buddhist empire of Majapahit in east Java, until its demise in 1527. Thanks to the presence of intensive rice cultivation that allows for the economic surplus required for empire-building, this Javanese political entity was quite similar to the powerful Burmese, Thai and Khmer realms found in the plains of mainland Southeast Asia, where Islam never managed to make any significant inroads.

One reason for the sketchy impressions of early Islamic state formation on Java is the absence of reliable contemporaneous indigenous sources and the particular focus of foreign accounts by Portuguese and Dutch navigators, which concentrate on the political and economic aspects of their ambitions rather than religion. As a result, researchers have only been able to piece together a fragmentary picture. Finally, there is the additional challenge posed by the emergence of multiple centres, which requires a narrative covering a wide geographical spread while simultaneously maintaining some sense of a chronological order. Finding such a balance is further complicated by the interrelations between events in one area and their impact elsewhere.

The situation in the Islamic states of the Pasisir, centred on a string of settlements along the northern coast of central Java, and east Java's adjacent Gresik–Surabaya area, seems to have been an exception to the lasting religious plurality on Java, which was accommodative of a wide range of beliefs and practices. An explanation for the fact that the Islamisation process along the coasts bears a greater resemblance to developments in the Malay parts of insular Southeast Asia might be that the chieftains of the coastal fiefdoms found themselves in a position very similar to that of their counterparts to the northwest: ruling entrepôts directly connected to the mercantile networks of the Indian Ocean and the South China Sea. Facing the additional threat of political domination from the intensive rice culture-based powers in the interior, the Pasisir's outward and seafaring outlook drove the coastal settlements and fiefdoms towards a more decisive conversion to Islam so as to be accepted into the wider Muslim ecumene. This impression is also conveyed in the research conducted by de Graaf and Pigeaud, whose survey of the principalities and kingdoms is still the seminal work on sixteenth-century Islamic statehood on Java.

Temporally wedged between pre-Islamic Majapahit and Mataram, the new inland power which began expanding its influence from the 1580s onward, the sixteenth century was the heyday of the Pasisir sultanates and their uncompromising fidelity to the Islamic faith – at least in comparison with the contested Muslim identities of the subsequent Mataram era.

Aside from the late fourteenth-century tombstones found in the Trowulan–Troloyo area, the earliest manifestations of proselytising Muslims on Java are associated with the so-called *Wali Songo*, the semi-legendary 'Nine Saints' credited with facilitating the early spread of Islam on Indonesia's most populous island. Different sources give different lists of names, while the saints' life stories are also more myth than history – dates are almost impossible to verify, whereas 'facts' often fall short in terms of certainty or even veracity. The information about these figures that has reached us is recorded in sources of much later date, which were very likely compiled and composed with the purpose of creating a particular impression of how the Islamisation of Java came about. So while before the end of the sixteenth century there is little or no incontestable evidence of what exactly transpired, the relevance and significance of the transmitted *Wali Songo* stories rests on what they can tell us about the outlook of Java's Muslims on their own past.

According to this body of legend, the first preachers to bring Islam to Java were two brothers of mixed Arab–Cham parentage: Raja Pandita and Raden Rahmat. In terms of time frame, their arrival from Champa is thought to have been between the 1440s and 1470. While Raja Pandita settled in Gresik, Raden Rahmat moved to Surabaya. Posthumously referred to as Sunan Ngampel

Denta, or Sunan Ampel, the latter is generally regarded as the oldest of the *Wali Songo* (de Graaf and Pigeaud 1974: 19–21, 138). In some versions Raden Rahmat is also called Maulana Malik Ibrahim al-Samarqandi, but others report that this was the name of his father, who is remembered as Sunan Gresik in those texts – making him – rather than his son – the oldest of the *Wali Songo*. It seems that after this initial episode, for a while the Gresik–Surabaya area receded into the background, only to regain prominence in the early seventeenth century, when it became a centre of resistance against the expansionist ambitions of the new inland power of Mataram, which was trying to establish itself as an empire of the same standing as pre-Islamic Majapahit.

The initial centre of gravity for the further spread of Islam on Java was located on its north coast – more specifically in Demak. While it is unclear when exactly the 'state' of Demak was established, the event is attributed to one Raden Patah (Fatah), who is sometimes given as the son of Bra Wijaya of Majapahit, and in other instances as a former resident of Gresik, or even a Chinese immigrant. As a trading post, Demak had a very mixed population, including a sizeable contingent of expatriate Muslims composed of different ethnicities. Demak's reputation as an increasingly important centre of Islamic learning was connected with its central mosque and the alleged involvement of a number of *Wali Songo* in its early activities.

This mosque was probably established around 1507 with Demak's ruler at the time, Tranggana (d. 1546), present at its inauguration. On this occasion he also received investiture as Ahmad Abd al-Arifin at the hands of another one of the *Wali Songo*, Sunan Gunung Jati (1450?–1569?). Sunan Ampel makes a brief reappearance in these reports of the event as well, featuring as the father of the mosque's first imam, Sunan Bonang, who is also included in the *Wali Songo* fraternity, and whose sister is said to be the ancestor of the subsequent four imams. Also featuring in the congregation of *Wali Songo* at Demak is Raden Sahid, a nobleman from east Java credited with carrying Islam into the eastern parts of the Indonesia archipelago and who became known as Sunan Kalijaga. It is reported that when Raden Sahid visited the mosque, he magically received a garment worn by the prophet and endowed with supernatural powers. Known as Anta Kusuma, the garment was passed on to the fourth imam of the Demak mosque, Rahmatullah of Undung. Notwithstanding Anta Kusuma's protective qualities, the imam was nevertheless martyred in a battle against Majapahit (de Graaf and Pigeaud 1974: 94).[6] At the instigation of Sunan Gunung Jati, Rahmatullah was succeeded by his son Japar Sidik or Ja'far al-Sadiq (a name with a Shi'i ring to it), who went on to become one of the *Wali Songo* as well, under the posthumous name of Sunan Kudus.[7]

The young imam was credited with inflicting final defeat on Majapahit, an achievement which heralded the extension of Demak's influence in both western and eastern directions, at the expense of other centres of Islamic piety, such as

Cirebon, Banten and Gresik–Surabaya. From Demak, Islam was also carried overseas into southern Borneo. Demak's expansion of political power was coercive and violent. So while Islam may have made its first inroads into Southeast Asia in a peaceful manner, the further Islamisation process also involved belligerent rulers and militias of committed Muslims led by religious leaders, such as Ja^{c}far al-Sadiq, referred to as *panghulu* in the Javanese sources. De Graaf and Pigeaud have suggested that these forces may have been modelled after earlier armed groups of pious militants recruited from the expatriate Muslim merchant communities, who had taken control of the Pasisir ports in the course of the fourteenth and fifteenth centuries. It is also illustrative of the two trajectories towards Islamic state-building on Java: the usurpation of political control by a Muslim 'middle class' and the conversion of 'pagan' rulers (de Graaf and Pigeaud 1974: 27).

After the death of Tranggana/Ahmad Abd al-Arifin, the Demak realm began to fragment again, allowing semi-autonomous Cirebon, Banten, Gresik and Surabaya to become effectively independent principalities. However, in the course of a bloody succession war, Demak's fourth ruler, Susuhunan Prawata, who had studied with both Raden Sahid (Sunan Kalijaga) and Sunan Kudus, presented himself as a protector of Islam. A Portuguese traveller described him as having the ambition of becoming a 'segundo Turco' – a reference to Sulayman the Magnificent (1520–66) and his successes against the Habsburg dynasty in Europe (de Graaf and Pigeaud 1974: 76). However, Prawata was soon assassinated, allegedly at the instigation of his own teacher Sunan Kudus, who is said to have acted out of envy of the ruler's simultaneous mentoring by Sunan Kalijaga.

Generally speaking, the authority of imams of the Demak mosque was more religious than worldly, although there was a clear symbiosis with the rulers through teaching and patronage. In terms of their standing and legitimacy as Muslim rulers, the Demak sultans benefitted from their close associations with multiple *Wali Songo*. While the latter also acquired immediate political significance through their involvement in the founding of other Islamised states, such as Cirebon, Banten and Gresik–Giri, the exploits of *panghulus* such as Sunan Kudus added a martial dimension to their religious reputation. As evinced by his questionable behaviour towards Sunan Prawata, this violent streak was not confined to outward expansion alone. Although Sunan Kudus eventually left Demak, withdrawing from politics and reinforcing his standing as a pious Muslim by founding a new mosque at Kota Tajug, he turned against other religious scholars, or *ulama*, whose viewpoints he considered heretical. Among other things, this resulted in the execution of Seh[8] Lemah Abang and Seh Maolana of Krasak-Malang, as well as the death of a disciple of Seh Jangkung, whose own life was saved by the intervention of Sunan Kalijaga (de Graaf and Pigeaud 1974: 99). The figure of Sunan Kudus foreshadowed a recurring feature in subsequent centuries: a combination of piety and militancy that would often translate into religiously motivated violence.

The mosque established by Sunan Kudus at Kota Tajug was named after him and is still known as Masjid Menara Kudus. Alternatively, it is also referred to as Al-Masjid al-Aqsa. The names refer to Jerusalem – al-Quds in Arabic – and its Al-Aqsa mosque. According to one legend, this is a reference to Sunan Kudus's acquisition of a stone from Jerusalem while making pilgrimage to Mecca. Together with the Demak mosque, Menara Kudus is considered a sacred site with an influence that radiates across the archipelago. It also forms the basis for a separate dynasty of 'saintly lords', styled after the founder's *Wali Songo* title: Sunan Kudus. The word *menara* is also Arabic in origin and refers to the mosque's colossal minaret. Its structure and that of the mosque complex in general are reminiscent of the Hindu *candis* and Buddhist *chedis* found all over Java. It constitutes an example of the cultural fusion that was tolerated by some of the *Wali Songo*; mixing Islamic and pre-Islamic building styles in Javanese mosque or palace (*kraton*) architecture, as well as the employment of an artistic medium like *wayang* (puppet theatre) for the sake of propagating Islam.

Towards the end of the sixteenth century, Demak's political power may have been on the wane, but there are indications that the speed of its demise may have been exaggerated by seventeenth- and eighteenth-century Javanese histo-riographers wanting to enhance the fame of inland principalities such as Pajang, but especially their own patrons: the Mataram dynasty. In search of an ally in its fight against Portuguese Malacca, Aceh still made overtures to Demak in 1584. However, a few years later Demak's sultan had to flee; first seeking refuge in Malacca, before moving to Banten and the protection of its ruling house to which he was related.[9] However, the religious prestige of Demak's central mosque and that of the descendants of the royal house continued to matter well into the nineteenth century.

Aside from Demak and Kudus, there are some other localities along Java's northern coast with *Wali Songo* associations. These include Japara to the north, Cirebon and Banten to the west, and Tuban, Gresik–Giri and Surabaya to the east. Demak's relationship with Japara was symbiotic in nature. While the latter had superior port facilities, it had less easy access to the interior than Demak. During part of the sixteenth century, Japara had a female ruler in the person of Ratu Kali Nyamat, who succeeded her deceased Chinese husband. Childless, she was related to the royal houses of Demak and Banten, becoming a kind of matriarch to both dynasties during her lengthy reign. As the powers of Cirebon and Banten grew, the political influence of Japara declined, and – like Demak and Kudus – it fell victim to the onslaught of the new power that was on the rise in Java's interior: Mataram.

The story of Cirebon and Banten's subsequent Islamisation is tied up with the saint who became known as Sunan Gunung Jati. Different legends give his personal name as Nurullah, Ibn Molana, Maulana Shaykh Madhkur and Sa'id Kamil, but nowadays there is consensus that his proper name was Syarif Hidayatullah. It is said that he originated from Pasai in Aceh (others put him in Egypt), but that after returning from hajj in 1524 he did not go back to his homeland, which was then under threat from the Portuguese, deciding to settle on Java instead. The *Sejarah Banten* reports that, during his studies in Arabia, Sunan Gunung Jati was inducted into the Sufi order of the Kubrawiyya at the hands of Najmuddin al-Kubra (d. 1221) himself (Bruinessen 1994a: 305). The evident temporal discrepancy between the two can perhaps again be explained in the same way as in the case of Mas'ud al-Jawi. De Graaf and Pigeaud surmise that Sunan Gunung Jati's first-hand experience of the incorporation of the *Haramayn* – the holy cities of Islam, Mecca and Medina, both located in West Arabia's Hijaz region – into the Ottoman Empire by Selim I (r. 1512–20) inspired his earlier mentioned investiture of Tranggana as ruler of Demak and his injunction to reign over Demak as a pious Muslim monarch. Not long after that, Sunan Gunung Jati travelled further west to bring Cirebon and Banten into the fold of Islam and to install his sons Pangeran Ratu and Hasanuddin as respective rulers. According to the *Sejarah Banten*, Sunan Gunung Jati remained in Banten until 1552, before finally settling in Cirebon, where he died in 1570 and was buried on 'Teak Mountain' or *Gunung Jati*, from which the saint's posthumous name is derived.

The Banten region covers an area in west Java that also encompassed Sunda Kelapa, at that time the main port serving the inland Sundanese kingdom of Pajajaran. The establishment by Sunan Gunung Jati of an alternative Muslim stronghold for religion and maritime trade in Banten came at Pajajaran's expense and involved a fair degree of coercion and use of force, for which the saint received military support from Demak. To reflect the importance of this event for the Islamic cause, Sunda Kelapa was renamed Jayakarta (Jakarta) – *jaya* meaning 'conquest'. In 1529, Sultan Tranggana of Demak donated a large cannon to Banten, which had been forged by a Portuguese renegade and convert called Zain al-Abidin. Known as *Ki Jimat*, it remained on display in Banten until the early 1900s (de Graaf and Pigeaud 1974: 119). Legend has it that the first Sultan of Banten, Sunan Gunung Jati's son Hasanuddin, then married daughters of both Tranggana of Demak and Sunan Kalijaga, thus giving Banten's royal family a double connection with the *Wali Songo*. While no further incursions were made into the Pajajaran territories of the interior under Hasanuddin, he did expand his influence across the Sunda Straits into Lampung in southern Sumatra, not only for religious but also for economic reasons – namely, to tap into the lucrative pepper trade. However, in 1579, Hasanuddin's son Yusup (Yusuf) went on to conquer the capital of Pajajaran, Pakuwan, located near present-day Bogor (called Buitenzorg during Dutch colonial times), with the assistance of an Arab Muslim scholar named Molana

Joedah. Sixteen years later, his successor Molana Ibrahim perished in an expedition initiated to extend Banten's influence into the Palembang area to the north of Lampung. The comparatively violent way in which Muslim Banten spread its influence has given this sultanate a rather martial reputation and resulted in a more politicised role for its *panghulus*. Family relations aside, this may have contributed to the decision of the last ruler of Demak, Pangeran Mas, to seek refuge in Banten, after an initial exile in Malacca following the conquest of Demak by Mataram. Also in the case of Banten, it is appropriate to note that the title 'sultan' was awarded posthumously to its rulers in chronicles such as the *Sejarah Banten*. The first ruler of Banten to actually receive formal investiture as sultan was Abdul Kadir (Abd al-Qadir) (r. 1596–1651), and this only occurred in 1638, after obtaining the necessary permission from the Grand Sharif of Mecca (Azra 1992: 365; Bruinessen 1995: 167; Ricklefs 2006: 50). By that time this did not mean very much any more in real political terms: Dutch designs to turn Jakarta, now renamed Batavia, into the base of VOC operations, meant that already by 1619 Banten had lost much of its political independence – although it benefitted from Dutch protection against Mataram and threats issuing from Palembang (de Graaf and Pigeaud 1974: 124–5).

Little is known of neighbouring Cirebon's pre-Islamic history, other than that its Sundanese literary culture disappeared as a result of Javanese conquests, not making a comeback until the eighteenth and nineteenth centuries. It makes the Cirebon region a transitional zone of Javanese and Sundanese cultural influences. According to the Portuguese Tomé Pires, Cirebon's original Muslim founders belong to the same Chinese family from which the rulers of Demak also descended. In contrast to Banten, Cirebon's political significance was limited and at the end of the sixteenth century its dynasty was forced to accept the suzerainty of the new political power rising in Java's interior: Mataram. However, the religious prestige attached to its lineage and the presence of Sunan Gunung Jati's shrine made it into an important Islamic centre. By the time Sunan Gunung Jati's direct successor died in 1650(!), a new political actor had appeared on the scene: the Dutch VOC. When the Mataram Sultan of Surakarta (Solo) ceded Cirebon to the Dutch in 1705, the VOC retained Sunan Gunung Jati's descendants as paid regents until the middle of the twentieth century.

Located to the east of Demak, the locality of Tuban features prominently in the *Wali Songo* legends. Sunan Ampel's wife, and the mother of his son Sunan Bonang (the first imam of the Demak mosque), is said to have been a daughter of Tuban's ruler, Adipati Wilatikta. Sunan Bonang was also buried in Tuban and his shrine remains a centre of Islamic worship and pilgrimage.

Further away, facing the island of Madura, are Gresik and Surabaya, two centres of commerce dominated by overseas Chinese since the fourteenth century. As discussed earlier, these places are also the location where the oldest tombstones on Java have been found, as well as of the landfall of the first Muslim preachers. However, it is not possible to establish their exact connection to the later 'sunans of Giri', the title by which the Muslim rulers of Gresik and Surabaya became known during the sixteenth century (de Graaf and Pigeaud 1974: 138). It is again the Portuguese travel writer Tomé Pires who provides the earliest available information about two competing '*patis*' in Gresik around 1500: Cucuf, a scion of the Malacca royal family, who controlled the port, and Zeinall, who was confined to the interior and said to have had good relations with Demak. Javanese sources reporting the appearance of the Muslim preacher Raden Paku, who became known as the eponymous Sunan Giri, all date to the seventeenth and eighteenth centuries. His birth story resonates with that of the biblical (and Qur'anic) Moses: a foundling born to a princess from Java's eastern-most kingdom, Blambangan, and either an Arab scholar or Malaccan prince (depending on which legend one follows). Raden Paku was adopted by a noblewoman from Gresik and then sent to Surabaya to be educated by Sunan Ampel, alongside the latter's son, Sunan Bonang. Upon his return to Gresik, he settled on a mount (Giri), taking the name Prabu Satmata. His decision to build such a retreat ties in with the many holy mountains featuring in pre-Islamic religious lore on Java.

The stories of the second sunan of Giri, Sunan Dalem, also consist mostly of legends, including the transformation of the sunan's pen into a powerful dagger or *kris*, Kalam Munyeng, which was used to fend off a violent attack by Gajah Mada, the chief minister of Majapahit; and a report of his brief interim reign after the fall of Majapahit in 1527. Following the rise of Demak, it seems that Gresik's independence under the sunans of Giri was respected and that it was allowed to flourish until the early seventeenth century. Refraining from interference in central Javanese politics, Gresik's rulers held both political and religious influence throughout the eastern parts of the island. During the lengthy reign of Sunan Prapen, Gresik was involved in both trade and spreading Islam to Lombok, Sumbawa, Bima and what the Dutch called the 'Grote Oost' – the islands scattered between Sulawesi and New Guinea.[10] There are also stories that the sunans of Giri provided religious instruction to Sultan Zain al-Abidin of Ternate (r. 1486–1500) and to a Minangkabau named Dato ri Bandang, who then took the message of Islam to eastern Borneo and to Makassar in southern Sulawesi (de Graaf and Pigeaud 1974: 152–3). Compared with other principalities founded by the *Wali Songo*, such as Cirebon and Kudus, Gresik–Giri's political and economic significance in the eastern parts of Indonesia seems to have been more or less on par with that of Demak in central Java.

Power shift to the interior: the Mataram Empire and Islam
With the demise of Demak, the preponderance of political power shifted back to Java's interior: first to the minor state of Pajang, but in the final decade of the

sixteenth century to the new contender Mataram, which would establish itself in the course of the seventeenth century as the most powerful state in central Java. Mataram's dynastic history is messy, but as increasingly experienced political operators capable of forging ever-changing alliances, its rulers and descendant cadet branches in Yogyakarta and Surakarta have managed to survive centuries of Dutch colonial intervention, a lengthy independence struggle, and postcolonial republicanism – retaining prestige, state support and even recognition of special autonomous status until today.

The groundwork for the rise of Mataram was laid by Panembahan Senapati (also spelled Senopati), who is said to have converted to Islam in 1576 (Ricklefs 2006: 33). Eight years later, he was awarded the title Senapati Ingalaga by the King of Pajang, but in the Javanese traditions he is simply known as Ki Gede Mataram. Supposedly at the instigation of Sunan Kalijaga, one of Ingalaga's first actions was to build a brick defence wall around his palace (de Graaf and Pigeaud 1974: 225). During the next fifteen years, he challenged his former patron and then Pajang's former vassal states, including Cirebon, Demak and Japara, before turning his attention to east Java. Legends attribute the Senapati's successes to the possession of the Anta Kusuma heirloom which was bestowed on the new ruler by descendants of Sunan Kalijaga, who were known as the religious lords of Ngadi Langu.

The real empire builder of Mataram, however, was its third ruler, Hanyakrakusuma, who went into history as Sultan Agung (r. 1613–46) – the 'Great Sultan'. As had been the case with his counterpart in Banten, he was only recognised as Sultan Abdul Muhammad Maulana Matarani toward the end of his reign in 1641, after sending a mission to Mecca and receiving formal authorisation from the sharif (Ricklefs 2006: 51). Between 1625 and 1634, Sultan Agung brought the Pasisir states and the Houses of Sunan Giri and Sunan Ampel in Gresik and Surabaya to heel, usually reconciling with them through intermarriage. As to the ruler's religious inclinations, Javanese chronicles report a pilgrimage to the shrine of Saint Sunan Bayat at Tembayat in 1633 and the creation of a unique *Anno Javanico* – adopting the Islamic lunar months but retaining the numerals of the Javanese Saka year calendar (Ricklefs 2006: 39).[11] These indigenous sources also retain 'prominent features of pre-Islamic origins', including the sultan's mystical marriage with Ratu Kidul, the Goddess of the Southern Sea. Ricklefs characterises Sultan Agung as a 'reconciler' between early Javanese religious beliefs and Islam, but the evidence for the latter depends largely on a body of eighteenth-century texts composed on the occasion of the centennial of his Tembayat pilgrimage, and which will be discussed in more detail below (Ricklefs 2006: 43). In fact, it is contemporaneous Dutch sources that describe him as a pious Muslim who attended the mosque.

In the decades after Sultan Agung's death in 1646, the situation in Mataram became increasingly chaotic. More often than not proponents of Islam, or –

perhaps more accurately – rulers and noblemen intent on upholding their own credentials as pious Muslims, were in outright opposition to the Mataram royals. Until 1680, Agung's successors Amangkurat I (1646–77) and Amangkurat II (1677–1703) were confronted by a formidable alliance consisting of Trunajaya, the ruler of West Madura; Raden Kajoran, the keeper of the Sunan Bayat Shrine; and the sunans from the Gresik–Surabaya area. Having killed most of his opponents, Amangkurat II took possession of the Kris Pusaka Kalam Munyeng and declared an end to the rebellion, which 'the *babads* described as holy war (*sabilolah, aprang sabil*)' (Ricklefs 2006: 65). From the 1660s until 1682, Banten too was causing trouble, up to the point when the Dutch VOC intervened by sending its ruler Sultan Ageng (Tirtayasa) and his religious mentor Shaykh Yusuf of Makassar into exile on Sri Lanka. This brings Ricklefs to the conclusion: 'That so much of the anti-Mataram rebellion rested upon Islamic appeals is testimony to the progress of Islam as a definer of identity in the Javanese heartland' (Ricklefs 2006: 67).

However, also during the next half a century, as a result of continuous dynastic infighting and the compromising impact of the dependency of rulers and claimants to the throne on VOC support, the Mataram rulers' actual relationship with Islam remained ambiguous. During the course of five consecutive reigns, Islam was mobilised for political purposes during two Javanese succession wars, occurring in 1703–8 and 1719–23 respectively. In both instances, foreign Muslim preachers of allegedly Arab extraction were considered as key instigators. Encik Abdullah, who claimed to be a Meccan shaykh and who sided with the perpetrator of a massacre of VOC officers at the *kraton* in 1686, was krissed to death by Commander Govert Cnoll in 1708.[12] A wandering Hadhrami *sayyid*, named Maqallawi, was killed in a stand-off with the VOC in the Mataram capital of Kartasura during the 1719 celebrations of the Prophet Muhammad's birthday – *Mawlid al-Nabi* in Arabic, *Garebeg Mulud* in Javanese. During these decades of chaos and confusion, the Mataram *pusakas* or sacred heirlooms went missing. Upon his surrender, Amangkurat III had handed over fakes to the VOC, and the originals were only returned to Java in 1737 by his descendants after the ruler's death during his exile in Sri Lanka.

The formation of an Islamic intellectual tradition in Indonesia

In the previous chapter we saw how a revised date for the death of Hamzah Fansuri, whose work is considered the oldest surviving example of a developing Malay-Muslim writing culture, pushes the emergence of a Southeast Asian Islamic cultural and intellectual tradition further back in time. What is known about Fansuri's life from his writings also makes clear that this literature is not a local product in the sense that it is not the outcome of experiences that are culturally or geographically confined to Southeast Asia, but rather the result of extensive travel and wide-ranging cultural interactions. Combined with occasional anecdotal evidence of the even earlier existence of figures such as Mas'ud al-Jawi, this would mean that Southeast Asian participation in Islamic intellectual networking is much older than what can be learned from the advances made since the 1990s in mapping these connections and analysing the resulting body of texts, because these data only go back to the seventeenth and eighteenth centuries. Fansuri's death in 1527 would also make him a contemporary of some of Java's *Wali Songo* – provided the dates relevant to their life stories can be relied upon in the first place. However, apart from a few sixteenth-century texts, in the case of Java, the parallel development of a Javanese Islamic literature has only survived in eighteenth-century texts that are presented as recompositions of earlier versions from a century or more before. Here too, notwithstanding the abundance of Javanese cultural tropes, the substance of the narratives is derived from the traditions of the wider Muslim world, thus creating a new genre of Javanese religious writing.

These emerging Indonesian Muslim writing cultures are not only of literary interest, they are also media for the introduction of Islamic learning – doctrinal, philosophical, legal, spiritual and otherwise – to Indonesia, and its subsequent further adaptation and development through the transmission of indigenous interpretations and engagement with the resulting tradition. Aside from a linguistic-literary medium, this also required an institutional infrastructure, consisting of an education system, Sufi orders and other means for facilitating this intellectual networking both across space and over time.

Emergent Muslim writing cultures in Indonesia

Students of Malay-Muslim literature, such as Anthony Johns, underscore the distinction between the 'crude' Malay chronicles of Sumatra and the much richer Javanese accounts (Johns 1963: 46). Such differences are an indication of the varying modalities at work in the Indo-Malay Archipelago. The richness of the Javanese chronicle traditions, as well as their dimension of what Alatas calls the 'fantastic', are 'of great significance both in themselves and as evidence of acculturation' (Alatas 1997: 32; Johns 1963: 46). Johns also adds the observation that this significance must be seen more in terms of what it tells us of the Javanese worldview, its 'cosmic classifications', and the consequences for the integration of Islam in Javanese society, rather than as an evaluation of concrete historiography (Johns 1961: 150)

Syed Naguib al-Attas's research into the earliest period of Malay-Muslim – or *Jawi* – writing forms part of his theoretical work on Southeast's Islamisation and his argument that its origins lie in West Asia. It also constitutes a counternarrative to the – in his view – disproportionate amount of attention paid to Java by especially earlier Dutch Indonesianists, which appears to have been a constant irritant to him. Based on his literary-historical investigations, al-

Attas argues that the affinities between the literary traditions of the Arabs and Persians and the emergent Malay-Muslim literature provide convincing evidence for an Islamisation process that directly connects insular Southeast Asia with Muslim West Asia, making him the strongest advocate of the 'Arab theory' of Islamisation (Azra 1992: 33). This theory is grounded in a 'history of ideas as seen through the changing concepts of key terms in Malay language in the 10th/16th and 11th/17th centuries', using primary materials in Malay 'of a literary nature in the fields of religious law and jurisprudence (*shariʿah* and *fiqh*), philosophy or rational theology and metaphysics (*ʿilm al-kalām* and *tasawwwuf*)' (Attas 1969: 1).

Based on these studies, al-Attas contends that the influence of Islamic concepts on Malay culture has been greater than that of the earlier Indic traditions, claiming that in translations from the Hindu and Buddhist religious literatures, 'the philosophical expositions, so important in the original, suffered great neglect' (Attas 1969: 3). In the case of Islam, the coming of the Qur'an to Southeast Asia had a tremendous impact on Malay culture. The effects of this influence were threefold; instilling an awareness of the importance of language; stimulating a tendency towards a greater clarity of language; and effecting a transition from oral to written literary traditions. This attention to the linguistic, literary and philosophical implications of the coming of Islam serves also as a correction of what he considers the manifestly erroneous tendencies of historians and other scholars to reduce the revolutionary changes brought about by Islam to external phenomena, namely commercial, political or artistic motivations.

Using the work of Hamzah Fansuri as a case study, the important contributions by al-Attas emphasise both the formal and substantive aspects of Arab and Persian Muslim influences on the development of a Malay literary and Islamic intellectual tradition. His discussions of Arabic and Persian prosody feed into an argument for Hamzah Fansuri as the originator of the Malay *shaʿir* (from *shiʿr*, the Arabic for 'poetry') as a distinct poetic form, thus 'establishing a new name for a new *genre*' (Attas 1968: 37).[13] Braginsky and Riddell emphasise the appropriation of Arabic-Persian prosody into Malay poetry as part of a translation process, whereby literal translations from the Arabic original into Malay, through active interventions by representatives of the recipient culture, progressed towards a remarkable transformation and intermixing of religious and literary traditions.

The repeated emphasis placed by al-Attas on what he calls the 'rationalistic' aspects of the substance of Islamic thought stand in strange contrast to the overwhelming mystical and theosophist contents of Hamzah Fansuri's *oeuvre*, which are best articulated and systematised in his prose works: *Asrar al-ʿarifin* ('The Secrets of the Gnostics'), *Sharab al-ʿashiqin* ('The Drink of Lovers') and *Al-Muntahi* ('The Adept') (Attas 1969: 21, 30, 809). To my mind, the allegedly 'tremendous influence of the *Shayku'l-Akbar – the Doctor Maximus* among the Sūfīs

– Muhyi'l-Dīn ibnu'l-ʿArabī of Spain (638/1240)', as well as 'the marked influ-ence of the thoughts and ideas of ʿAbdu'l-Karīm al-Jīlī (832/1428)', highlighted by al-Attas, are at odds with rationalist strands of Islamic thinking drawing on the Aristotelian tradition, as represented by a figure such as Ibn Rushd, who had little regard for either the theological approaches of al-Ghazali or what he con-sidered the obscurantism of ancient philosophers (Attas 1968: 54–5).[14] Be that as it may, the impact of the theosophies of Ibn al-ʿArabi and al-Jili's thinking – especially the earlier mentioned notion of the 'Unity of Being' or *wahdat al-wujud*, which is central to what is also referred to as *Akbari* thought – continued to be reflected in later Malay-Muslim writing. It would become the subject of fierce intellectual debates in seventeenth-century Aceh. Before turning to these debates, it is opportune to first briefly survey parallel literary developments taking place on Java.

Early evidence of a Muslim writing culture on Java is limited to three texts that date from the sixteenth century. The date of the next surviving body of texts can only be traced to the third decade of the eighteenth century, although the authors are adamant that their writings are based on preceding texts dating back almost 100 years. Two of the sixteenth-century Javanese texts were brought back to Europe by the first Dutch expedition to Indonesia in 1597. While this is certain proof of their existence at the end of the sixteenth century, a key author-ity on Javanese Islamic literature, Merle Ricklefs, notes that 'their age at that point and their provenance is uncertain' (Ricklefs 2006: 21).

The Islamic discourse of the first text, called a *primbon* or divination almanac, evinces the influx of Arabic words, technical terms and expressions into the Javanese vocabulary (Drewes 1954). Their occurrence side by side with Javanese jargon suggests an 'accommodation between older and newer religious concepts in Java' (Ricklefs 2006: 23). The second treatise has become known under the title of *The Admonitions of Seh Bari* (Drewes 1969). While its linguistic and cultural context is Javanese, the 'intellectual frame of reference is [. . .] wholly Islamic', because it consists of the denunciation of false doctrines that are all Islamic in origin, including esotericism (*batiniyya*), Qarmatian doctrines and writings by Ibn al-ʿArabi (Ricklefs 2006: 23). The origins and age of the third text are much less certain, as the existing document is a copy from 1860. It has been presented under the title *An Early Javanese Code of Muslim Ethics* by the same editor as the other two (Drewes 1978).

Widening and deepening Islamic learning

The levels of sophistication in these early surviving instances of an emergent Islamic discourse show that, by that time, maritime Southeast Asia was already well integrated into the intellectual networks of the wider Muslim world. As the forward post in the Indian Ocean zone, by the early seventeenth century

Aceh in particular had established a reputation as a centre of Islamic learning, to which scholars flocked; not only from other places further east in the archipelago, but also from the west.

Debating theosophy in Aceh: *wahdat al-wujud* vs *wahdat al-shuhud*

The reigns of Aceh's *roi soleil*, Iskandar Muda, and his successor were not only the heyday of the sultanate's political fortunes, but during that time the court was also the scene of vibrant religious and intellectual activities, including debates concerning the controversial doctrine of *wahdat al-wujud* or 'Unity of Being', which came to a climax in the 1630s.[15]

Wahdat al-wujud is at one and the same time an emanation theory of realities with echoes of the Neoplatonist Plotinus, as well as an inverse path of spiritual attainment for Sufis, culminating in a mystical experience of ultimate truth. There are two strands to the theosophical theory: one distinguishing five grades of Being, traceable to Ibn al-ᶜArabi and al-Jili; and a later one structured around seven stages, attributed to the Indian scholar Muhammad Fadl Allah al-Burhanpuri (d. 1620). While Hamzah Fansuri's writings contain references to the five stages associated with Ibn al-ᶜArabi, those of his alleged disciple, Shams al-Din al-Sumatrani or Shamsuddin of Pasai (1575–1630), subscribe to al-Burhanpuri's seven stages – the doctrine that became known as *martabat tujuh* (seven stages or grades). Not much is known of Shams al-Din's life other than that he held a very senior position at the Aceh court, including that of *Shaykh al-Islam* during the reign of Iskandar Muda, whom he reportedly initiated into the order of Naqshbandiyya Sufism. He is best remembered for his major work, *Miᶜrat al-Muᶜminin*, which contains the most detailed discussion of the seven-graded Unity of Being (Riddell 2001: 110–11). It is surmised that the substitution of Fansuri's version, based on Ibn al-ᶜArabi and al-Jili's five stages, was a result of the influence of a text written around 1590 by al-Burhanpuri, entitled, *Al-Tuhfa al-mursala ila ruh al-nabi* or *The Gift Addressed to the Spirit of the Prophet*.[16] Containing a detailed explanation of al-Jili's theory of the 'Unity of Being', with an alternative breakdown into seven stages, this text began exercising great influence on South and Southeast Asian Muslim scholarly circles around the turn of the sixteenth to seventeenth century. Also it has been suggested that the difference between Fansuri's five- and Shams al-Din's seven-stage theosophies could be explained by the revised date of Fansuri's death in 1527, which creates the temporal distance during which al-Jili's theory was adapted by al-Burhanpuri and then left its mark on Shams al-Din's writings of the early seventeenth century.[17]

Highlighting the relation between the *wahdat al-wujud* and *insan kamil*, in both his original works and commentaries on the poetry of Hamzah Fansuri, Shams al-Din al-Sumatrani's writings suited Iskandar Muda's desire to enhance the perceptions of his kingship. Operating under his patronage, the influence of

Fansuri and al-Sumatrani's ideas thus received official sanction on the part of the ruler. However, this was not to continue after the sultan's death, with the arrival of Nur al-Din al-Raniri (d. 1658) at the court of his successor Iskandar al-Thani.

While Nur al-Din's *nisba* of al-Raniri refers to the town of Ranir in Gujarat, this scholar was actually of Hadhrami descent and a member of the Hamid clan – whose familial ties criss-crossed the Indian Ocean, connecting Yemen to the Hijaz, Gujarat, the Maldives and Aceh (Laffan 2011: 17). However, al-Raniri had a double connection with South Arabia's Hadhramaut through his initiation into Sufism at the hands of another Hadhrami scholar, Sayyid Umar al-Aydarusi (Riddell 2001: 116; Azra 2004: 54). Although he spent only seven years (1637–44) at the Aceh court, he left an indelible mark – not least because of his challenge of Shams al-Din al-Sumatrani's understanding of *wahdat al-wujud* as heretical. Al-Raniri's objections are laid down in a treatise entitled *Hujjat al-siddiq li-dafᶜ al-zindiq* as well as other texts. All these have been very influential, even leading to the burning of Shams al-Din's writings. Although the details need not detain us, the focal point of al-Raniri's critique revolves around the distinction that must be made between two groups of *wujudiyya* adepts: one group, which includes Ibn al-ᶜArabi, regards the Being of God as that upon which all other beings depend for their existence.[18] According to this group, this represents a true – and therefore, orthodox – Unity of Being. The other group conflates the existence of these other beings with God's Being, claiming that nothing exists but God. This constitutes a heresy, to which – according to al-Raniri – both Fansuri and Shams al-Din had succumbed.[19]

Al-Raniri's critique foreshadows the influences of Islamic reformist ideas about tolerable and unacceptable forms of learned Sufism (*tasawwuf*) expressed in the dichotomy between *wahdat al-wujud* and *wahdat al-shuhud* – 'unity in witnessing'. Advocating a tempered form of Islamic mysticism, the latter is often referred to as 'Neo-Sufism'.[20] A possible early connection with Egypt and the mosque-university of al-Azhar, signalled by Michael Laffan, also offers further insight into how the *wujudiyya* debate is embedded in intellectual developments involving the wider Muslim world. As mentioned earlier, trade connections between Southeast Asia and the Arabic-speaking parts of the Muslim world had also resulted in the adoption of Ayyubid and Mamluk regal styles. There is also evidence of the hosting of Egyptian scholars by the Aceh court in the sixteenth century. In 1643, al-Raniri was ousted from his position at the Aceh court following the arrival of an ethnic Minangkabau named Sayf al-Rijal (d. 1653), who was a student of one of the victims of al-Raniri's inquisition – a local scholar named Kamal al-Din. Sayf al-Rijal also called himself Sayf al-Din al-Azhari. Such events suggest an initial opening up of Aceh to scholarly debates that had been emerging in Cairo from the sixteenth century onward around the Sufi interpretations by Ibn al-ᶜArabi's followers, who were referred to as the *muhaqqiqun* or 'men of realisation'. These debates were the result of the double influence of Persian ideas carried by Kurdish and Azeri scholars fleeing the expanding Shi'i Safavid state and of the work of early logicians from the Arab West introduced by Moroccan scholars, like Muhammad ibn Yusuf al-Sanusi (d. 1495). Confronted with the dangers of 'ignorant pseudo-Sufis' engaging with theosophical ideas they could not comprehend, Cairo's scholarly scene responded by advocating the 'orthodox' rigour vested in Egyptian juridical authority that underpinned institutionalised *tarīqā* Sufism, which 'had become a crucial part of the social fabric under Ottoman rule' (Laffan 2011: 15). These ideas now also travelled to Southeast Asia through al-Sanusi's Sufi primer, *Umm al-barahin* ('Mother of Signs') and responses to queries from Acehnese Muslims by, for example, Muhammad al-Manufi (d. 1663). There they would continue to circulate in the *jawi* world through sustained scholarly networking in the centuries to come.

The Acehnese *wujudiyya* polemic was not the only instance of Indonesian debates featuring accusations of heresy. One of the most well-known stories circulating on Java involves the inquisition of Seh Siti Jenar by the full assembly of the *Wali Songo* and his subsequent execution at the hands of Sunan Kalijaga personally.[21] Also set on Java is a report in an eighteenth-century text about another Islamic teacher facing charges of heterodoxy, which will be discussed in more detail below.[22]

Aside from his involvement in the *wujudiyya* debate, other writings by al-Raniri, including *Sirat al-Mustaqim* and *Bustan al-Salatin*, evince broad religious learning in other disciplines than *tasawwuf*, encompassing law and theology, as well as politics and history. His *Sirat al-Mustaqim* is still used in Indonesian Islamic schools as a reference work on Islamic ritual, while *Bustan al-Salatin* is not only valuable for the history of Aceh, but also functions as a 'mirror of princes' (Riddell 2001: 117–19). The catholicity of al-Raniri's learning, including a familiarity with religious renewal (*tajdid*), prefigures the contributions of the next important scholar from northern Sumatra, Abd al-Ra'uf al-Singkili (1615–93).

Wandering students and itinerant scholars

Al-Singkili's significance lies not just in his prominent position in Aceh, but perhaps even more in his reputation as a scholarly networker acquiring religious knowledge that was both wide and profound, through decades of travel and study at centres of Islamic learning across the Muslim world.

Syed Naguib al-Attas's philological studies and Anthony Johns's work on the role of Sufis in the spread of Islam, as well his introduction of the concept of the Indian Ocean as an Arabic-speaking Mediterranean, have been very important for raising scholarly awareness of the significance of networking in the dissemination of Islamic learning in Indonesia, while the more recent discoveries by the duos Guillot–Kalus and Feener–Laffan provide tantalising indications that these connections may actually be centuries older. Maintaining such a shared Islamic tradition depends not only on individual and communal scholarly effort, but also on established mechanisms of authorisation and transmission. Insight into these matters has greatly benefitted from the mapping of these *ulama* networks in the seventeenth and eighteenth centuries by Azyumardi Azra and Peter Riddell. Their findings not only provide the architecture of the lines of transmission, they also evince that mystical traditions of trans-regional Sufi orders were complemented by other disciplines of Islamic learning, thus forging a cohesive and integral Muslim society in Southeast Asia. Azra's painstakingly detailed collection of data on the biographies and scholarly production of the participants in these networks has also advanced the knowledge about how Islamic renewal, reformism and – eventually – modernism reached insular Southeast Asia.

Following the establishment of Ottoman control over Egypt and the Hijaz, the security situation in the Western Indian Ocean and Red Sea also improved, allowing hajj traffic to intensify. Numerically, the Muslims from Southeast Asia soon formed the most important contingent in the increasing numbers of hajj pilgrims and expatriate students in the Haramayn. While Hamzah Fansuri, Shams al-Din al-Sumatrani and Nur al-Din a-Raniri all spent time in Mecca and Medina, with Abd al-Ra'uf al-Singkili, more sustained and verifiable documentary evidence of the presence of *jawi* scholars become available in terms of both their studies and their own innovative contributions.

Probably of mixed Arab–Malay origin and a native of Singkil near Barus, Abd al-Ra'uf ibn Ali al-Fansuri al-Singkili left Sumatra around 1642, not to return for almost twenty years.[23] On his way to the Hijaz, he studied briefly in Qatar, followed by several years in Bayt al-Faqih and Zabid in Yemen, before arriving in Mecca and finally settling in Medina.[24] In Medina two scholars were of particular significance, not just for al-Singkili's career, but for the expansion of Islamic learning among the *jawi* Muslims in general. Ahmad al-Qushashi (d. 1660) and his student and disciple Ibrahim al-Kurani (1614–90) gave real momentum to the scholarly nexus between West and Southeast Asia. While al-Qushashi's fame rested on his reputation as a Maliki jurist, shaykh of the Shattariyya order and initiate in several other *tarekat*, al-Kurani was regarded as an all-round genius, considered by many of his peers as the *mujaddid* or renewer of the eleventh century of the Islamic era (Azra 2004: 18).[25] Al-Kurani's influence was not limited to completing al-Singkili's training in Sufism following the latter's initiation by al-Qushashi into the Shattariyya and Qadiriyya orders. In order to resolve the confusion affecting Muslims in Aceh in the wake of al-Raniri's attacks on Hamzah Fansuri and Shams al-Din, al-Kurani also wrote an influential commentary on Burhanpuri's *Gift Addressed to the Spirit of the Prophet*, possibly at the personal behest of al-Singkili.[26]

Both al-Qushashi and al-Kurani are considered as exponents of the earlier mentioned Neo-Sufism. This 'rapprochement between the shari'ah-oriented

ʿulamāʾ (more specifically, the fuqahāʾ) and the Sūfīs' forms in Azra's opinion a 'salient feature' in seventeenth- and eighteenth-century scholarly networking (Azra 2004: 33). Al-Singkili also subscribed to this more sober form of Sufism advocated by his teachers. In his own writings on the subject he too rejected the strand of *wujudiyya* condemned by al-Raniri as heretical, while a commentary he wrote on Ibn al-ʿArabi evinces the influence that al-Kurani exercised on his thinking. The reconciliation between the study of Islamic law (*fiqh*) and mysticism (*tasawwuf*) is also reflected in al-Singkili's preoccupation with wider Islamic learning. He was the first Muslim scholar from Indonesia to produce a work on *fiqh muʿamalat* – Islamic law dealing with the domain of Muslim daily life as opposed to acts of worship. In addition, he is the author of *Tarjuman al-mustafid*, the first Malay commentary (*tafsir*) on the complete Qur'an, mainly drawing on the *Jalalayn* of al-Mahalli (d. 1459) and al-Suyuti (d. 1505). In terms of building his own following in Indonesia, among al-Singkili's most important disciples are the 'Tuanku of Ulakan' – a Minangkabau known as Burhanuddin (1646–92) – and the west Javanese Shaykh Abd al-Muhyi.[27] Ending his days as a leading scholar in Aceh, al-Singkili is remembered as the 'Shaykh of *Kuala*' – a reference to his shrine near the Kuala Aceh or 'Aceh River' (Azra 2004: 85–6).

While al-Singkili was a kind of *Homo universalis* or Renaissance Man, his contemporary Yusuf al-Maqassari (1626/7–99) was mainly interested in Sufism, although he is primarily remembered as a political intrigant due to his earlier mentioned involvement in the Banten rebellion of the early 1660s. As a militant Sufi he prefigures individuals such as Usman dan Fodio (1754–1817) of the West African Sokoto Caliphate, the Dagestani Imam Shamil (1797–1871) and Sudan's Muhammad Ahmad al-Mahdi (1845–85). Probably a native of Makassar, Shaykh Yusuf brought Sulawesi into the orbit of Islamising Indonesia. After initial studies on Borneo, he married into the royal family of Gowa in South Sulawesi, only to leave again for Aceh, with the intention of studying with al-Raniri. Because the latter had already left Aceh, Yusuf al-Maqassari continued his journey to Gujarat in order to catch up with Aceh's former Shaykh al-Islam. It is claimed he became the first Indonesian to be initiated in the Qadariyya order – allegedly by al-Raniri himself. From Gujarat, he probably continued on Singkili's trail to Zabid in Yemen, Mecca and then Medina, where he too joined the circle of al-Qushashi and al-Kurani. Along the way he added inductions into the Naqshabandiyya, Ba al-ʿAlawiyya and Shattariyya to his repertoire of *tarekat* initiations (Feener 1998/9: 118–19). Laffan suggests that this spiritual-intellectual trajectory connects al-Maqassari to the earlier mentioned *muhaqqiqun* (Laffan 2011: 20). Unlike al-Singkili, Yusuf al-Maqassari did not immediately return to Indonesia, but travelled first to Damascus to study with Khalwatiyya shaykhs. In due course, this resulted in the emergence of a Khalwatiyya-Yusuf Sufi branch in al-Maqassari's native Sulawesi (Bruinessen 1991: 251).

Probably returning to Indonesia sometime between 1664 and 1672, al-Maqassari did not return to his home country of Gowa, because he was sceptical of the sultan's support for the Islamic cause, opting instead to settle in Banten, where he had been before. Joining the circle of Sultan Ageng Tirtasaya by marrying one of his daughters, he was not only involved in introducing Sufi teachings, but also became caught up in the earlier sketched rebellion against the VOC.[28] Arrested in 1683, he was initially sent into exile in Sri Lanka, but when the Dutch noticed that this did not stop al-Maqassari from continuing his machinations by passing on writings via visiting pilgrims, he was moved to their Cape colony in 1693, where attempts to isolate him failed again. In fact, Yusuf al-Maqassari is still celebrated by South African Muslims for bringing Islam to the Cape (Feener 1998/9). Initially buried at Faure in 1699, his body was transferred to Gowa in 1705 – making al-Maqassari a Sufi saint with shrines in both Sulawesi and South Africa.

With Sulawesi now firmly embedded into the *Dar al-Islam* through Yusuf al-Maqassari's multiple *tarekat* connections, in the course of the eighteenth century the religion also gained a more solid foothold in east Sumatra and southeast Borneo (Laffan 2011: 31). The key figures during this stage in Indonesia's Islamisation process are Abdussamad of Palembang or Abd al-Samad al-Palimbani (c. 1704/19–88/9)[29] and Muhammad Arshad al-Banjari (1710–1812?). Both spent an extraordinarily long time in the Haramayn – in the case of al-Banjari almost thirty-five years, while al-Palimbani stayed even longer, never to return home.

Like Abd al-Raᶜuf al-Singkili, Abd al-Samad al-Palimbani was said to be of Arab ancestry and received a thorough and well-rounded Islamic education. His mystical disposition and studies with Muhammad ibn Abd al-Karim al-Samman (d. 1775), a guardian of the shrine of the Prophet and one of Medina's most influential eighteenth-century scholars, led to al-Palimbani's induction into the new Sufi order founded by al-Samman. Fusing elements of the Qadiriyya, Naqshbandiyya and the North African Shadhiliyya orders with those of the Khalwatiyya, the Sammaniyya is actually considered a sub-branch of the latter, because it is the only lineage, or *silsila*, acknowledged by al-Samman himself – in spite of also having *ijaza* or authorisation to pass on the teachings of other orders into which he had been initiated. This then resulted in the introduction of the Sammaniyya in the Palembang area by Abd al-Samad al-Palimbani's returning students and later in the financing by the Sultan of Palembang of a Sammaniyya lodge (*zawiya*) in Jeddah. Its popularity was not least due to al-Samman's reputation as miracle worker, of which the reports (*manaqib*) were translated into Malay and circulated widely throughout Indonesia (Bruinessen 1994b: 8–9).[30] Aside from his role as a Sufi *khalifa* with authority to induct other adepts into various *tarekat*, al-Palimbani's intellectual significance lies in his contributions to Sufi scholarship; in particular, his reconciliation between the theosophy of Ibn al-ᶜArabi and the tempered Sufism of al-Ghazali. For this purpose, he wrote tracts in both Malay and Arabic. While the former were used as a didactics for wider audiences, the latter dealt with more controversial topics – including Ibn al-ᶜArabi's *Fusus al-hikam* ('Bezels of Wisdom'), al-Jili's *Al-insan al-kamil*, and the writings of al-Burhanpuri and al-Kurani. By writing them in Arabic, al-Palimbani sought to avoid confusing less well-educated Muslims or exposing them to the temptations of heresy (Azra 2004: 131–2).

Abd al-Samad al-Palimbani's contemporary from Borneo, Muhammad Arshad al-Banjari, shared the intellectual-religious outlook of his Sumatran counterpart. Under the patronage of his future father-in-law, Sultan Tahlil Allah (1700–45) of Banjarmasin, al-Banjari went to study in Mecca and Cairo. Upon his return, he wrote – on royal instruction – an expansion of al-Raniri's *Sirat al-Mustaqim* under the title *Sabil al-muhtadin* ('The Path of the Guided'). In contrast to al-Palimbani, al-Banjari never mentions Muhammad Fadl Allah al-Burhanpuri, Shams al-Din al-Sumatrani or Ibrahim al-Kurani, instead relying on 'sober Egyptian scholars such as al-Suyuti and al-Shaᶜrani' (1493–1565). Yet at the same time, like Yusuf al-Maqassari a century before, both al-Palimbani and al-Banjari situated themselves in the 'lineage of the *muhaqqiqun*' (Laffan 2011: 30). This is less contradictory than it may seem because – although critical of the Medinese tradition and opposed to the influx of Persian-Turkish Sufi influences in Egypt – figures like al-Suyuti and al-Shaᶜrani were not averse to Sufism and were in fact themselves initiates in several orders.

By far the most prominent scholar from the Palembang Muslim community, Abd al-Samad al-Palimbani's standing as a prominent scholar in the Muslim world at large is also reflected by his inclusion in Arabic biographical dictionaries.[31] During his lifetime (although he was himself physically absent most of the time), Palembang overtook Aceh as the centre of Islamic learning on Sumatra, while Patani reached a similar position on the Malay Peninsula. Under Sultan Mahmud Badr al-Din (r. 1724–57), Palembang prospered economically thanks to pepper and tin exports, while his successor Ahmad Taj al-Din (r. 1757–74) became an important patron of Islamic learning, sponsoring the translation of Wali Raslan al-Dimashqi's (d. 1145) *Fath al-rahman* ('Triumph of the Merciful') – a text offering an 'accurate expression of the latest form of orthodoxy encountered in Mecca or Cairo' (Laffan 2011: 28).

Finally, it must be noted that, although never actively involved in politics, Abd al-Samad al-Palimbani shared Yusuf al-Maqassari's militant outlook. This becomes clear from his writings on *jihad*. Texts such as *Fada'il al-Jihad* reflect not simply a more radical reformist stance, but also demonstrate al-Palimbani's opposition to Dutch interventions in Indonesia, advocating a decidedly activist stance against colonialism. Azra notes that the leading nineteenth-century scholar of Islam, Christiaan Snouck-Hurgronje, insisted that *Fada'il al-Jihad* has inspired many *jihadi* epistles and pamphlets during the Netherlands' protracted war in Aceh at the end of the nineteenth century (Azra 2004: 140).

Al-Palimbani's anti-colonial interventions were not limited to scholarly writings; as will be seen below, he also wrote letters to rulers with injunctions to fight the European infidels in the name of Islam.

Texts and power at the Mataram court

A century after Aceh's *wujuddiya* debate, the Mataram court on Java was the scene of a comparable but inverse exchange concerning the 'relationship between devout Sufism and Java's rich pre-Islamic cultural heritage' (Ricklefs 2006: 116). It is found in a text called *Serat Cabolek*, of which the oldest existing version only dates to the nineteenth century, but which records a doctrinal debate that took place in Kartasura in 1731. It involved two Islamic scholars, Ketib Anom of Kudus and Kyai Haji Ahmad Mutamakin, in which the latter stands accused of revealing secret knowledge to the uninitiated and is also mocked for his reliance on Arabic texts rather than indigenous and indigenised learning. Although Mutamakin's position was condemned, he was not executed for heresy – as had been the case with Kamal al-Din in Aceh. At the same time, *Serat Cabolek* reflects an implicit acceptance that the wisdom contained in Javanese and originally Indian texts, such as *Bima Suci*, *Arjunawiwaha* and the *Ramayana*, could also be considered *ngelmu* (*ᶜilm* in Arabic), or Islamic mystical knowledge; no less authoritative than scholarship in Arabic. Even though – in the end – Islam was considered the prevailing religious category, there was no question of having to make exclusive choices between cultural and religious loyalties; instead, both influences were absorbed into Javanese Islamic civilisation.

This is also true for four other texts produced around 1730 – although they too are presented as recompositions of earlier versions that allegedly already existed in the time of Sultan Agung. They offer a record of a religious and intellectual condensation which Ricklefs refers to as 'mystic synthesis' (Ricklefs 2006). Written at the direction of Ratu Pakubuwono, the queen dowager dominating the Mataram court after the death of her husband Pakubuwono I in 1719, they were intended to enhance the religious credentials of the latter's successor and grandson, Pakubuwono II.[32]

Although recast in a Javanese cultural setting, the *Carita Sultan Iskandar* and *Carita Yusuf* retell the Qur'anic episodes about Alexander the Great and the biblical figure of Joseph. Used as 'vehicles for uplifting tales of adventure, heroism, beauty, and piety, the two tales [are] peppered with moral and mystical aphorisms' (Ricklefs 2006: 108). After their completion, at the end of 1729, a start was made on the composition of what is the most 'Javanese' work of the quartet. Entitled *Kitab Usulbiyah*, it deals with issues that are without an obvious foundation in the Qur'an and probably also without Malay predecessors, which had provided the basic material for the Iskandar and Yusuf texts. Merle Ricklefs has characterised *Kitab Usulbiyah* as a 'thaumaturgical work [. . .] a powerful magical tool in the campaign to Islamize the *kraton* more fully and thus to perfect it'

(Ricklefs 2006: 115). As Javanese cultural synthesis features more prominently, Islamic orthodoxy recedes into the background. The fourth and final text, *Suluk Garwa Kancana*, is a straightforward work of religious didactics and pedagogy. Also set during the reign of Sultan Agung, its 'reconciliation of Javanese martial traditions of kingship with Islamic traditions of mystic piety' is further evidence of the domestication of Islam at the Mataram court (Ricklefs 2006: 49).

Ratu Pakubuwono had ordered the writing of these texts as a means to assist in moulding her grandson Pakubuwono II (1726–46) into a pious Sufi king. With this objective of perfecting the reign of a Javanese king, the books became *pusakas* – heirlooms with supernatural powers – that were to be closely guarded and could only be handled by qualified individuals, such as Ratu Pakubuwono. Reflecting the simultaneous catholicity and eclecticism of Javanese Sufism, the purport of the texts is captured by a metaphor that likens Arabic and Javanese literature to 'a person's right and left eyes' (Ricklefs 2006: 127).

Javanese religious practice and culture

Aside from stimulating the development of a new indigenous religious literary tradition, the Islamisation of Java also had wider societal effects. As was the case with Muslim state formation, in the interior this process followed its own trajectory, but Java's Muslim population too was increasingly drawn into the networks that connected it to Muslims elsewhere.

One of the most conspicuous elements of the Islamisation of the court was the introduction of select aspects of Islamic law and more ostentatious displays of religious practice. These included the prohibition of gambling for money and the use of opium, while cockfighting continued to be condoned and even the consumption of alcohol was tolerated (the latter featured prominently in maintaining relations with the VOC). However, the enforcement of the Islamic penal code, including the imposition of *hudud*, or death penalties, was reserved for the religious court at the capital only. In 1732, Pakubuwono II also began attending the Friday prayers in the mosque. Prior to that, the ruler's participation in such congregational prayers had been limited to his attendance at court celebrations – once every eight years in the Javanese calendrical cycle – on the occasion of the Prophet's birthday – a festivity known as *Garebeg Mulud Dal*.[33] At the same time, Pakubuwono II was also known to engage in ascetic practices on Gunung Lawu, one of Java's ancient sacred mountains; practices that were maintained under successive, more Islamised, Javanese monarchs of the late eighteenth century.

Little is known to what extent this type of Islamic identity formation and display of piety moved beyond the court into wider Javanese society. However, Ricklefs notes that 'there are hints that the European presence fed Islamically defined xenophobia' (Ricklefs 2016: 123). During the reign of Pakubuwono II, Raden Adipati Natakusuma became the new Islamic strongman at the court. Under his direction, figures such as Kyai Hajji Mataram and Sayyid Alwi – a name suggesting a connection with the Hadhramaut – were admitted to the court as part of the prince's entourage. Although their exact credentials remain obscure, they did obtain influential religious positions and created a fair amount of suspicion among VOC officials. Between 1741 and 1743 it seemed as if the Muslim camp would emerge victorious from the power struggle at an increasingly disintegrated Mataram court. After ejecting Sayyid Alwi and Hajji Mataram from his court and making amends with the VOC, which exiled many of the Islamic agitators to Sri Lanka and South Africa, the embattled Pakubuwono II's final years coincided with the beginning of a third and protracted Javanese succession war (1746–57). Its eventual outcome was a split of Mataram into the Sultanates of Yogyakarta and Surakarta, agreed by the 1755 treaty of Giyanti between the VOC, Prince Mangkubumi and Raden Mas Suryadi – who would go on to reign as Sultan Hamengkubuwono I (r. 1749–92) and Susuhunan Pakubuwono III (r. 1749–88) respectively – though hostilities dragged on for another two years. An accompanying feature of this partition of Mataram was a parallel split of power within Surakarta between the susuhunans and a junior lineage of princes known as the House of Mangkunegoro.

It was the ruler of newly established Yogyakarta, Hamengkubuwono I, who emerged from this power struggle as the most important Javanese ruler of the late eighteenth century. The first monarch since Sultan Agung to again use the title 'sultan', his reign also constituted a new stage in Java's ongoing Islamisation process. However, at the same time it is important to remain aware of the enduring relevance of the 'variety in Javanese religious sensibilities' (Ricklefs 2006: 156). For example, in the courtly writing tradition that had developed under the direction of Ratu Pakubuwono, during the second part of Hamengkubuwono's reign, his son and later successor oversaw the writing of the *Raja Surya* – according to Merle Ricklefs, 'the most spiritually potent book of Mangkubumi's reign' (Ricklefs 2006: 160). Also it is said that one of his daughters possessed a Javanese version of al-Burhanpuri's *Gift Addressed to the Spirit of the Prophet* (Ricklefs 2006: 164). In Surakarta, the title holder of the junior lineage, Prince Mangkunegoro I (r. 1757–95), rose to grow into the most 'publicly pious figure among the late-eighteenth-century elite' and a staunchly Islamic competitor of the susuhunan (Ricklefs 2006: 165). This is partly attributed to the influence exercised by one of his wives, who descended from the caretakers of the Muslim shrine at Tembayat. At the same time, the links with pre-Islamic religious sites and associated practices were also retained in Surakarta, even though Java became increasingly integrated into the Islamic networks that connected Muslim Indonesia with other parts of the Muslim world.

Amidst these variegating styles of Islamising Java, it seems that self-identification as 'Muslim' grew increasingly firm, developing into a religious identity without any 'serious alternative' (Ricklefs 2006: 155). Earlier mentioned Malay-speaking figures of great standing and leading initiates in multiple Sufi orders, such as Abd al-Samad al-Palimbani and Muhammad Arshad al-Banjari, also played a role in bringing the Javanese-speaking heartlands of central and east Java under the sway of more sober forms of Sufism and within the ambit of wider Islamic religious learning. In addition, scholars such as al-Palimbani directed their calls to defend the Islamic faith against the infidel colonisers to the three Muslim rulers in Yogyakarta and Surakarta.[34]

In the wake of such admonitions, another prince from Surakarta's Mangkunegoro dynasty, Wiryakusuma, began profiling himself as a distinctly Islamic ruler after his return from exile in South Africa. In the subsequent chronicles of his reign, he is referred to as a *waliyolah* – or 'friend of God' – that is to say a saint – who acquired the *ngelmu* (religious knowledge) of kingship from various religious teachers (Ricklefs 2006: 182). A spiritual seeker all his life, after ascending the throne of Surakarta as Pakubuwono IV (1788–1820), he began replacing the old court officials 'with his new favourites, collectively known as *santris* – "students of religion"' (Ricklefs 2006: 175).[35] Within this segment of the Muslim populace, a certain hierarchy can be discerned. At the top stood the teacher-scholars, known as *kyai* or *guru*. Next came those who had performed the pilgrimage to Mecca and were now referred to as *hajji*.[36] Then there were the lower-ranking religious officials in villages who were called *kaum*. The lowest rung on this ladder was occupied by the *pradikan* or *perdikan*– residents of pious villages in specially designated tax-exempt areas (Carey 2014: 19).

While it has been suggested that this signalled a very early influence of the Arabian reformer Muhammad ibn Abd al-Wahhab (1703–92) in Java, this seems very doubtful, not least because the *santris* continued to engage in shrine visits and laying claims to supernatural powers – practices that are roundly rejected in Ibn Abd al-Wahhab's puritan interpretation of Islam that came to be referred to as Wahhabism. Corroborative evidence can also be gleaned from a Javanese text called *Wicara Cras*, in which Pakubuwono IV's *santri* entourage is depicted as a deviant group associated with the Shattariyya order. The *kraton* elite in Surakarta also engaged in the same practice as Ratu Pakubuwono of composing religious texts as magically empowered heirlooms. Thus, in 1791, court scribes began producing new versions of the *Carita Iskandar* and *Carita Yusuf*. Creating a third instance in which Islamic texts were mobilised for their supernatural powers, the stage was set for the next phase in the Islamisation of Indonesia – characterised by concerted efforts to use Islam as a means of resistance against existing indigenous power structures and to counter increasingly intrusive European colonial interventions, leading to the formation of a political entity, and an alternative oppositional model, that begin to resemble what is presently known as Indonesia.

Islamic education and learning: institution and curriculum

Aside from tempering Sufism, while at the same time calling on Muslim rulers
to resist infidel schemes for political dominance in Southeast Asia's Muslim territories, Abd al-Samad al-Palimbani and Muhammad Arshad al-Banjari were
also instrumental to the development of an indigenous Islamic education system
in Indonesia – in terms of both institutions and curriculum formation. The
vehicle through which this curriculum was transmitted is what the Javanese
call *pesantren* and the Malays refer to as *pondok*.[37] This 'Islamic boarding school'
is a typical Southeast Asian institution, which – along with the Sufi *tarekat* – has
been the key medium for carrying Islamic learning into rural peasant milieus.
VOC monopolisation of especially external trade combined with the surveillance of travelling Muslims presented a combination of economic and religious
restrictions that drove Islam from cities into the countryside. With rural *pesantren*
becoming the new centres of religious learning, the Islamisation of Indonesia's
agrarian societies was able to gain pace, because it largely took place beyond the
gaze of the colonisers. As the power base of the *ulama*, who consider themselves
the 'Heirs of the Prophet', the *pesantren* milieu became Indonesia's custodian of a
tradition of Islamic learning preserved by the so-called *Ahl al-Sunna wa'l-Jamaᶜa*
('People of the Tradition and Community', in Indonesian also often rendered as
Ahlussunnahwaljamaah). Since then, the *pesantren* have functioned as incubators for
generations of Muslim leaders and intellectuals, including the first democratically elected president.

This '*pesantren* world' continues to exist today and remains an important component of now partly urbanised 'networks of agrarian Islam' (Lombard 1990:
II, 110). Although there is anecdotal evidence from European sources for the
existence of Islamic schools in the seventeenth and possibly even the sixteenth
centuries as far east as Makassar and Ternate, the first mention of *pesantren* on
Java date only to the first half of the eighteenth century. However, even then a
specialist like Merle Ricklefs remains suspicious of the claim 'that Pakubuwana
II later established the great pesantren of Tegalsari, near Pomogoro, in quest of
renewed spiritual power after his defeat in 1740' – during the war of the VOC
against expatriate Chinese, which also included a substantial Muslim contingent
(Laffan 2011: 26). Oral histories from Banjarmasin relate the establishment of
an 'Islamic educational institution' by Muhammad Arshad al-Banjari and his
Bugi colleague Abd al-Wahhab al-Bugisi (Azra 2004: 119). This has led Michael
Laffan to surmise that the establishment of this educational complex may have
been inspired by the founders' acquaintance with the *madrasa* of Cairo during
their studies in Egypt (Laffan 2011: 30).

Although most present-day *pesantren* were founded relatively recently, they
still betray a set of features from the past, which also point up some similarities
with pre-Islamic religious learning and practice in Indonesia, often of Indian
origin. There is fragmentary evidence from the Majapahit time of the existence

of ashram-like retreats for indigenous asceticism (called *tapa* in Javanese or *peta-paan* in Malay). Like the *pesantren*, these were located away from populated areas and structured around a paternal relation between the teacher (*guru* or *kyai*) and the student (*murid*). Finally, the *pesantren* world also emulated another India-inspired phenomenon: the figure of what in German is called the *Wanderstudent*, who seeks knowledge in a number of places and at the feet of different teachers.

In the wake of the scholarship and sober Sufism brought to Palembang, Banjarmasin and Banten through translations into Malay of the tempered writings of al-Ghazali by Abd al-Samad al-Palimbani, Muhammad Arshad al-Banjari and other eighteenth-century scholars associated with the Sammaniyya order, Laffan notes also that: 'the scholarly diet of Javanese Muslims was becoming ever more stable and bound to standards set in Mecca and perhaps at Cairo's al-Azhar mosque, led between 1794 and 1812 by Abdallah al-Sharqawi' (Laffan 2011: 27).

The programme of study in the *pesantren* or *pondok* began with the memorisation of the Qur'an – probably in reverse order, starting with the thirtieth *juz'* or section, consisting of the shorter Suras at the end of the Qur'an. Dedicated students could complete this by age twelve and then move on to the more challenging study of Islam's dogmatic and doctrinal foundations: law texts would be drawn from the Shafi'i *madhhab*, one of the four surviving authoritative schools of Sunni Islamic law and the prevailing one in Egypt, coastal South Asia and in Southeast Asia. Questions related to *kalam* or theology would be taught through *Umm al-barahin*, the earlier mentioned primer compiled by al-Sanusi, which reached its widest circulation by the end of the nineteenth century. Beginnings of the substantive study of the Qur'an would be made through al-Singkili's Malay translation of the *Jalalayn*. Thus prepared, the more advanced students could then engage with the inner (*batin*) meanings that complement the outer (*zahir* in Arabic, *lahir* in Indonesian) meanings of the text. All this required close guidance, whereby the intense teacher–pupil relationship was often, but certainly not always, replicated in the intimate connection between Sufi master and disciple. It is equally important to note also that the sobering influence of Sammani reformism did not make itself felt everywhere, and that the Shattariyya and its associated texts, including al-Singkili's *Tarjuman* and al-Burhanpuri's *Tuhfat*, remained influential on Java and in Sumatra's interior.

In terms of pedagogy and didactics, Zamakhsyari Dhofier points out that a distinction needs to be made between the *pesantren* proper and what he calls *pengajian*. The distinction between the two is in the level of Islamic education provided and the teaching methods that are used. The *pengajian* cater to novices and beginners, offering basic training called *sorogan* – intensive one-on-one tutoring requiring 'devotion, industry, discipline, and most importantly, patience' (Dhofier 1999: 11). Only after sufficient exposure to this type of training are students considered ready for the more advanced didactical methods used in the *pesantren.* There, intermediate and advanced students progress through a learning system called *bandongan* or *weton*, where students attend lectures by the *guru* or *kyai* in groups (called a *halaqa*, which can range from five to 500), independently taking notes on the text that is being discussed.

Concluding remarks

Research conducted in the last few decades has rendered available increasingly detailed knowledge of the varying dynamics that have been at work in Indonesia's continuing Islamisation process since the religion's initial introduction. Islamicists, Indonesianists, and a rare breed of historians and linguists with backgrounds in both Middle Eastern and Southeast Asian studies have provided important new insights into contacts among religious scholars (*ulama*), who participated in the networks that criss-crossed the Indian Ocean. In the course of the seventeenth and eighteenth centuries, these activities led to scholarly interaction of increased intensity and frequency, stimulating the exchange of Islamic learning; the development of new Muslim writing cultures in Southeast Asia that employed regional and local languages; new modes of legitimising political rule and of royal patronage for religious learning; and the emergence of an indigenous Islamic education system, but also the contestation of religious identities. All these elements continue to inform the further Islamisation process in Indonesia, while, simultaneously, its peoples have to come to terms with the increasingly intrusive colonisation by Europeans and the concomitant introduction of what the latter call 'modernity'.

CHAPTER 3

Islam as resistance

The exposure of Indonesian Muslims to seventeenth- and eighteenth-century Islamic reformism and contestations of Muslim identity formation also constitute ingredients in what I will call 'Islam as resistance' – which may be directed against both domestic and external challenges affecting Muslims in Indonesia. As was the case with the emergence of Islamic networks across the Indian Ocean, the mobilisation of religion as a political tool in the course of the nineteenth century must be seen in the context of developments in the wider Muslim world, but increasingly also as a reaction against ever more invasive intrusions by non-Muslims as European colonialism enters the age of high imperialism.

Around the turn of the eighteenth to the nineteenth century, two disasters befalling the Ottoman Empire also foreshadowed dramatic changes in Muslim Southeast Asia. First of all, the Sublime Porte was confronted with Napoleon's invasion of Egypt in 1798. Not even a decade later, Istanbul temporarily lost control of the Hijaz and the Haramayn with the occupation of Mecca and Medina by Arab forces united in an alliance consisting of a dynasty of chieftains from the Central Arabian region of Najd and descendants of the reactionary reformer Muhammad ibn Abd al-Wahhab – namesake of the puritan form of Islamic revivalism that became known as Wahhabism. These two events not only heralded the decline of Ottoman power, but they were also the beginnings of a new phase in European expansion across the world, as well as of the parallel development of more vigorous efforts towards Islamic reform – two trends that would be increasingly at loggerheads with each other as the nineteenth century progressed.

Napoleon's influence was also felt more directly in Indonesia. In the course of his European conquests, the Netherlands were first occupied and then completely annexed into the French Empire. Initially cutting off the metropole from its overseas colonies, the Southeast Asian possessions were first administered by Marshall Herman Daendels (1808–11), a military officer loyal to the French, and then placed under an English lieutenant-general (1811–15) after French fortunes took a turn for the worse and Britain invaded Java. Following Napoleon's defeat in 1813, the former Dutch Republic emerged from this period as a kingdom under Willem I (r. 1813–40) and, in 1815, the Netherlands' overseas possessions were restored to Dutch sovereignty in accordance with the Anglo-British Treaty of 1814. Nicknamed *Coning Koopman* ('King Merchant'), the newly crowned monarch exploited the effective bankruptcy of the VOC in 1796 and the impact of the Industrial Revolution to lead a complete overhaul of Dutch colonial policy, turning what now became the Netherlands East Indies into the mainstay of the metropole's economic prosperity.

The first two sections of this chapter, dealing with early nineteenth-century warfare in the Minangkabau region of Sumatra and in central Java, serve to illustrate the transition from the Islamic order shaped by centuries of network-ing to a new phase in Indonesia's Islamisation process, when Muslims were confronted with the onslaught of modernity in the guise of European high imperialism. The final sections of this chapter discuss how this challenge was met by transforming the existent Muslim ecumene of the Indian Ocean into a sense of Islamic nationhood and by emergent strands of proto-nationalism in Minangkabau, Java, Aceh and elsewhere; forging new multilayered identities in which Islam featured as one of the constituent elements.

The early Padri movement in west Sumatra's Minangkabau region (1803–25)

Scholarship has given much attention to the allegedly Wahhabi inspirations for the so-called Padri Wars, creating the impression that the conflict was an early exponent of the spread of eighteenth-century Arabian Islamic revivalism.[1] Since the early 2000s, the association of the Padris with Wahhabism has been reinforced through the identification of its leaders as progenitors of Salafism in Indonesia by some Muslim activists operating on that side of the Islamic spec-trum. The involvement of three returning *hajjis* with first-hand experience of the Saudi-Wahhabi occupation of Mecca and Medina (1803–13) in the politico-religious turmoil erupting in the Minangkabau during the first decade of the nineteenth century, makes it tempting to project such a light on these events. But as one authoritative voice on Minangkabau history and culture observes: 'Coincidence is not proof [. . .] and in no Padri War-era Minangkabau text do we find mention of Wahhabism' (Hadler 2008: 979).

Therefore, the conflicts affecting the Minangkabau region should not be narrowed down to an unprovoked, spontaneous eruption of religious zeal, nor should the influence of other Islamic tendencies than Wahhabism be ignored. Instead, the wars during the first decades of the nineteenth century are better understood when placed within the wider context of drastic economic and social changes affecting eighteenth-century Minangkabau, which then led to confron-tations between different political forces employing competing politico-religious discourses.

For more than thirty years, the mountainous Minangkabau region would be the scene of continuous violence. Initially, the conflict was confined to a confrontation between the old elite, consisting of Minangkabau nobility and traditional chiefs, on the one hand, and ambitious religious enthusiasts, on the other. But subsequently, as the theatre of operations expanded and other parties became involved, things became more complicated. Therefore, it is important to appreciate regional variations in the unfolding of the conflicts within the Minangkabau itself, and to recognise the distinction between the early and later phases of the war, which also differ in terms of the extent and intensity of Dutch intervention.

Prelude: the Minangkabau at the eve of the nineteenth century

As noted earlier in this book, the complexity and diversity of the Minangkabau world (*Darat* or *Alam Minangkabau*) also extends to its religious landscape. In spite of formal allegiance to Islam, Christine Dobbin has rightly noted that: 'Over the centuries the Minangkabau exhibited towards foreign religions an attitude typical of many mountain-dwellers towards the religions of the civilized world: they remained largely impervious to them, whether they came by way of the eastern or western lowlands' (Dobbin 1983: 7). This observation resonates with the work of James C. Scott on upland populations and other agrarian societies in Southeast Asia. His analysis and theorising of an anarchist streak among these subaltern peoples and of resistance under the aspect of 'hidden transcripts' in books such as *The Art of Not Being Governed: An Anarchist History of Upland Southeast Asia* and *Domination and the Arts of Resistance: Hidden Transcripts*, also bear relevance to the narrative of this chapter.

Consequently, indigenous religious and cultural features persisted well into the nineteenth century – including a continuing role for the 'spirit doctor' (*pawang*) and the survival of the respective Minangkabau customary law (*adat*) traditions of Bodi Caniago and Kota Piliang. However, transformations in the socio-political structure under the influence of drastic shifts in the economic fortunes of key social actors in the Minangkabau world eventually led to 'a period of religious enthusiasm and frenzy' during which a 'particular regional variant of Islam [. . .] briefly suffused and transformed an entire society' (Dobbin 1983: 7). What had happened?

Until the 1500s, Minangkabau international commerce had been part of the Indian Ocean and archipelagic mercantile networks involving Malays, Acehnese, Chinese, Indians, Arabs and Minangkabau middlemen for many centuries. That all changed with the arrival of the Europeans and their increasingly interventionist ways of colonising Asia. Regional actors were under increasing pressure when, by the mid-seventeenth century, the political and economic power of both Malacca and Aceh had receded and the Dutch began monopolising trade on Sumatra's west coast. The Dutch turned the southern port of Padang into their main emporium, taking control of the supply of textiles in exchange for gold and pepper, while trying to stamp out the local production of cotton, which was regarded as unwelcome competition. The VOC's intrusive trade policies forced indigenous middlemen into becoming Dutch agents or had them replaced by Chinese.[2] More changes were under way when, in the course of the eighteenth century, the English East India Company and free traders operating in its orbit also became increasingly involved in Sumatra's west coast commerce with Bengal, the Coromandel and Malabar Coasts. With the establishment of a British colony in Penang in 1786, the English also began syphoning off trade in cassia and gambir via the Malacca Straits. A growing global demand for coffee from the 1790s onward saw American traders make an appearance in the archipelago as well.

Thanks to this new interest, domestic coffee producers in the Minangkabau hill villages began to prosper too. Unlike the rice fields of the valleys, which were held as communal property of matriarchal lineages, economic activity on higher elevations added to the personal wealth, or *harta pencarian*, of the male producers (Dobbin 1983: 128; Hadler 2009: 7). Meanwhile, the decline in gold exports as a result of the depletion of the Minangkabau mines in the 1820s and 1830s had a negative impact on the economic fortunes of both miners and the traditional lineage elites, who had historically dominated the trade in this precious metal.

This forms the background to the inroads made by Islamic reformist ideas into the Minangkabau world at the end of the eighteenth century. All these changes and the accompanying shifts in power created a combustible mix with political repercussions, in which religion became an operative tool for the actors involved. Apart from remaining alert to the wider socio-economic context, a further word of caution is in place here. Most of what we know about the Padri Movement comes from Dutch sources. While they provide quite detailed information on what was a primary colonial concern, economics, data on the role of Islam are generally presented as part of an emergent colonial surveillance literature. And while the objective of that type of inquiry is to peer at the goings-on behind what James Scott calls the 'hidden transcripts' of resistance, the challenge of investigating such discourses is exactly that: they are hidden and therefore seldom documented in the colonial archives. Consequently, what we can learn from this literature is not only incomplete, but also refracted through a particular lens of observation. However, there are also two indigenous sources that chronicle the unfolding of the Padri Wars. The first one is the *Hikayat Jalal al-Din* by Jalal al-Din Ahmad of Samiang, nicknamed *faqih saghir* ('the little jurist'), and a disciple of one of the main protagonists in the early stages of the conflict.[3] Composed in the 1820s, it not only offers insights into late eighteenth-century Islamic reformism and the history of the Padri Wars, but also introduces a new genre into the Malay-Muslim writing culture: the autobiography (Hadler 2009: 18). The other one is the *Naskah Tuanku Imam Bondjol*, the memoir of another protagonist of the Padri Movement, named Peto Syarif (1772–1864), who gained notoriety with the Dutch and fame among the Minangkabau as Imam Bondjol.[4]

As a religion that is urban in origin, Islam's infiltration of rural societies, with their own agrarian cycles and accompanying cultural and religious practices, has always proven cumbersome. Also in the Minangkabau, such indigenous customs continued to flourish well into the nineteenth century. Consequently, it was in Sumatra's west coast ports, such as Ulakan and Pariaman, where Islam found its first and also most lasting footholds, although – until the second half of the eighteenth century – even there conversion remained largely restricted to the broker or middlemen families. Islam penetrated the interior via both the west and east coast rivers, where it primarily caught on with those involved in the gold trade; in particular, the Minangkabau royal family with its close relations to Malacca. Outside gold-producing villages, the prestige attached to Islam was only modestly reflected in the incorporation of a religious functionary known as *malim* (from the Arabic *muᶜallim*, 'teacher') into the entourage of the lineage chiefs or *penghulus*. But this was only for decorum and the *malim* had no influence in the lineage council (Dobbin 1983: 118).

One institution that did provide an opportunity for Islam to enter into the Minangkabau world proper was the *surau*. Originally this referred to 'the house where young men lived after puberty away from the lineage house' (Dobbin 1983: 120). However, in the course of the Islamisation process this locale became the Minangkabau equivalent of the *pesantren* or *pondok* and – with that – a key link in the chain of transmission of Islamic learning. As in many other places in the archipelago, in the Minangkabau the other important institution for this Islamisation process was the Sufi brotherhood or *tarekat*. Both were instrumental in facilitating the blending of Islam into the cultural settings of the Minangkabau, while exposing the students to the universally shared core of Islamic doctrine. As elsewhere, also in the Minangkabau, learning Arabic and studying *fiqh*, or Islamic jurisprudence, formed the mainstay of the Minangkabau *surau* curriculum. At the same time, the simultaneous presence of the Naqshbandiyya, Qadiriyya and Shattariya orders resulted in the spread of varying strands of *tasawwuf* or Sufi learning and practice. The Shattariyya tradition had been introduced at Ulakan by Burhanuddin, a follower of the Aceh-based Abd al-Raᶜuf al-Singkili. From there it travelled inland into the Agam Valley, where the Kota Tua area especially was turned into a major centre of Islamic learning, becoming known as the base of the so-called *Empat Angkat*, or 'four exalted ones' – a reference to four locally influential Shattariya Shaikhs (Dobbin 1983: 125). As discussed in the previous chapter, what set the curriculum of the Shattariyya *surau* apart from those associated with other Sufi brotherhoods was its focus on the *martabat tujuh* – the doctrine of 'seven stages' outlined in al-Burhanpuri's *Tuhfat*.

In spite of tensions between the different *tarekat* – for example, due to the opposition especially of the Naqshbandiyya to the 'seven stages' doctrine – until the end of the eighteenth century, the presence of *surau* and *tarekat* did not pose a challenge to the wider society of the Minangkabau. However, with the expansion of cassia and coffee exports, and the resulting influx of new wealth, things started to change. Growing prosperity enabled more Minangkabau Muslims to make the pilgrimage to Mecca, but booming trade also led to an expansion of local and regional markets and with that to a rise in the problems associated with the dark side of such concentrations of people and money, ranging from banditry to dangers to public morality in the form of gambling (cock fighting), prostitution, and the consumption of *tuak* (an alcoholic brew made from palm trees), tobacco and – most worryingly – opium. Whereas the *penghulu* councils of the traditional matriarchal lineage system struggled to respond effectively to disputes arising in this changing environment, as centres of expertise in Islamic law, and thanks to the general commercial flair exhibited in the *sunna* or Islamic tradition, the *surau* and its teachers were much better equipped for dealing with such legal and moral issues.

It is therefore not surprising that, from the 1780s onward, the spirit of Islamic reformism suffused the Shattariyya of Kota Tua and – even more so – the Naqshbandiyya based in neighbouring Cangking, leading to an ever more vigorous call for a return to the *shariᶜa* in the Agam Valley. Bearing this in mind, even with the arrival of pilgrims returning from a Wahhabi-occupied Hijaz, Michael Laffan is right to suggest that 'rather than seeing a Wahhabi genesis in West Sumatra', it is more helpful to understand the Padri Movement as having grown up around scholars of a reforming Shattari tradition in the interior, who rejected the authority of the incumbent masters based in the lowland town of Ulakan (Laffan 2011: 41).

Economic transformation, Islamic reformism and political change

How these various modalities of Islamic revivalism and reformism were at work in early nineteenth-century Minangkabau is best illustrated by comparing three emblematic figures who dominated the beginning of the Padri Wars.

The first one to confront the challenges posed by increased trade and the accompanying influx of money and people was Tuanku Nan Tua (d. 1824), the leading Shattari teacher, 'who had attracted literally thousands of pupils to Kota Tua' (Dobbin 1983: 125). He transformed himself from a political quietist preoccupied with spiritual attainment into a guardian of public morality and dispenser of law and order. Not opposed to commerce as such (*surau* needing to be self-sufficient were very much engaged in economic activity), he campaigned against banditry and sent out missions of students to convince leaders of surrounding villages to conduct trade in accordance with Islamic law. Thanks to the success of these efforts, Tuanku Nan Tua became known as the 'patron of traders', and his campaign was expanded outside the *Empat Angkat* by his chief disciple, 'the little jurist' Jalal al-Din (Dobbin 1983: 127).[5] Although this expansion did not go unchallenged by the traditional elite, a more serious threat to these domestic Shattari reform efforts was indeed posed by the return of pilgrims from Wahhabi-occupied Mecca, who favoured a more militant form of Islamisation seemingly inspired by witnessing the revivalism promoted by Muhammad ibn Abd al-Wahhab.

The key representative of this alternative and, in regards to Minangkabau culture, uncompromising approach was Tuanku Nan Rinceh (d. 1832), who took as his protégé the most prominent of the returning pilgrims, Haji Miskin. Both the Tuan and the Haji were former pupils of Tuanku Nan Tua and had also been involved with Jalal al-Din's expansion efforts of the 'back to the shariᶜa' movement outside the Kota Tua area. Although initially they continued to have their mentor's support, when the campaign of enforcing their own strict interpretation of Islam took the level of violence to a whole new degree, this resulted in an irreparable split. Consequently, Tuanku Nan Rinceh has been characterised as 'the archetypical Padri'; the name under which these puritan zealots became known – although they referred to themselves as *orang putih* or 'white ones' – meaning truly pious Muslims (Dobbin 1983: 131; Laffan 2011: 41). Tuan Nan Rinceh managed to build up his own support base, which not only consisted of followers such as Haji Miskin, but also received the patronage of the leading Shattari shaykh of the whole Agam Valley, Tuanku Mensiangan, who had been won over from his initial quietism to the principle that forcible conversion was permitted if everything else had failed.

The final show-down between the two camps occurred during a debate in 1815, where Tuangku Nan Tua condemned the large-scale violence in which one village was set against another, while Tuangku Nan Rinceh expressed his frustration over the futility of low-intensity skirmishes between armed crowds. Losing the argument, Tuanku Nan Tua and Jalal al-Din were denounced as *Rahib Tua* ('old Christian monk') and *Raja Kafir* ('King of Infidels') respectively, whereas Tuanku Mensiangan was hailed as the *Imam Besar* or 'Great Imam'. Tuanku Nan Rinceh himself, together with his entourage of seven *malim*, became known as the *harimau yang delapan* (*harimau nan salapan* in Minangkabau); the 'Eight Tigers' (Dobbin 1983: 134; Hadler 2009: 26). The forceful imposition of Islamic judges (*qadi*) on villages still administered through *penghulu* councils, the introduction of Arabised dress codes, and the unleashing of unrestrained deadly violence, revenge killings and capturing of booty from the defeated, do indeed invite comparisons with the Saudi-Wahhabi campaigns in Arabia.

However, continued coffee consumption and veneration of Sufi saints – practices eschewed by the followers of Ibn Abd al-Wahhab – make such Wahhabi parallels tenuous at best. Moreover, as the 'Eight Tigers' mobilised their followers against Tuanku Nan Tua's camp, there are plausible indications of *tarekat* competition. Not only was Tuanku Nan Rinceh joined by someone called Tuanku di Samani (suggesting a Sammaniyya connection), his chief spokesman, Tuanku Nan Salih, made a specific point of highlighting and condemning the opposition's persistent adherence to the Shattari doctrine of 'seven stages'. This unleashed a wave of violence against those suspected of continued allegiance to the Shattariyya tradition: their villages were attacked, mosques burned and *ulama* killed, while women (married and unmarried alike) were kidnapped and married off to the invading Padris. This has led to speculation that what was really going on was a take-over of the Agam Valley by the 'more globally salient Naqshbandiyya brotherhood' with greater affinity to reformist Islam (Laffan 2011: 42). Aside from ideological incentives, personal grievances and cold political calculation should not be discounted either: not only was Tuanku Nan Salih the son of one of Tuanku Nan Tua's victims in earlier purification campaigns, the 'Eight Tigers' also manipulated poor villages without ancient lineages against the Minangkabau elites, and intentionally turned Padris previously adhering to the Bodi Caniago *adat* tradition against Kota Piliang villages.

Pragmatic considerations seem also to underlie the 'introduction of Padri principles into Tanah Datar' – the valley southeast of Agam (Dobbin 1983: 136). Here one Tuanku Lintau features as the third emblematic figure of the early Padri uprising. This rich coffee-trader-turned-warlord appears to have entertained rather opportunistic motives. After pursuing Islamic studies in the coastal port towns, upon his return in 1813, he managed to obtain the patronage of the Raja Alam of Minangkabau for the sake of the moral improvement of Tanah Datar along the lines of Tuanku Nan Rinceh's teachings in the Agam Valley. Two years later, still facing resolute opposition from most of the *penghulu* establishment and feeling dissatisfied with the Raja Alam's lack of strength, Tuanku Lintau ambushed and massacred most of the royal family. To vindicate these actions and legitimise his now unassailable position, he married the daughter of the last Raja Ibadat and eventually took over the offices of Raja Ibadat and Raja Adat himself. Tuanku Lintau and his *hulubalangs*, or war chiefs, were more renowned for their martial skills than their piety or religious learning, and it seems that economic considerations ruled paramount in their subsequent campaigns. To compensate for the land lost to coffee cultivation, they expanded their power into rice-growing lowland areas, while labour shortages were resolved by enslaving the subjugated populations. It was these sorts of practices that earned Padris the near universal hostility of the valley population. As a result, and in contrast to the highlands, the plains remained by and large unconverted to the Padri cause.

While it was not possible to bring all hill villages under a unified administration, even independently, villages involved in the Padri uprising shared certain features, including impressive mosque compounds surrounded by moats or ponds; heavy fortifications, often extending into joint defence works with other villages; and a male population that was on an almost constant war-footing. While battlefield encounters out in the open remained rare, Padri warriors were notorious for their intimidatingly aggressive challenges during hostilities. In this context, there is another aspect of Padri warfare that is certainly at odds with puritan interpretations of Islam but a common feature among militant Sufis: invulnerability cults, in which magical incantations and the astrological determination of auspicious days for battle by religious teachers allegedly rendered the *hulubalangs* invulnerable to lethal injuries (*bertuah*).[6]

The varying dynamics of the Padri movement in Agam, Tanah Datar and Limapuluh Kota Valleys found yet another manifestation north of these Minangkabau heartlands, gravitating around the village of Bonjol in the Alahan Panjang Valley and its eponymous leader, Imam Bondjol.[7] He has not just come to be regarded as *the face* of the Padri Movement and a 'trope of resistance' against Dutch colonialism (Hadler 2008: 975);[8] in 1973, he was included in the official pantheon of national heroes of the Indonesian Republic, where he features together with only two other nineteenth-century Muslim leaders: the Javanese Prince Diponegoro and Teuku Umar of Aceh.

The future Imam Bondjol – then still known as Peto Syarif – had also been a pupil of Tuanka Nan Tua, but was pulled into the orbit of the Padris after a visit by Haji Miskin and one of the local rulers, Datuk Bendahara, yet another former student of Tuanku Nan Tua, who himself had switched sides because he found the teachings of Tuanku Nan Rinceh more attractive. In spite of such support, the Padri teachings met with much local resistance, not only on religious grounds, but also because of the influence they gave to people of modest origins, such as Peto Syarif. As a result, the movement set up its own community apart from mainstream Minangkabau society. After the assassination of Datuk Bendahara in 1806 and an encouraging personal visit by Tuanku Nan Rinceh, Imam Bondjol developed into a successful Padri war leader, further aided in building his position by the growing economic prosperity that resulted from Bonjol's much improved trade relations. Between 1812 and 1825, Imam Bondjol rose to become the undisputed leader of what originally had been a quartet, known as the *tuanku yang berempat*, 'the four tuanku'. By the mid-1820s, Bonjol's influence extended to the west coast ports of Tiku and Air Bangis that had previously belonged to Aceh. Another wing of the Padri forces took the movement's influence further into the interior, even conquering part of the Batak lands of northern Sumatra.

The Dutch reoccupation of Padang in 1819, however, blocked a southward expansion of the Padris along the coast, forcing Imam Bondjol to change tactics. With the restoration of independence and the foundation of the Kingdom of the Netherlands, a new factor was added to the complexity of the Padri Wars: an increasingly intrusive Dutch economic policy, bringing with it drastic changes to the Minangkabau's administrative system. Having benefitted economically during the relatively benign English interregnum, from the 1820s onward, the Padris were confronted with the newly designed colonial policy of King Willem I. Seeing a confluence of their own interests with those of the traditional Minangkabau elite, the Dutch made common cause with the royal family by establishing a military alliance, based on a treaty signed in 1821 with Sultan Alam Bagagar Syah, the nephew of the last Raja Alam of Minangkabau. As will be seen in the next section, in line with similar policies that had been imposed in Java, the Dutch appointed Sultan Alam and Tuanku Nan Tua's nephew, Tuanku Samit, as regents of Tanah Datar and Agam respectively. At the same time, however, the Dutch also tried dismantling the matrilineal *penghulu* system and replacing it with Dutch-paid village and district heads (called *kepala negeri* and *kepala laras*). *Benteng* or fortresses were established in Tanah Datar (Fort van der Capellen) and Agam (Fort de Kock) to support the monitoring of Padri activity and movements by the Dutch colonial army (Dobbin 1983: 151–2).[9]

The Dutch return to Sumatra in 1819 also inaugurated their first large-scale armed intervention against the Padri Movement, in the course of which Haji Miskin became one of the early casualties. Aside from Minangkabau royalty and the *penghulu* class, Muslim leaders such as Tuanku Nan Tua also began to see the advantages of Dutch support. Meanwhile, Padri leaders such as Tuanku Nan Rinceh, Tuanku Lintau, Tuanku Nan Saleh and also Imam Bondjol, feeling secure enough owing to the opening of an alternative trade channel via newly established Singapore or Aceh, were willing to accepted status quo agreements proposed by the Dutch, whereby Padri authority and their right to promote their religious system in the areas under their control were tolerated in exchange for accepting a Dutch presence in Padang and the areas occupied in the military campaigns between 1821 and 1825. At that point in time, the Padris felt they were negotiating from a point of strength, because Dutch attention was now consumed by concerns over another uprising in Java that constituted a graver challenge to their hold over their colonial possessions.

From mystic synthesis to Islamic millenarianism: Diponegoro and the Java War

While reformist Islamic influences acquired a foothold in Sumatra in the first decades of the nineteenth century, in the course of the same time frame, the Javanese Islamic synthesis reached its apotheosis at the Yogyakarta court in the person of Prince Diponegoro (1785–1855) and his leadership during the Java War. What interests us here is how Islam coloured this indigenous Javanese response to Dutch colonisation. But, in order to be able to assess this properly, and also appreciate the wider importance of this confrontation between the Javanese and their Dutch colonisers, which would define the colonial relationship for its remaining century, it needs to be contextualised within a setting of relevant aspects of imperial history. For this, three issues need to be addressed: the circumstances leading to the outbreak of violent hostilities; the figure of Diponegoro; and the composition of his support base and the reasons for the eventual breakdown of his alliance of forces.

The political context: a new kind of colonialism

The Java War erupted on the back of the formation of the Concert of Europe at the Congress of Vienna in 1815. Both are part and parcel of an emergent new world order, in which Napoleon's empire made way for a new balance of power in Europe and for industry-driven European imperialism on an unprecedented scale elsewhere in the world. Prefiguring the notion of 'glocalisation', which was coined by Roland Robertson to characterise a much later worldwide phenomenon, the effects of the new colonial drive behind nineteenth-century empire-building manifested themselves globally as well as locally, because the Concert of Europe and the Java War also reflect a redefinition of power relations between European countries, as well as within their overseas possessions in Southeast Asia, with the Netherlands having to surrender primacy in the Indian Ocean to Britain and Yogyakarta being forced to come to terms with the definitive demise of the Majapahit–Mataram legacy. Glimpses of this increasingly invasive and repressive Dutch presence have already been signalled in the previous section, but, before other parts of the Indonesian archipelago were affected in the course of the nineteenth century, Java was first to bear the full brunt of this development in a prelude lasting from 1808 until 1815.

The redefinition of the relationship between central Java's courts and Batavia began under Napoleon's appointee as governor-general, Herman Daendels (1762–1818). It was during his tenure (1808–11) that the foundations were laid for the modern colonial state of the Netherlands East Indies. His strategy consisted of breaking the connection between the courts and the Pasisir, combined with securing access to the economic resources of the courts' own territories in central and east Java, including forest produce, cash crops, labour and rice-producing districts, while also executing a more detailed border demarcation between the Yogyakarta and Surakarta sultanates. He also intended to exercise tighter military and political control through the centralisation of colonial administration, which included new edicts for ceremony and protocol that greatly upset the etiquette-conscious Javanese court elites. According to a key scholarly authority on the period, '[t]his was not just about changing a few archaic practices, a little tinkering at the edges to bring the East Indies [sic] Company into the modern world. This was root and branch change [. . .] it was clear that Java had entered a new age' (Carey 2014: 85–6).

Some members of the Yogyakarta royal family would not take this oppression lying down. Foreshadowing the more significant Java War orchestrated by his distant but more senior relative Diponegoro (a grandson of the second and son of the third sultan), Raden Ronggo Prawirodirjo III (1779–1810) led a brief revolt against Daendels in 1809–10. In contrast to Diponegoro, who would cast himself as a distinctly Islamic leader, Raden Ronggo can be considered as Java's 'Old Order's last champion' (Carey 2014: 91). Although Raden Ronggo too may have regarded himself as a *Ratu Adil* or 'Just King', there was an important difference with Diponegoro's future undertaking: despite his extensive connections with the east Javanese Islamic communities, there was nothing in Ronggo's rebellion which distinguished the 'people of Islam' from the European *kapir* and Javanese 'apostate'. Instead, the spirit of the Hindu-Javanese shadow play (*wayang*) and the ghost of Sultan Mangkubumi hovered over his enterprise (Carey 2014: 103).

The abortive revolt did little to derail Daendels's policies. The reigning Sultan Hamengkubuwono II (1750–1828) was unceremoniously shoved aside while his son (Diponegoro's father) and serving crown prince, Raden Mas Surojo (1769–1814), was appointed as a figurehead regent. This Dutch-orchestrated palace revolution opened the way for the annexation of Yogyakarta's borderlands with the north coast and the cancellation of the traditional payment of *strandgeld* or 'rent' by the Dutch to the court for the use of the Pasisir.[10] Faced with an impossible political situation, Yogyakarta teetered on the brink of civil war, but a brief reprieve came when – in May 1811 – Daendels was replaced as governor-general following the annexation of the Netherlands into Napoleon's empire almost a year earlier. However, within months Java was invaded and conquered by a British army from India. During a temporary breakdown in law and order after the bloody battle between Franco-Dutch and British forces at the stronghold of Meester Cornelis, a reckoning also took place at the Yogyakarta court. While the prince regent was spared and again appointed as crown prince, the reinstated Sultan Hamengkubuwono II ordered the assassination of the corrupt chief minister who had treacherously taken advantage of Daendels's fiscal policies. The incident is relevant in that when explaining the minister's 'dispatch' to the British, the sultan included the defamation of Islam among the charges (Carey 2014: 122).

Eventually, Britain took control of Java and placed its administration in the hands of two key figures from nineteenth-century British imperial history in Southeast Asia: Thomas Stamford Raffles (1771–1826) as Lieutenant-Governor of Java and John Crawfurd (1783–1868) as British Resident in Yogyakarta. Unfortunately, 'the despoliation of Yogya treasure' and 'evisceration of the south-central Javanese courts' started under Daendels simply continued during the British interregnum (1811–15), when the latter showed themselves as the 'world's champion colonial asset strippers' (Carey 2014: 91, 114). Within half a year of their arrival, relations between the British and the sultan broke down. This resulted not only in the latter's second removal from the throne and the appointment of the crown prince as Hamengkubuwono III (r. 1812–14), but also in the full-scale pillage and plunder of the *kraton* by British and Bengali troops. Neither Yogyakarta nor Surakarta would ever again pose a threat to European rule. For that reason, Peter Carey suggests that '1812, rather than the end of the Java War, should perhaps be seen as the date when the new colonial era dawned in Java' (Carey 2014: 135). From then on support for challenges of colonial hegemony would come from outside the court tradition. Eventually more an inspirational than a political success, the five-year-long war that ravaged Java between 1825 and 1830 depended on its leader's ability to get the Islamic religious communities and the Javanese peasantry behind his cause.

In this Diponegoro was unwittingly aided by both British and Dutch colonial policies of the ensuing two decades. Although Raffles and Crawfurd's esteem for indigenous culture and learning contrasted with the policies of the philistine Daendels and many post-revolutionary Dutch colonial administrators, their relations with select members of the Javanese elite were no less exploitative and manipulative. Aside from replacing Hamengkubuwono II with Crown Prince Raden Mas Surojo, they curtailed the latter's power by appointing his uncle Notokusomo (1764–?) as an independent prince with his own army under the title Pakualam I (1813–29) – thus replicating the same divide-and-rule scenario that the VOC had directed in Surakarta through the Treaty of Gyanti of 1755. The new treaties imposed on Yogyakarta in August 1812 were nothing short of a political revolution, as the ruler's armed forces were disbanded and more territories were annexed, while the abolition of the office of provincial or district *bupati* (roughly comparable to a governor) left many members of the royal family destitute. The introduction of a cash tax scheme meanwhile delivered the peasantry into the hands of Chinese moneylenders, which caused increasing ethnic tension throughout central Java. Finally, a new judicial system placed all foreigners and Javanese born outside the principalities under the jurisdiction of the colonial government, thus curtailing the role of the religious courts or *surambi*. All these measures contributed to the future rallying of the religious communities and peasantry behind Diponegoro. As his father's chief political adviser, the prince was further alienated when – after the third sultan's unexpectedly early death in 1814 – Raffles appointed the corrupt Pakualam I as regent of Diponegoro's half-brother, the child sultan Hamengkubuwono IV (1804–23, r. 1814–22).[11] Although he tried to actively involve himself in his younger sibling's education, Diponegoro could only watch the court's further degradation during the remainder of the British interregnum and the subsequent return of the Dutch, whose new colonial policy was every bit as interventionist and subverting to the standing of Yogyakarta. In Peter Carey's assessment:

> The roots of the sultanate's descent in the moral abyss, pithily described by Van Hogendorp in his reference to the Dutch transformation of the *kraton* into 'a brothel', can be traced to this period. So too can Diponegoro's implacable conviction that Yogyakarta should be destroyed, and the apostate Javanese rulers stripped of their political power for a new moral order based on Islamic precepts and traditional Javanese values to be established. (Carey 2014: 161)

Javanese elite resentment of the Dutch deepened when the sexual exploitation of Javanese women by depraved Dutch officials was widened to family members of the nobility, while Diponegoro's personal anti-Dutch sentiments further intensi-fied as a result of the persecution and exile of Kyai Murmo Wijoyo, a respected Islamic religious leader with close ties to his father.

Although the first governor-general appointed by the newly founded Kingdom of the Netherlands, Godert van der Cappellen (1778–1848, in office 1816–26), was of the opinion that Dutch colonialism could not continue without protecting the local population from excessive exploitation, this was not the view of *Koning Koopman* Willem I. He saw colonies as *wingewesten* (areas for making profit) that could restore the economic fortune of the impoverished metropole. This attitude was shared by the influx of veterans from the Napoleonic wars, post-revolutionary colonial administrators, and plain fortune seekers; 'newcom-ers' (*baroe datang*) despised by Batavia's creole elite (Carey 2014: 169). Van der Cappellen was a man decades ahead of his time, because only with the intro-duction of the *Ethische Politiek* (Ethical Policy) in 1901, would safeguarding the welfare of colonial subjects become recognised as a government responsibility.

In the meantime, Diponegoro's resolve only hardened to return Java to the political order existing before Daendels – when Dutch and Javanese had respected each other's sovereignty. The new Dutch administration not only sought to acquire land for settlers, it also imposed yet again a new set of tax regu-lations enabling unscrupulous Yogyakarta courtiers and Chinese merchants to take advantage of the common people. The resulting social and economic malaise led to a string of millenarian movements: in 1817 a villager named Umar Mahdi – claiming to a be soldier of the Ottoman sultan and having the support of one of the *Wali Songo*, Sunan Bonang – called on his followers to expel Chinese and Europeans from Java. They were all quickly arrested. The same year, 4,000 Javanese from the Madiun area congregated at a place associated with the so-called Joyoboyo Prophecy as the locale where the 'Just King' would manifest himself. In 1819, a similar event occurred in Malang, while in Blitar, a holy man known as Iman Sampurno ('Sage of the Perfect Faith') predicted the coming of a plague, which eventually materialised in 1821 in the form of a wide-spread cholera epidemic. As part of his prophecy, he proclaimed that Muslims could ward off the danger by returning to their true faith. All these incidents resonate strongly with what eventually transpired in the Java War.

Diponegoro's messianic mission

This then forms the setting in which Diponegoro would eventually unleash a full-blown uprising against the Dutch. But aside from having an understanding of the political context, to appreciate the nature of this rebellion, the personality of its leader requires closer scrutiny too.

The prince's birth name was Bendoro Raden Mas Mustahar. As per Javanese royal tradition, when he turned twenty in 1805, he was given his adult name Raden Ontowiryo. Seven year later, he finally received the princely title of

Bendoro Pangeran Arjo Diponegoro from his father on the occasion of the latter's ascension to the throne as Hamengkubuwono III.[12] Although he was the
first-born of a future sultan, who in turn was the oldest grandchild of the founder
of the Yogyakarta lineage, Mangkubumi, the fact that Diponegoro's mother
was an unofficial wife (*garwa ampeyan*) formed a hindrance to his succession to
the throne. In spite of her modest status at the court, his mother Raden Ayu
Mangkorowati (1770?–1852) could claim descent from Kyai Ageng Prampelan,
a retainer of the founder of the Mataram dynasty, as well as from one of the *Wali
Songo*: Sunan Ampel of Gresik. This pedigree certainly fed into Diponegoro's
sense of predestination.

In the *Babad Diponegoro*, the memoir he eventually wrote during his twenty-
five-year exile on Sulawesi, Diponegoro recorded that when he was presented
to the ageing Mangkubumi, the latter foretold that this child would cause the
Dutch even greater trouble than he had done himself, but that its outcome
would only be known to God. This resonates with another prediction ascribed
to the seventeenth-century Sultan Agung: that after the end of his reign in 1646,
the Dutch would rule Java for 300 years, during which time just one Mataram
descendant would rise up, only to be defeated. Diponegoro's sense of destiny
was very much shaped by the recollection of these and other prophesies, contained in the *Aji Soko* tales and the *Serat Joyoboyo*, in which early Javanese lore and
Islamic allusions are interwoven into a narrative of mystic synthesis (Ricklefs
1974: 242–4; Carey 2014: 60, 201–2). During meditation retreats at various
stages of his life, Diponegoro also had his own immediate spiritual experiences,
involving mystical encounters with both the Javanese spirit world and Islamic
saintly figures. These included an 1805 pilgrimage to the south coast, as part of a
Javanese aristocrat's rite of passage into adulthood. For Diponegoro this lengthy
spiritual wandering turned into a seminal event of life-changing significance,
similar to that of his great-grandfather Mangkubumi and the latter's brother-in-
arms Raden Mas Said, the later Mangkunegoro I.

By way of preparation for this episode as a *satria lelono* or wandering knight,
Diponegoro visited a number of mosques and religious schools in the Yogya area,
while also shaving his hair, dressing in a white robe, putting on a green turban,
and calling himself Seh Ngabdurahim (Shaykh Abd al-Rahim). Adopted for the
sake of anonymity, the Arabic name – together with his changed appearance
and mosque visits – evince a distinctly Islamic component in what is very much
a deeply Javanese practice. Eventually, retreating from the inhabited world
(*tirakat*), in the course of this period of solitude, Diponegoro had a visitation by
Sunan Kalijaga while meditating in the cave of Song Kamal. This instilled in
him a conviction that he was not only destined to be a temporal leader, but also
to become a *wali* in his own right– a 'spiritual overseer of the Javanese sover-
eigns' (Carey 2014: 52). Marking the symbiosis between the Islamic and ancient
Javanese traditions in this spiritual quest, he then continued to Imogiri, the royal

gravesite of the Mataram dynasty. There he visited the shrines of Sultan Agung, Mangkubumi and Ratu Agung, before continuing to the coast for an encounter with Ratu Kidul – the Goddess of the Southern Sea. Although as a devout Muslim, Diponegoro resolutely rejected the goddess's offer of supernatural assistance, he would retain a lifelong fascination with this pagan figure. The last visitation of this early spiritual journey occurred at nearby Parangkusumo, where he experienced a foretelling of the destruction of Yogyakarta and the ruin of Java. He was also instructed to look after his father, the future Hamengkubuwono III, not to accept the office of crown prince, but instead to remain on the lookout for a sign in the form of an arrow named 'Sarutomo'.

Finally, Diponegoro changed his name from Ngabdurahim to Ngabdulkamit. A corruption of Abd al-Hamid, it has been suggested that this new Muslim name was a reference to Sultan Abd al-Hamid I (r. 1773–87), the first Ottoman ruler to explicitly claim the title 'caliph' and actively use it to legitimise his rule (Ricklefs 1974: 241). It also conjures up associations with the Sultan of Ngrum (Rum), which is not only mentioned in the Aji Soko legends and Joyoboyo prophecy, but which – as discussed in earlier chapters – has been a persistent motif in Southeast Asian Islamic lore, in particular in relation to establishing the credentials of Muslim rulers. The sign of the arrow 'Sarutomo', meanwhile, recalls an episode involving Arjuna, the hero of the Mahabharata-inspired Javanese shadow play. The figuring of Sunan Kalijaga and Sultan Agung, alongside Arjuna and the rejection of Ratu Kidul, provide a quartet of motifs that gave Diponegoro 'a clearer sense of his prophetic destiny and place in Javanese history', at a point in time when the old regime was crumbling under the imposition of a new colonial order (Ricklefs 1974: 228).

These experiences also illustrate Ricklefs's caution – later repeated by Carey – of measuring Diponegoro against some kind of universal Islamic standard or characterising him as a 'purifier' of Islam:

> That is not to suggest that Dipanagara [Diponegoro] was not a Muslim. [. . .] If one is to understand Dipanagara's views, one's first task must be to understand what were the traditions and beliefs which he inherited, rather than what were the beliefs of coreligionists living thousands of miles away. (Ricklefs 1974: 228; quoted in Carey 2014: xxxviii)

Religion, and Islam in particular, is of central importance for understanding Diponegoro and his significance for Indonesian history, because as Ricklefs added: 'It was where everything began' (Ricklefs 1974: 229). This beginning was at Tegalrejo, the country estate of his great-grandmother, Mangkubumi's widow Ratu Agung, where Diponegoro spent his childhood years – sheltered from the court intrigues for which he developed a lifelong aversion.[13] Compared with the later visionary experiences, here Diponegoro also had a more conventional exposure to Islamic learning. Female relatives played an important role in

Diponegoro's early religious upbringing. Aside from Ratu Agung, these included also his paternal grandmother Ratu Kedhaton, who came from Madura – an island renowned for its Islamic intellectual tradition, in particular in the fields of Arabic grammar and prosody. Eventually, Diponegoro inherited Tegalrejo and it became his main residence and retreat, resulting in lengthy absences away from the *kraton* that irritated both his grandfather and father. While Diponegoro would attend the courtly *Garebeg* ceremonies on the occasion of the Prophet's birthday and the celebrations of the end of the fasting (*Eid al-Fitr*) and the pilgrimage (*Eid al-Adha*), he found their particular format – which he considered more Javanese than Islamic – sinful.

Tegalrejo's rural setting not only enabled Diponegoro to become intimately acquainted with the lifestyle of Java's peasantry, it also offered an entry point into the *pesantren* world of Java's 'students of religion' or *santri*. In fact, Diponegoro's first wife and mother of his oldest son was the daughter of a *kyai* or religious teacher. This future Prince Diponegoro II (d. before 1856) would eventually change his name to Raden Mantri Muhamad Ngarip in 1830. In his own memoir, *Babad Dipanagara Surya Ngalam*, he remembered his mother as 'a devout woman who took pleasure in accompanying her husband in his religious duties' (Carey 2014: 25). Aside from these village contacts, Diponegoro's religious orientation also stimulated relations with members of the Yogyakarta court who shared his Islamic interests, as well as with prominent non-Javanese Muslims in the Tegalrejo area, such as Shaykh Abdullah al-Ansari – an Arab from Jeddah who had married into the family of the first sultan's son. According to reports from another one of Diponegoro's sons, Raden Mas Alip, the shaykh and his son-in-law Ahmad were among Diponegoro's leading advisers in the run-up to the war in 1825.

The Tegalrejo estate was also in the vicinity of the so-called *pathok negari* or 'pillars of the state' – a reference to Yogyakarta's 'four main centres for scholars of Islamic law' (Carey 2014: 17). During the Java War, Diponegoro would marry the daughter of a revered *kyai* from one of these centres, Kasongan, and employ the services of the sons of another based in Melangi. This was Kyai Taptojani, a scholar originating from Sumatra, who had a reputation as an able translator of particularly difficult Islamic texts. By then Kyai Taptojani had moved to Surakarta and – in very old age – he played a role in the first round of peace negotiations during the Java War. In Diponegoro's younger years, Surakarta was more important as a religious centre than Yogyakarta thanks to the generous patronage extended by Sunan Pakubuwono IV. Its *Garebeg* ceremonies drew *santri* from all over Java, whereas those in Yogyakarta remained very much local affairs. This was also a reason for his deeply religious son, Diponegoro II, to decide to study with another Surakarta-based scholar, Kyai Mojo (d. 1859). The tensions that would later develop between Diponegoro's supporters from among the Yogyakarta aristocracy and those drawn from Surakarta *ulama* circles can partly be attributed to the appointment of Kyai Mojo as the prince's most prominent *santri* adviser.

In fact, at least four of Diponegoro's sons would receive a *pesantren* education and become ardent Muslims, undoubtedly stimulated by their father's own interest in Islamic learning. His own lack of a formal education would affect not only Diponegoro's writing style, which remained hesitant and ungrammatical throughout his life, but also the informal way he spoke. However, records show Diponegoro's exposure to broad Islamic learning. He studied Burhanpuri's *Tuhfa* and other works on *tasawwuf*, as well as Javanese *suluk*, Qur'anic exegesis, histories of the prophets (*sirat al-anbiya*), *usul al-din* and Islamic jurisprudence, and works on Islamic political philosophy, including *Sirat al-Salatin* and *Taj al-Salatin*. In addition, he read adaptions from Arabic and Persian tales about kingship and statecraft, alongside Javanese versions of texts on Indian heroes such as Rama and Arjuna, famous cycles of *wayang*, the *Serat Menak* – the epic of Amir Hamza (the Prophet Muhammad's uncle) – and texts on cosmogony and agricultural myth. The resulting understanding of Islam, also corroborated by his autobiography and surviving notebooks from his later exile, 'show[s] that he was more a typical Javanese mystic than an orthodox Muslim reformer' (Carey 2014: 33).

Peter Carey, who is among the foremost expert scholars who has closely studied Diponegoro's writings, explains that the latter's mystical view of *tokid* or *tawhid* – the absolute unity and unicity of God, an understanding of which can only be attained through a fourfold path traversing faith (*iman*), gnosis (*ma'ripat*) and true *islam* – is 'typical Javanese *primbon* (divination almanac) material'. Even the mention of *tarekat* must not be understood as pointing to the Sufi orders, but as a reference to the Shattariya as 'a receptacle for many old-fashioned mystical teachings'. Consequently, he concludes that '[t]here was nothing in Diponegoro's visions which involved the creation of an Islamic society along the lines of the Padri reformers' (Carey 2013: 35).

The Java War: a final Javanese–Dutch showdown

Diponegoro's final realisation of his millenarian role and the critical developments leading up to its eventual fulfilment converged in a three-year run-up to the outbreak of the actual war in 1825.

With the unexpectedly early end in 1822 of the morally corrupt reign of a still young Hamengkubuwono IV, a very reluctant Diponegoro was appointed as one of four guardians to the next child-sultan. Meanwhile the volcanic eruption of Yogyakarta's Mount Merapi at the end of the same year gave a further sense of foreboding. Adding to Diponegoro's personal frustration was intense disappointment at being passed over again for succession, whereas in neighbouring Surakarta the son of a concubine was allowed to ascend to the throne as Susuhunan Pakubuwono VI (r. 1823–30). At the same time, the Yogyakarta treasury was dealt its final blow, when Governor-General van der

Cappellen tried to sabotage Willem I's new policy favouring direct coffee cultivation by Dutch planters by decreeing that all European- and Chinese-held lands should be returned to their original owners. However, the effects of this measure were the *kraton*'s effective bankruptcy, because it could not meet the indemnity payments to the affected lessees. In the concomitant breakdown in law and order, villagers and estate workers resorted to settling scores with hated foreign masters, while bandits and other criminals also took full advantage of the ensuing chaos. In this state of near anarchy, the already very tense relationship between Diponegoro and his stepmother (mother of the late Hamengkubuwono IV) broke down completely over substituting the incumbents of critical courts positions with pliable but unsuitable replacements and her insistence on throwing in the royal family's fortunes with the Dutch. Diponegoro's subsequent maltreatment and insults at the hands of the equally incompetent Dutch Resident in Yogyakarta and his deputy led to the complete severance of his relations with the court in February 1824.

Against this background, Diponegoro sought refuge in spiritual contemplation, inaugurating a crucial fifteen-month period of visitations and dream occurrences which he later carefully documented in his autobiography. The two most crucial episodes concern the final premonitions of his role as 'Just King' (*Ratu Adil*). Recorded in great detail in his *Babad Dipanegara*, the most telling passages deserve to be cited in full. Both occurred at similarly auspicious moments, namely during the so-called *Layla al-Qadr* – the night toward the end of the month of Ramadan when Muhammad received the first revelations of the Qur'an in 610 CE. In the first one, in May 1824, Diponegoro is summoned by a man dressed like a *hajji*:

> The prince had not the strength to know
> or to look upon the countenance
> of the Ratu Adil, whose brilliance
> indeed eclipsed the sun.
> Only his clothing was closely observed
> by the prince in its entirety.
> His Turban was green
> [and] he wore a white *jubah* (tabard)
> white trousers [and] a red shawl.
> He faced the northwest [direction of the *qibla*, CK]
> [. . .]
> Ah, you Ngabdulkamid
> the reason I have summoned you
> is for you to set my army fighting.
> Let Java be conquered immediately!
> If anyone
> should ask you
> for your mandate, it is the Qur'an (Carey 2014: 215–16)

The second vision was preceded by three recurring dreams of the late Hamengkubuwono IV's mother, in which she received an instruction that her son's widow should marry a *wali wudhar*. Interpreting this as a reference to Diponegoro, the prince was duly approached, but because of the soured relation with his stepmother, the attempt evidently failed. However, Diponegoro consulted Kyai Rahmanudin, the former *penghulu* of Yogyakarta, as to the meaning of these dreams. The latter explained that, although *wali wudhar* was often taken to be a reference to the *Wali Songo*, it actually referred to six key Qur'anic Prophets (Adam, Noah, Abraham, Moses, Jesus and Muhammad), Sunan Giri and Sultan Agung, suggesting that Diponegoro might be the ninth. This very Javanese reading is heretical, in the sense that Islamic tradition considers Muhammad as the 'Seal of the Prophets' (*khatim al-anbiya'*), meaning that divine prophecy ended with him. Rahmanudin's reading of the queen mother's dreams also holds the clue to Diponegoro's ultimate pre-war vision during the fasting of 1825:

> You have been given the title
> by the Almighty
> of Sultan Ngabdulkamid
> Erucokro Sayidin
> Panatagama of Java
> Kalifat Rasulullah (Carey 2014: 221)

Seeing these various Islamic and non-Islamic designations side by side makes this a very powerful stanza. 'Just King' (*Erucokro*), 'Lord of Faith' (*Sayidin*), 'Regulator of the Faith' (*Panatagama*), and 'Caliph of the Messenger of God' (*Kalifat Rasulullah*) underscore the multilayered and multifaceted aspects of religious identity formation, as well as its dynamic character; identity is not fixed but constantly evolving, as is the very process of Islamisation. This pile-up of titles also strengthened Diponegoro's resolve not only to drive out the Dutch, but also to replace the defiled court and see to the fulfilment of his war-time call to be recognised as the 'Regulator of the Faith' – the one demand he refused to give up even when the war was lost and he was facing the certain prospect of exile or worse. While his claims as 'Just King' and adjudicator of Javanese-Islamic law served as the rallying call for the *santri* communities to side with Diponegoro, his aristocratic mission of establishing a new *kraton* alienated them and would eventually contribute to a split with Kyai Mojo and his followers. Aside from this 'class' dimension and the regional rivalry between Yogyakarta and Surakarta that has been alluded to earlier, the breakdown of trust between Diponegoro and Kyai Mojo, in 1827, was also precipitated by the latter's insistence on a division of political authority:

> Mojo, according to Diponegoro's account, challenged the prince's position as Sultan Erucokro by asking him to divide his sovereignty into four parts, that of

ratu (king), *wali* (apostle of religion), *pandita* (one learned in the law) and *mukmin* (the believers), suggesting that Diponegoro should choose one of these functions. If he chose that of *ratu*, Mojo implied that he himself would take that of *wali* and enjoy undisputed religious authority. (Carey 2014: 254)

Not surprisingly, Diponegoro refused. Given that Kyai Mojo was the ideological driving force on account of his intellectual superiority, the breakdown of relations undermined Diponegoro's standing with the *santri*, thereby fragmenting the 'unique social breadth and religious fervor' of the prince's alliance consisting of aristocracy, peasantry and pious Muslim communities (Carey 2014: 256). Meanwhile, the renaming of Diponegoro as Ngabdulkamid pointed not just at the well-known trope of the 'Sultan of Rum' in Southeast Asian Muslim literatures. On a more mundane level, it also served as an inspiration to organise his army along the same lines as the Ottoman military: his most senior field commander Sentot (1808–55), the teenage son of the late Raden Ronggo, received the title *Ali Basah* (Ali Pasha or 'High Commander'), while various units were named after regiments from the Janissary Corps (Carey 2014: 60).

The actual unfolding of the Java War has been the subject of multi-volume studies by Dutch military historians and need not detain us here.[14] What is of interest though is that – after the Dutch had besieged and destroyed the Tegalrejo estate – Diponegoro proclaimed a 'Holy War' (*perang sabil*) with himself acting as the 'head (*imam*) of the Islamic religion in Java', while issuing authorisations (*piagem*) to princes and other members of the court elite (*priyayi*) to act as local commanders. Noblemen elsewhere in Java were also eager to receive such mandates, regarding them as an opportunity to serve their own regional interests, which would eventually compromise the war effort. Such tensions between the differing objectives of the various actors involved in the rebellion would eventually also affect Diponegoro's relationship with his *santri* support base. Aside from Java's aristocracy and their peasant levies, the Muslim communities had formed the second support base of the rebellion in terms of both ideological motivation and manpower. They consisted of pious Muslims from the Yogyakarta court, *pesantren* and tax-free villages (*pradikan* or *perdikan*), but included also some Arabs and mixed-blood Chinese converts, as well as the forces mobilised by the abovementioned Surakarta-based Kyai Mojo.

It was the religious character of the Java War – exemplified by Diponegoro's continued insistence on being recognised as 'Protector and Regulator of the Faith' and its reliance on mobilising the *santri* constituency of the population – that convinced his Dutch opponents of the threat this posed to 'the foundations of the Christian West's authority in Java, distinguishing it from the dynastic struggles of previous centuries' (Carey 2014: 251). This meant that the solution to such past conflicts – a nominally independent kingdom along the lines of those given to Hamengkubuwono I, Mangkunegoro I or Pakualam I – was out of the question. Consequently, after Diponegoro's dramatic surrender to General de Kock at Magelang in 1830, he was shipped off into exile on Sulawesi: the first three years in Manado, the capital of the heavily Christianised northern province of Minahasa, then for the remainder of his life as a virtual prisoner in Makassar's Fort Rotterdam. Here, while his physical environment contracted, Diponegoro's spiritual world expanded as he first wrote down his memoirs and then prepared for the end by what in the Javanese Shattariya tradition is called *plawanganing pati* ('[opening] the gateway to death') (Carey 2014: 321). Assessing the significance of Diponegoro and the Java War, Peter Carey writes:

> Diponegoro fought both for the restoration of an idealized Javanese past, and the establishment of a new moral order in which the teachings of Islam, especially its legal precepts, would be upheld. This was the essence of his popular appeal for the religious communities and his importance for the future, his style of 'mystic synthesis' forming one of the key strands of Islamic piety in post-1830 Javanese society. (Carey 2014: 328)

From religious purification to 'Minangkabau nationalism'

Post-1830 Sumatra was also confronted with reinvigorated Dutch colonisation. When the Dutch became distracted by the start of the Java War in 1825, Padri leaders in Lintau and Bonjol had felt sufficiently emboldened to increase their raids. With the appointment of King Willem's confidant, Johannes van den Bosch, as the new governor-general of the Netherlands East Indies (1830–3) and the introduction of a more invasive colonial economic policy, Padris and the Dutch were set on a new collision course. Like Java, by the early 1830s, Sumatra's Minangkabau too had experienced more than a decade of Dutch interference in their polity. The various causes of their dissatisfaction were similar to those of the Javanese: new tax regimes; direct Dutch involvement in coffee cultivation; the obligation to provide coolie services; the insult of quartering Dutch troops in mosques; and administrative changes that undermined the *penghulu* lineage system in much the same way as comparable measures on Java had done to the authority of the *priyayi* (Dobbin 1983: 196). The second phase of conflict and confrontation in west and central Sumatra would even feature some of same *dramatis personae* as the Java War.

In the course of the five-year lull in Padri–Dutch hostilities, the situation in Minangkabau underwent another significant change. During this period, a noticeable laxity had developed in the observance of Padri-imposed regulations, such as the prescription of female dress codes and prohibition of the use of tobacco and chewing betel. Given the earlier scepticism expressed over the characterisation of the Padri Movement as a Wahhabi-inspired phenomenon, interpreting this relaxation of rules as a manifestation of disenchantment on receiving news from returning pilgrims about the Saudi-Wahhabi defeat in

1818 at the hands of an Ottoman-Egyptian expeditionary force is not convincing. A more plausible explanation for this lessened puritan fervour in the intervening years is that it had worn down due to the persistent rejection of the Padri Islamisation efforts by the traditional Minangkabau elite and their followers, combined with the military pressure exercised by the Dutch since the early 1820s and enforced with new energy after the end of the Java War. Eventually such opposition forced the remaining Padri not just to make compromises regarding the enforcement of their religious edicts, but also to come to an understanding with the Dutch.

By 1831, the Dutch conquest of west Sumatra entered its second phase with the sending of an expeditionary force that took control of the Minangkabau heartlands. The deaths of Tuan Lintau and Tuan Nan Rinceh in 1833 also robbed the Padri Movement of two of its most important leaders. It now fell to Imam Bondjol's 10,000-strong army to make the last defiant stand against the Dutch. However, with military defeat unavoidable and imminent, the village of Bonjol also gave in to the same spiritual malaise that had affected other parts of the Padri world, as the Imam too began having second thoughts about uncompromising Islamic revivalism and puritan reform. In the case of Imam Bondjol, some researchers have suggested a link with 'stale news' – as Laffan puts it – of the collapse of the first Saudi-Wahhabi state in Arabia (Laffan 2011: 44). However, as other Padri leaders went into oblivion, Imam Bondjol has managed to do the same as Diponegoro by writing an autobiography: namely, to sustain the image of an Islamic activist who remained defiant in the face of a more powerful adversary, by turning defeat and disillusion into a heroic stance, enabling future generations of Minangkabau – and later Indonesians in general too – to reinvent Imam Bondjol as what Jeffrey Hadler calls a 'trope of resistance' against Dutch colonialism (Hadler 2008: 975). Hadler's close reading of *Naskah Tuanku Imam Bondjol* situates the protagonist's significance within the context of post-1830 colonial Sumatra. The text comprises three distinct parts: the autobiography proper; a memoir of Imam Bondjol's son Naali Sutan Caniago; and reports of meetings held in the Minangkabau highlands between 1865 and 1875 – a not uncommon format for Malay manuscripts. Nevertheless, the *Naskah* is a 'single polyvalent text', providing material for an exercise in intertextuality that brings to light the varying functions of this body of writings (Hadler 2008: 992). It is the different political purposes for which it has been used since its inception that 'gives the story of the Tuanku such potency' (Hadler 2008: 989).

There is another incident from the second phase of the Padri Wars that deserves consideration. By 1832, Dutch military action seemed very much like a 'mopping-up' campaign, until an unexpected flare-up in the hostilities in January 1833, when – barely four months after occupying the village – the Dutch garrison in Bonjol was massacred. Retaining much of its 'magical aura', because of its resilience and dogged resistance, Bonjol was considered '*negeri sakti*, a village endowed with supernatural powers. It was also given the title *kompeni darat*, the company of the Minangkabau interior, indicating that it had proved itself a match for the Netherlands Indies government' (Dobbin 1983: 205). While it would become the last Minangkabau Padri centre to hold out until 1837, the 1833 rebellion represented a broader front of Minangkabau resistance to Dutch colonisation. For Christine Dobbin, this is reason to posit the term 'Minangkabau nationalism'. For this she takes her cue from the historiography of French West Africa and writings about emergent nationalism in colonies by scholars such as Eric Stokes, which challenge a neat categorisation into primary resistance, post-pacification revolt and modern nationalism. Suggesting instead 'a permanent, underlying "ur-nationalism", manifesting its hostility to the European presence in a distinct series of historical forms', Dobbin proposes to also understand the 1833 rebellion in those terms, because it brings together a variety of anti-colonial actors (Dobbin 1983: 194).

While it would be the last time that members of the Minangkabau royal family featured at the head of an anti-colonial resistance, Islamic leadership maintained its position, which by then had become a constant feature since the first attempts of *tarekat* leaders to oust the VOC from Padang in the 1680s and early 1700s. As will be seen below, the Shattariya order in particular – helped by certain *penghulu* lineages – would demonstrate remarkable resilience in staying at the forefront of a religiously inspired resistance against the Dutch until the 1908 Tax Revolt. Similarly, it is possible to discern a geographical continuity, with the Agam and Tanah Datar Valleys remaining the epicentres of resistance well into the twentieth century. Aside from Bonjol, Padri leaders were also involved in uprisings in Rao and Kamang. However, in the latter district, another charismatic figure rose up in 1834, who called himself *daulat*. When cursing the *kepala laras* who had sided with the Dutch, he appealed to 'the pre-Padri magical tradition of the *tarekat*' (Dobbin 1983: 204). Although he managed to mobilise a significant following with the help of several *penghulu* lineage chiefs, a Dutch expedition snuffed out their resistance in 1835.

More surprising was the appearance on the Minangkabau scene of a Javanese warrior: Diponegoro's former field commander Sentot, who had gained notoriety as Ali Basa Prawirodirjo. Having cut a deal with the Dutch in 1829, he was given the rank of lieutenant-colonel, a salary and money to maintain his own army. However, Governor-General van den Bosch thought Sentot might be usefully employed against the Minangkabau. Thus, in 1831, he was shipped off to Sumatra together with Dutch reinforcements commanded by Colonel Elout, who had also earned his laurels in the Java War. Although Sentot was now also provided with a rice-growing district with more than 5,000 peasants that gave him a standing similar to that of Surakarta's Mangkunegoro, he thought this was below his dignity as a Yogyakarta royal. Contacts with the local Padris rekindled his contempt of the Dutch and religious zeal as a practising Muslim. Considered a useful figurehead by his new allies, Sentot's own aspiration was to become the overlord of the Minangkabau highlands. Rallying the support of the remaining Padris in northern Agam and Lintau, he then called on the valley *penghulus* to recognise him as their supreme commander. Taking the titles Raja Jawa and Sultan Alam, he also changed his name to Muhammad Ali Basa Abdul Mustafi. After Sentot had failed to unite his Minangkabau supporters into an efficient fighting force, in the summer of 1833, the Dutch eventually got him to abandon his highland base and he ended his days under virtual house arrest in Bengkulu.

Attempts by Minangkabau royalty, such as the Regent of Tanah Datar, Sultan Alam Bagagar Syah, and Raja di Buo, who tried to emulate Sentot's attempts to put themselves at the head of the 1833 uprising, also ended in failure. Bagagar Syah died in 1849 in Batavia, while Raja di Buo found himself roaming the eastern Minangkabau periphery until his death in 1880. While they had managed to secure some Padri support, their resistance was lacking in coordination and was no match for the now well-established Dutch colonial regime. In addition, some Padri leaders had reconciled themselves with the new situation under the Dutch, with one Tuanku Nan Cedok even accepting the position of Regent of Limapuluh Kota. Once Bonjol had been subjugated in 1837, the final Minangkabau revolts were no longer commanded by Padris. Instead, they were uprisings led by what Dobbin has described as secular figures who had originally benefitted from the first Dutch–Minangkabau treaty of 1821, but who became increasingly dissatisfied with the economic and political effects of the Dutch incursions. The latter continued their annexation with the capture of Inderagiri (1838), Singkil, Barus and Siak (1839–40). The brief rebellion of the Regent of Batipuh, Kali Raja, and his nephew the Pamuncak, in 1841 would be the last Minangkabau uprising until 1908.

In the final analysis I side with Laffan and Dutch scholars from the past such as Kielstra and Schrieke, who all conclude that the Padri Wars were not quintessentially Wahhabi. As signalled by Dobbin, their later phase appears to foreshadow an emergent Minangkabau nationalism that would eventually merge into a sense of Indonesian nationhood with Islam featuring as one of its constituent elements.

Islam in the Netherlands East Indies after 1830

Peter Carey may have suggested considering 1812 as the *annus horribilis* for the fortunes of central Java's monarchs, but Merle Ricklefs has a point when proposing that – for the rest of Java, and indeed Indonesia at large – the wider consequences of the introduction of the *Cultuurstelsel* (Cultivation System) by the new Governor-General van den Bosch makes 1830 into a watershed year of even greater importance. It is against the background of the unfolding of this next phase in European imperialism, and its concomitant production of new regimes of knowledge, that any strict and clear-cut dichotomy between colonial overlords and their Muslim subjects must be critically examined and called into question.

While I continue to discuss the Islamisation of Indonesia in the remainder of the nineteenth century under the rubric 'resistance', it is important to underscore its symbiotic aspects instead of conceiving of resistance in purely antagonistic terms, as this would suggest a binary of indigenous Muslims vs non-Muslim colonisers that is inaccurate and incomplete. Muslims certainly continued to confront the Dutch, but the strategies and tactics they employed were often also informed by borrowings derived from that very encounter. Earlier indications of such complexities could already be discerned in the preceding sections on the Padri and Java Wars. Moreover, in the course of the nineteenth century, differences between Muslims themselves became more pronounced, leading to polarising trends which, in turn, resulted in acts of resistance among Muslims against those other Islamic strands and tendencies they happened to disagree with. For these reasons it is more accurate to regard Muslim colonial subjects as interlocutors, whose further understanding and continued mobilisation of their own religious tradition signals agency. This is manifested through intellectual exchange in which Orientalism does not merely produce a certain kind of knowledge of non-Western peoples on the part of European colonisers; it also plays a mediatory role in intercultural exchange in general, and – more germane to this book – in varying interpretations of Islam. Awareness of such diversity should help in making sense of the different voices that compose this discourse of resistance and which may – at times – even become cacophonous without such an interpretative framework.

Islamic education

Aside from new factors causing unprecedented change, there were also elements of continuity that affected the Islamisation process in nineteenth-century Indonesia. Shifting attention back from the political transformations during the first four decades to what we ended with in the previous chapter, the 1830s and 1840s saw an expansion of the influence of the *pesantren* and *pondok* as religious scholars moved away from the courts. Rendered economically and politically impotent, the latter were no longer in a position to offer patronage to the arts and learning on the scale they were used to. However, 'rather than sending Islamic institutions in decline, the wholesale annexation of Java may actually have proved a blessing', working to the benefit of those with stakes in that system (Laffan 2011: 46). While the full-scale imposition of the Cultivation System by the Dutch caused much hardship for peasants forced to grow cash crops, it also allowed the emergence of a minority of indigenous landowners (other than the *priyayi*), including Islamic religious teachers and their dependants, whose economic prosperity grew; thus also enhancing their overall social standing.

Improved communications, introduced for the sake of the efficient trans-portation of agricultural produce, added further to the prosperity of religious schools with advantageous locations along these new economic arteries and facilitated their transformation into 'key nodes of intellectual exchange' (Laffan 2011: 47). They also provided springboards for advanced study in cosmopolitan places such as Surabaya and Singapore, or even further travel to the centres of Islamic learning in the Middle East. This also solidified the position of Mecca-based scholars originating from Java – the most important one being the *mufti* of the Shafi‘i school, Ahmad bin Zaini Dahlan (1816–86) – but also *ulama* from outer islands, who continued to direct the cross-Indian Ocean network-ing that had evolved in the preceding centuries. Even without surviving records of their individual contributions to scholarship and curriculum development on par with those by eighteenth-century Malay-writing scholars such as al-Palimbani or al-Banjari, there is some evidence of Javanese efforts to replicate and emulate Acehnese and Meccan models for the reworking of Shafi‘i texts in earlier centuries. A comparable dynamic seems to have been at work in 'post-Padri' Sumatra, where 'the surau continue to play an important role in educat-ing Minangkabau youth throughout the nineteenth century' on both the village level and in the formation of distinctly important centres of learning. However, aside from disseminating doctrinal orthodoxy, *pesantren*, *pondok* and *surau* also remained important as sites of Sufi activity (Dobbin 1983: 241–2).

Sufi orders between popularisation and rivalry

The continued and even growing significance of established religious institu-tions was – to a degree and for a while – also applicable to the *tarekat* or Sufi orders. In his study of Islamisation in the Minangkabau between the end of the Padri Wars in 1837 and the 1908 Tax Revolt, Werner Kraus has mapped the role of the *tarekat* in the remainder of the nineteenth century. Aside from the presence of transnational Sufi orders, such as the Naqshbandiyya, Qadariyya, Samaniyya and Shattariya, he has also identified a number of local brother-hoods, which distinguish themselves by a continuing emphasis on indigenous animist beliefs and practices, the use of talismans and amulets (*jimat*), and a variety of forms of magical knowledge (*ilmu*). In contrast to the widespread attrac-tion of the Shattariya to various social layers of Southeast Asia's Muslim popula-tion, the Naqshbandiyya appealed more to educated Muslims who appreciated the 'rational' undertones of the order's reformed orthodoxy. Not only that, historically the Naqshbandiyya itself had adopted a conscious strategy of reach-ing out to those with political power – making 'worldliness' into one of its basic tenets alongside inwardly directed piety. These aspects favourably disposed Naqshbandiyya doctrine to becoming an 'elite ideology' (Kraus 1984: 92–3). Consequently, the Naqshbandiyya was able to make inroads among the pious members of the traditional Minangkabau leadership, as it had also managed to do at the Bugi-Malay court of Johor and in the Sultanate of Pontianak in Borneo.

As noted earlier, Michael Laffan has suggested that already during the Padri Wars there are indications that the Naqshbandiyya was making its influence felt among 'Shari°a-minded' Muslims across the Padri–traditionalist divide. In the 1860s, for example, Ahmad ibn Jalal al-Din – one of the sons of the *faqih saghir* – returned to Cangking as an initiate of the Naqshbandiyya order. He can be considered an exponent of an emergent *nouveau riche* of committed Muslims, who – until the early 1900s – saw the Naqshbandiyya as a vehicle for gaining more influence in their villages and towns, before shifting allegiance to another group of reformists who became known as the *kaum muda*, or 'new generation' – in contrast to the *kaum tua* or 'old generation' (Kraus 1984: 92; Laffan 2011: 42).[15] In regards to the Minangkabau, Kraus and Laffan then seem to confirm Dobbin's observation that, for the remainder of the nineteenth century:

> Much of the energy of the *tarekat* leaders became reabsorbed in mutual squabbles. The period after 1847 right down to the 1890s was marked by a reflorescence of the Naksyabandiyah *tarekat* and by attacks made by its leaders on the Syattariyah as heretical. (Dobbin 1983: 242)

Outside the Malay-speaking parts the archipelago, Sufi orders also remained relevant, with especially the Naqshbandiyya actually gaining ground. In Java, two branches of the Naqshbandiyya became active in the second half of the nineteenth century. The first one, belonging to the Khalidiyya branch, was introduced by followers of Shaykh Isma°il Minangkabawi, who was based in Singapore and Riau (east Sumatra), after returning from Mecca in 1850. The other one, combining Naqshbandi and Qadiri practices, was the creation of Ahmad Khatib of Sambas in West Kalimantan, who died in Mecca around 1875.[16] Both branches put more emphasis on adhering to the Five Pillars of Islam (creed, prayer, fasting, almsgiving and pilgrimage) than the Shattariya.

In Java, as in the Minangkabau, globally operating Sufi orders functioned alongside local and regional manifestations of mysticism. Kartawidjaja (1850–1914), a *priyayi* from a respectable lineage of Muslim scholars whose hybrid upbringing included exposure to *pesantren* training and Christian missionary teachings, reports of a simultaneous presence on Java of Naqshbandiyya, Shattariyya and 'the "Tarek Moehamaddia" (which he thought had been an invention of the Nine Saints)' (Laffan 2011: 48). The latter, referring to themselves as 'Akmaliyya', continued to compete with both Shattari and Naqshbandi shaykhs throughout the nineteenth century. As late as the 1880s, an Akmali known as Mas Rahmat, who claimed to be the son of one of Diponegoro's associates, was still roaming the *perdikan* villages of Java and Madura (Bruinessen 2000: 370; Laffan 2011: 52). Both Karawidjaja's own biography and the anecdotal records he provides are illustrative of the changes transpiring in Indonesia's diversified religious landscape, encompassing mystical groups with evident Islamic roots and antinomian sects, such as the *Wong Birai*. On the back of the turn of the century in 1871, according to the Javanese calendar, messianic movements abounded. Texts such as *Akhir ing Jaman* ('End of Times') which began circulating in the 1860s, and the *Palambang tanah Jawah* ('Prophesy of the Land of Java') from the 1880s, appealed again to the coming of the *Ratu Adil* and salvation of those who adhered to the tenets of Islam. Islamic millenarianism received a further boost from the start of the fourteenth Islamic century in 1882 (1300 AH), as well as from events elsewhere in the Muslim world, such as rumours of an anti-Christian plot being hatched by the then Sharif of Mecca, Abd al-Mutallib (d. 1886), and the Mahdi Uprising (1883–98) in the Sudan (Ricklefs 2007: 79).

Remaining more or less invisible to the authorities until their involvement in anti-colonial activities, next to nothing is known of the spread of the Sufi orders or the exact numbers of their adherents until the late 1880s. The Dutch only became alarmed after a minor incident in Madiun in 1886, involving members of the Shattariya, and a more serious uprising two years later in Banten, west Java. Here shaykhs of the Qadiriyya–Naqshbandiyya took the lead in the Cilegon massacre of 1888, and the same was the case with a major rebellion on the island of Lombok in 1891 by the Muslim Sasaks against their Hindu Balinese rulers. Although Laffan suggests that 'Cilegon is in fact more realistically seen as a localized uprising than as a popular jihad', given the unmistakably politico-religious dimensions of these uprisings, it is small wonder that the Dutch began regarding Sufi orders such as the Naqshbandiyya as a fifth column (Laffan 2011: 144). In the colonial surveillance literature, parallels were drawn with the Freemasons, while loyalist Muslims, such as Sayyid Uthman of Batavia (1822–1914), were employed by the Netherlands Indies administration to discredit the Naqshbandiyya teachings.[17] Together with memories of the persistent resistance by Imam Bondjol and of the unexpected uprising of Kali Raja in 1841, Dutch concerns growing out of the perceived 'unpredictability of the natives' led to measures like the exclusion of *tarekat gurus* in the Minangkabau from public office and – after the Cilegon uprising – the 1889 introduction of so-called *goeroe-lijsten* (*guru* records), meant to monitor the presence of Sufi order members. Somewhat ironically, the freedom of the *tarekat* was further curtailed under an in itself more liberal colonial policy of the early twentieth century by the even more restrictive *goeroeordonantie* (*guru* ordinance) of 1905, which obliged religious teachers to secure written permission to teach from the *bupati*; to keep a register of their students; and to submit to the supervision of a local committee chaired by a district officer (Kraus 1984: 111–12; Latif 2008: 77).

The importance of hajj and the impact of technology

Both the colonial surveillance literature and more recent scholarship have also identified the pilgrimage to Mecca as an increasingly central factor in the further Islamisation of Southeast Asia in the course of the nineteenth century. Already between 1829 and 1852 this had been a reason for the colonial authorities to impose a monitoring system, requiring prospective pilgrims to obtain a special '*hajj* passport', which they needed to have stamped along the route and submit again upon return as evidence of having indeed travelled to the Hijaz for the intended purpose. In the wake of the Indian Mutiny, a new surveillance system was put in place in 1859, according to which *bupatis* had to give permission to Muslim residents of their region to depart for Arabia and again interrogate them upon their return, before they would be recognised as *hajjis* and permitted to don the attire associated with that status.

When technological advances such as the introduction of the steamship and the opening of the Suez Canal in 1869 led to an increase in volume, speed and frequency of trans-Indian Ocean traffic, this also intensified the impact of the circulation of ideas that accompanied the pilgrims travelling back and forth between Southeast Asia and the holy cities of Mecca and Medina, as well as other centres of Islamic learning in the Middle East. By the 1890s, pilgrims from Southeast Asia even outnumbered those from India, and have remained the largest single contingent ever since. Aside from monitoring pilgrims through the passport and examination system, increased numbers also resulted in curtailing the movement of independent travellers as colonial authorities saw the advantage of giving in to the pressures exercised first by Hadhrami operators and later by European liner companies to grant them the exclusive rights of transporting pilgrims en masse to Jeddah. In 1898, Dutch regulations decreed that pilgrims had to travel by steam and could only board ships in Batavia, Padang, and Sabang in Aceh. The enforcement of that rule was further facilitated by more stringent colonial administration outside Java following a series of border demarcation agreements between the Netherlands and Britain (Tagliacozzo 2005).

Laffan makes a point of stressing that performing hajj was 'an "ambivalent" experience for the jawa; in the sense that it fostered seemingly contradictory ideas of both local and Islamic identities' (Laffan 2003: 33). In Mecca, they became aware of their belonging to that all-encompassing Muslim entity of the *umma*, while on the other hand also realising their difference from pilgrims from the Middle East, Central Asia or Africa. From the mapping of Islamic networks across the Indian Ocean discussed in the previous chapter, we know of the sustained presence of Southeast Asian *ulama* in Mecca and a wider community in the Hijaz. Detailed information only became available in the late nineteenth century on the basis of reports furnished by the Dutch consulate in Jeddah (pilgrims from Indonesia were technically Dutch citizens), but especially thanks to the efforts of the scholar and later adviser to the colonial government in the Indies, Christiaan Snouck Hurgronje, who managed to do fieldwork in Mecca in 1885.

Drawing on a careful analysis and interpretation of statistical material on the hajj traffic from the 1850s onward, Merle Ricklefs has distilled what seems at face value a counter-intuitive finding from the available data. Based on a comparison of numbers of pilgrims and the ratio between *hajjis* and religious scholars in different regions of Java, he concludes that while there is indeed an explosive growth of pilgrims with the advancement of technology, it also appears that they tend to come from areas where there are 'fewer established religious professionals'. Inversely:

> where the Islam of the *kyai* was strong – the teachings of pious men whose faith, in many cases, was close to the mystical synthesis of the aristocratic elite – the new ideas of Hajjis may have found a less cordial reception than elsewhere. (Ricklefs 2009: 122)

Ricklefs's findings regarding the ratio between *hajji* and *kyai* numbers points at a 'contest of ideas developing in Islamic circles, in which *kyais* and Hajjis tend to play separate roles' (Ricklefs 2009: 123). These findings therefore point at an increasingly prominent phenomenon: a polarisation of Indonesian society, affecting not only relations between Indonesians and foreigners, between Muslims and non-Muslims, but also among Muslims themselves.

Polarising the *umma* below the winds

Together with economic and political changes brought about by this colonial policy, which imposed the growing of cash crops for export onto the indigenous agricultural populations, the developments sketched above all contributed to different forms of polarisation in Indonesian society.

In the case of Java, the top levels of the *priyayi* class thrived and had never been so secure in their positions thanks to the role they were given by the Dutch in the administration of the Cultivation System, but the lower echelons of this elite lost out. An emergent middle class consisting of Chinese, Arab and indigenous Muslim traders benefitted too, but remained politically suspect. However, the welfare of the main generators of this new wealth – the peasantry and growing numbers of urban workers – went into decline. The economic and demographic effects brought about by the Cultivation System also impacted heavily on the intellectual and religious contexts.

Certainly, mystic synthesis remained part of the religious landscape in nineteenth-century Java. Evidence of that is provided by a court text known as the *Serat Centhini* and collections of mystical poems known as *Suluk*, which are purposefully prolix, paradoxical, obscure and multilayered in their meaning, as well as by the wisdom literature by figures such as Prince Mangkunegoro IV

(1809–81) of Surakarta. But rather than the dominant discourse, mystic synthesis now became one of several variants of Javanese adherence to Islam and continues to be so until the present day.[18] By the 1840s and 1850s, 'there existed significant numbers of professionally religious in Javanese societies – mosque officials, religious teachers, guardians of holy sites, students at *pĕsantrens* – who were collectively known as *kaum* (the religious folk) or *putihan* (the white ones)' (Ricklefs 2007: 49). In the Pasisir they were known as *santri*, while the Dutch called them *geestelijken*, meaning 'clericals'. This development led to a widening gap between Islamic and 'Javanese' knowledge, starting along the north coast due to the presence of larger numbers of Arabs and other foreign Muslims, but gradually also moving into the interior. Attached to such intellectual competition is also a question of religious authority. Citing from the writings of the colonial civil servant Emile Gobée (1881–1954) from 1928, Ricklefs points at the distinction between the teachings disseminated by *tarekat gurus* and *kitab gurus*, while another source, the Javanese aristocrat Raden Natarata, relates of his experience in the early 1870s when a 'shariʿa-oriented' scholar refused to teach him Sufism, because it is 'truly forbidden (*kula haramakĕn*)' (Ricklefs 2009: 123).[19]

Against the background of such rifts, in the second half of the nineteenth century, a new term enters the vocabulary on religion in general and Islam in particular. This is the word *abangan*, which is etymologically associated with the Low Javanese (*ngoko*) word for the colour red or brown, but which was first brought into circulation through Christian missionary sources and later gained greater currency through Clifford Geertz's seminal book, *The Religion of Java* (Geertz 1960). Based on his extensive knowledge of both Javanese and Dutch text materials, Merle Ricklefs is confident that – in contrast to the term *putihan* (white) – *abangan* was not used as a social category or reference to a group of people before 1855. Initially, it seems to imply a secular, profane attitude. Given the semantic baggage carried by words like secularity and secularism, I would suggest that it is perhaps more accurate to speak of a preoccupation with worldliness rather than piety. In any case, for the first few decades of its usage, the meaning of *abangan* remained rather fluid.

It is not until the ferment of the 1880s, with reformist ideas advocating closer observance of Islam's religious duties gaining wider circulation, that the polarity *abangan–putihan* becomes more fixed. Laffan has suggested that 'the Naqshbandis around Madiun may well have been the first Javanese to begin labelling their abusive neighbours as "the red ones" (*wong abangan*) in contradistinction to themselves, the truly spotless *putihan*' (Laffan 2011: 50). Those identifying themselves with the latter – although numerically a minority of Java's overall population – clearly attach a derogatory meaning to the former. Religious, cultural and also socio-cultural connotations now converged in a terminology that reflected a society that was drawing apart:

differences in approach to Islam mirrored more general social differences. The *putihan* were wealthier, active in business, better dressed, had better homes, seemed more refined in manners, avoided opium and gambling, observed the pillars of Islam, gave their children more education and disciplined them more. The *abangan* differed on these same points. They were poorer, were not involved in trade and did not provide their children with education. *Abangan* still observed some religious duties, but did so in the name of village solidarity. Whereas the *putihan* read Arabic works and discussed the Islamic world's affairs, the *abangan* watched *wayang* performances and attended lascivious entertainments. In the *wayang* in particular, Javanese spiritual forces were at work. The two groups mixed only with the like-minded. (Ricklefs 2007: 102)

The life story of Kartawidjaja, rumours of the sharif's anti-Christian plot circulating in the Indies through letters from the *jawi* community in Mecca, and the vivid interest of Christian missionaries in the *abangan*: all formed ingredients in the growing suspicions among the *putihan* of a Dutch plan to Christianise Indonesia; a concern that certain Muslim activists have continued to harbour until the present day.[20]

For more or less the period between 1870 and 1900, Michael Laffan draws attention to another kind of polarisation in Indonesian society. With the opening of the Suez Canal, Hadhrami migrants flocked in larger numbers to Southeast Asia, many of them from lower social classes than before. Because of their Arab descent, in Southeast Asia they were accorded higher status than at home – especially those claiming honorifics such as *sayyid* or *habib*, which signalled descent from the Prophet Muhammad. In addition, they played a role in continued *tarekat* propagation, while their extensive mercantile networks around the Indian Ocean enabled many of them to play a vital economic role as merchants and moneylenders, and therefore occupy a commensurate privileged social position (Kathirithamby-Wells 2015: 94–103; Laffan 2003: 43–4). These developments created resentment among the indigenous Muslims, who not only questioned the sanctity of the new arrivals, but also envied their commercial success. Under the adage of 'divide and rule', the Dutch encouraged such sentiments and used them to vindicate a new policy of obliging different ethnic groups to live in separate quarters. In addition, the Indies Dutch also sought to separate themselves further from the rest of society, eventually leading to an official ordinance by the governor-general in 1904, instructing the Dutch to abandon the imitation of local customs. As a result of this segregation:

The ethnic *mélange* created by the influx of Chinese and Arabs ultimately emphasized the position of indigenous Muslims as the absolute underclass. This was officially entrenched by a tripartite colonial division of society into Europeans and the Christian allies, the Foreign Orientals (*vreemde oosterlingen*) and Natives. (Laffan 2011: 45)

Although intended to secure Dutch political supremacy, such categorisations also had unintended side-effects. In the late 1870s, Sultan Abd al-Hamid II (r. 1876–1909) became the first Ottoman ruler since his namesake Abd al-Hamid I (r. 1774–89) to make active political use of the title 'caliph', and position himself as the patron of the Sufi orders – particularly the Naqshbandiyya (Laffan 2003: 41). This formed part of what is generally referred to as the Pan-Islamist agenda he is said to have adopted – partly at the instigation of the Iranian-born reformist and agent provocateur, Jalal al-Din al-Afghani (1838–97) – to fend off threats posed by the European powers against his crumbling realm.[21] In the final decades of the nineteenth century, but even more so in the run-up to World War I, both expatriate Muslims residing in the Netherlands East Indies and the remaining sultans in Borneo, Sulawesi and Sumatra – with Aceh in the forefront – began issuing increasingly urgent appeals to Istanbul for the protection of their interests by the sultan-caliph. Obviously, this only led to further Dutch concerns over the rising spectre of political Islam. As will be discussed in the next chapter, the 'zero-tolerance' repression of any, even perceived, expression of politicised use of Islam by the Dutch colonial authorities stimulated Muslims to explore alternative ways of safeguarding their interests.

Meanwhile, in Aceh . . .

After the successful annexation and occupation of Java and of south and central Sumatra, the coastal areas of Borneo and Sulawesi, and other outer islands in the eastern parts of the archipelago, the Netherlands set its eyes on the pacification of *Serambi Mekkah* – the Sultanate of Aceh:

> With the Anglo-Dutch treaty of 1871, and with both North Sea powers fearing intervention in Sumatra of a third force – such as France, the USA or Italy – the Netherlands began the process of the 'rounding off' (*afronding*) of its oceanic empire. (Laffan 2003: 39)

This ambition triggered the protracted Aceh War (1893–c. 1910), in which the Dutch colonial army (KNIL) became bogged down in a vicious and unwinnable armed conflict that can be regarded as the Netherlands' 'Vietnam'.[22]

According to James Siegel, Dutch failure to secure military success was in part due to their misconception of the composition of the opposition, even on the part of the colonial government's erudite adviser Snouck Hurgronje. Not dissimilar to the complex situation in West Sumatra, 'Atjeh was not a society bifurcated into Islamic and customary elements, but one divided into four groups – *uleebelang* [chieftains, CK], *ulama*, peasants, and the sultan and his group – each of which had its own view of the nature of Islam and *adat* [customary law, CK]' (Siegel 2000: 11). Less attached to place than peasants, sultans or chieftains, the religious scholars, who had to leave their villages in pursuit of knowledge, stressed qualities of men in accordance with common human nature rather than affixed social roles, whereas *uleebelang* power was based on coerced control of both rice- and pepper-growing populations and the trade relations through which these products travelled. The position of the sultan was different again. Based in the capital Bandar Aceh Dar al-Salam, he acted as regulator of relations in a cosmopolitan multi-ethnic society through the ideological employ-ment of Islam rather than as the head of an organic whole. Also, his influence on affairs in the interior was very limited, restricting his abilities to curb the rival powers of the *uleebelangs* by making them 'officers of the state' through the issu-ance of authorisation letters known as *sarakata* (Siegel 2000: 41). Siegel suggests that the sultan's relationship with the *uleebalangs* constituted a *modus vivendi* in which the *uleebelangs* subscribed to the 'myth' of Aceh as an Islamic state, making the sultan into a 'magical figure' but without effective power: 'That Islam did not become synonymous with a magical sultanate, however, was due to the pres-ence of another group in Atjehnese society, the *ulama*' (Siegel 2000: 47).

Just like the sultan and *uleebelangs*, the *ulama* too were 'encapsulated in their own worlds', but theirs was 'not a natural outgrowth of the rural scene' (Siegel 2000: 48). Not only were their *pesantren* physically separate from the villages, but the *ulama* were economically dependent on neither the peasantry nor the chief-tains. Since the roles of the latter two groups were so much attached to the land, only the *pesantren* world offered a window of opportunity for escaping the social obligations associated with village settlement and kinship ties. This constituted a *rantau* of sorts, because one could not become a student and scholar by studying in one's home region. The transformative itinerant *pesantren* experience led to contempt for the *adat* of one's home, putting the *ulama* at loggerheads as much with 'heretical practices of the village as they were against the immorality of the *uleebelang*' (Siegel 2000: 59).

Fragmented by appearance, because no one of the 'four encapsulated groups existing side by side [. . .] depended on his relationship with someone in another group for a basic concept of social identity', and because each entertained dif-ferent concepts of Aceh and Islam, Siegel proposes that nevertheless '[there] was general agreement that Atjeh was an Islamic society' (Siegel 2000: 68–9). That realisation only strengthened in the face of an exterior adversary. So although Islam was only one of the rallying factors in the proto-nationalism that moti-vated the Acehnese drive to retain their independence, securing support of the Sublime Porte on account of an appeal to Muslim solidarity could prove criti-cal to withstand the Dutch assault. In fact, aside from drawing on a history of diplomatic contacts in earlier centuries, in the wake of the Padri Wars, Aceh's sultan had already sent requests to Istanbul for Ottoman protection from the Dutch. After the Dutch annexation of Inderagiri (1838), Singkil, Barus and Siak (1839–40), Sultan Mansur Shah (r. 1838[57]–70[23]) had attempted to make contact with Istanbul in 1838, 1849, and again in 1868 or 1869 (Kadi 2015: 154, 159–62).[24]

The first Acehnese deputation to visit Istanbul after the outbreak of the war in 1873 was led by the Hadhramaut-born and India-educated Habib Abd al-Rahman al-Zahir al-Saqqaf of Samalanga (1832/3–1896), but failed under diplomatic pressures exercised by the Netherlands and other European countries (Kathirithamby-Wells 2015: 99). Although, within a year, Bandar Aceh fell to the Dutch, who made it the capital of the Dutch-controlled province of Aceh under the name Kota Raja, it appears that individual Ottoman officers had made their way to Aceh in the 1875 and 1876 to render military assistance. Ottoman–Acehnese communications continued during the reign of Abd al-Hamid II. These were not limited to contacts with Istanbul, but also extended to the Ottoman-controlled Hijaz; an attempt to call on a Turkish frigate visiting Singapore en route to Japan; and calls on Ottoman diplomats in Southeast Asia for consular protection, including the consul-general in Batavia. Many of these initiatives during the 1880s and 1890s continued to involve Hadhramis. However, due to a combination of factors – including distance, lack of knowledge and political muscle on the part of the Ottomans – in none of these instances did it result in effective support for the Acehnese.

In Snouck Hurgronje's assessment, the Aceh War was 'the great opportunity for the *ulama* to wrest power from the *uleebelang*' (Siegel 2000: 71). Indeed, aside from the Habib of Samalanga, Acehnese *ulama*, such as Teuku Umar (1854–99), but especially Shaykh Muhammad Samman (1836–91), better known as Teungku Cik di Tiro, surfaced as leading resistance figures after the collapse of the sultanate in 1874.[25] Their emphasis on the common human nature – regardless of kinship or their role as villagers – that united Acehnese of different social strata as Muslims was what appealed to the peasants in the message of the *ulama*. However, what makes this first Aceh War a *perang sabil* or *jihad* different from future conflicts is that:

> While the *ulama* envisaged a community of believers on earth, the effective symbol of their appeal in the Atjehnese War, and in the reform movements, was paradise. [. . .] It was not until the 1930s that men began to realize a new life in this world was possible. (Siegel 2000: 74)

Concluding remarks

Aside from the Muslim militancy witnessed during the Padri, Java and Aceh Wars, the sea change with which societies in Indonesia had to cope in the face of increasingly intrusive interventions and invasive incursions by the Dutch, drove the Islamisation process in different directions. In the face of repression, some opted for political quietism; withdrawing into the relative tranquillity and reassuring comfort of the *pesantren* and *tarekat* worlds. In other instances, new opportunities arose as Dutch imperialism rendered other social and political actors powerless, thus creating niches that could be occupied by growing numbers of practising pious Muslims whose awareness of and exposure to developments elsewhere in the Muslim world had increased thanks to advances in communication technology and changing social circumstances. Set in motion in the 1830s, these trends would continue to develop further and open up unprecedented perspectives as the nineteenth century turned into the twentieth.

CHAPTER 4

Islam and nation-building

The previous chapter has demonstrated that religious polarisation in Indonesian societies affected not only Muslim relations with non-Muslims and 'nominal' Muslims, but increasingly also the interactions among the *putihan* or *santri* – the segment of observant and practising pious Muslims themselves. This dimension of religious polarisation will be further explored here, as it bears relevance to the further trajectory of Indonesia's Islamisation. Another observable trend is that the confrontational encounters of the Padri, Java and Aceh Wars give way to strategies of avoidance, with *putihan/santri* Muslims embarking on a kind of *hijra* – re-enacting the migration of the Prophet Muhammad from Mecca to Medina in 622 CE in order to escape the persecution of his small community of followers by the Meccan elite. This distancing from colonial society was not an entirely novel development; when discussing the emergence of the Islamic education system, it was already mentioned that – historically – *pesantren* and *pondok* occupied a distinct space in the micro-geography of the Indonesian village or town, creating a physical distance in order to symbolise their standing apart from mainstream society.

At the same time, advances in communication technology – such as the development of the steamship and opening of the Suez Canal, but increasingly also the printing press –made contacts between Indonesia's Muslim population and the wider *umma* more frequent and intensive. The effects of these developments were paradoxical in the sense that Indonesian Muslims became more conscious of their simultaneous belonging to a Muslim ecumene and their distinctiveness from other Muslims in terms of language, culture and – although less clear and at times even outright ambiguous – ethnicity. This awareness translated into a sense of national belonging in which religious solidarity remained relevant, forming for some even its most important constituting element. This notion of 'Islamic nationhood' has contributed to attempts to forge an Indonesian Islam and the formation of a notion of 'religious nationalism' that has also remained part of the politico-religious vocabulary in postcolonial Indonesia. While some Muslim activists had the ambition of defining this into concrete political agendas, others opted for a more cautious approach. As political quietists they tried working toward Muslim emancipation and furthering Islamic interests through education and religious propagation (*da'wa* or *dakwah*).

The dynamics of Indonesia's ongoing Islamisation process from the turn of the century and throughout the early 1900s onward must also be seen in the context of a sea change in Dutch colonial policy. While the failings of the Cultivation System quickly became apparent because of the havoc it created to the welfare of the peasantry and of growing numbers of urban workers, it was not until 1870 that it was effectively abandoned. An important catalyst in discrediting the Cultivation System and bringing about a rethinking of colonial policy was a novel published in 1860 by a soon-to-be-former colonial administrator, Eduard Douwes Dekker (1820–87). Written under the pen name Multatuli (from the Latin *multa tuli*, 'I have suffered much'), the satire *Max Havelaar* exposed the inherent abuses and scandals brought about by colonialism in the Netherlands East Indies.

A formally defined alternative policy was not introduced until 1901. It became known as the *Ethische Politiek* ('Ethical Policy') and was named after the so-called *Ethici* – colonial administrators and intellectuals who were uneasy about the blatant exploitation of the colonies' general populace by European imperialism. They felt that there was also a responsibility on the part of colonial governments to look after the indigenous populations of their dominions and create opportunities for their development and 'progress'; a concept that – obviously – continued to be defined on the basis of and measured against externally imposed standards. During the days of the Cultivation System, education had only been provided for a miniscule number of individuals from the indigenous population; in Java predominantly recruited from *priyayi* circles and in Sumatra from the administrative personnel employed in the Minangkabau coffee industry.[1] Increased efforts by the Dutch colonial government to improve access to state-sponsored education for the indigenous population formed an important aspect of the Ethical Policy. Between 1900 and 1930, the number of children in Dutch-language schools rose from just over 21,000 to close to 135,000. During the same period, the number of pupils attending indigenous schools (often run by the Islamic mass organisations) increased more than tenfold to one and a half million. These figures include all levels of schooling, but concern predominantly primary education; student numbers in Dutch-language secondary schools form just a fraction of these totals, while access to tertiary education was first limited to dozens and never amounted to more than a few hundred individuals.

Proponents of this new policy also included figures such as Christiaan Snouck Hurgronje, who saw it as his task to orchestrate the shift from nineteenth-century 'pacification' to twentieth-century 'association' and 'emancipation' of Indonesia's Muslims. To achieve his objective, he devised a two-pronged approach. First of all, he advocated a *splitsingstheorie*, according to which Islam is divided into a political and a religious component (Latif 2008: 54). While the Dutch authorities respected the latter, manifestations of the former would not be tolerated. Secondly, he proposed co-opting certain figures from the Muslim elites to help facilitate the development of a new Muslim intelligentsia. Among those recruited as informants and collaborators were the eccentric Sundanese *alim* Hasan Moestapa (1852–1930) and – most importantly – the Hadhrami Sayyid Uthman, who has already been mentioned in the previous chapter. Both held – at one time or another – the position of Honorary Adviser on Native Affairs, while Sayyid Uthman could more or less be considered the 'unofficial' *mufti* of the Netherlands East Indies.

These varying and at times conflicting trends manifested themselves most emphatically in what can be considered a defining exponent of the Islamisation process in twentieth-century Indonesia: the founding of Islamic mass organisations (*organisasi massa*, or *Ormas* in Indonesian acronymic parlay). These movements also became incubators for Islamic political parties and a 'civil society' Islam spinning off what we nowadays call NGOs, as well as what the autocratic New Order Regime later referred to as *Organisasi Tanpa Bentuk* (OTB, 'Organisations Without Form'). However, not all Muslims bought into the Indonesian nation-building project that was set in motion during the final decades of colonialism and the formative years of the independent republic. On the contrary, some activists preferred alternative Islamically inspired political agendas informing both Pan-Islamist ambitions and instances of regional separatism that surfaced in the postcolonial period. Both tendencies posed a serious challenge for Indonesia during early independence, as it went through the process of redefining itself from a federation into a unitary state.

Meccan and Cairene reformism: *kaum tua* and *kaum muda*

Looking back at the developments sketched in the previous chapter, nineteenth-century Indonesia was a society in flux, throwing up challenges to which Muslims had to find a response. As discussed in the final sections of Chapter 2 and throughout Chapter 3, this required skilful navigating between safeguarding the integrity of Islamic doctrine and actively promoting wider learning, while simultaneously coping with the obstacles put in the way of that mission by an increasingly powerful colonial state. The religious polarisation and the resultant diversification in Islamic discourses can be attributed to these dynamics.

From the late 1800s and early 1900s onward, the direction and reforms which had been issuing from *ulama* circles in the Haramayn since the seventeenth century had to contend with a new trend coming from Cairo. With the mosque-university of al-Azhar already a centuries-old established centre of Sunni Islamic learning, the Egyptian capital now also became the centre for another more drastic reformist trend, sometimes referred to as Islamic modernism. In Muslim Southeast Asia it operated alongside, and increasingly in competition with, the continuing Meccan influences. For Michael Laffan, this is reason to talk of 'Cairene Reformism'; a term which I will also use in contradistinction to 'Meccan Reformism' (Laffan 2003: 116). It adds yet another aspect to Indonesia's already multifaceted Islamisation process. A detailed unpacking of these two discourses is all the more important because they have continued to shape, even dominate, the Indonesian Islamic landscape ever since.

Reform-minded *ulama*

The Indonesian expatriate community in the Haramayn remained key to the continuing influence of Meccan renewal initiatives. With the demise of figures such as Nawawi al-Batini (1813–97/8), a scholar originally from Banten in west Java, and the Shafiᶜi *mufti* of Mecca, Ahmad bin Zaini Dahlan (1816–86), a changing of the guard took place with the appointment of Ahmad ibn Abd al-Latif al-Minankabawi, alias Ahmad Khatib (1860–1915/16), as Shafiᶜi *imam* in Mecca, sometime between 1887 and 1892.[2] Although a less elevated office than Ahmad Dahlan's position of *mufti*, it did mean that the young scholar Ahmad Khatib 'joined the religious hierarchy of the Ottoman Hijaz, assuring his future prominence within the wider Jawi ecumene' (Laffan 2003: 106). As recently as 1983, Christine Dobbin still had to signal that:

> In the 1890s Minangkabau was swept by an orthodox reform movement, although, lacking adequate research on the subject, it is difficult to draw many conclusions about it. Its motivating force was Syekh Ahmad Chatib, a descend-ant from a Padri kadi and a native of the goldsmithing village of Kota Gedang near Bukit Tinggi. [. . .] His orthodoxy had much in common with that of the Padris. (Dobbin 1983: 242)

A quarter of century later, with more research having been done, a clearer and more accurate image is emerging of the achievements and significance of this Ahmad Khatib. Not only is he considered the last of the great Mecca-based *Jawa ulama* of the late nineteenth and early twentieth centuries, 'for historians of Indonesian nationalism and reformism, Ahmad Khatīb is the most famous ᶜālim to have been born in the Alam Minangkabau' (Laffan 2003: 106). But there is more to Ahmad Khatib than that. While Nawawi was respected as a guardian of the tradition, even though some considered him a disseminator rather than a contributor, Ahmad Khatib was a more liminal figure. Having had some exposure to Western-style education, he 'functioned as a bridge between tra-dition and innovation', acting as 'a midwife' between what in the Malay and Minangkabau contexts are called the *kaum tua* (old generation) and *kaum muda* (young generation) (Latif 2008: 76).

Ahmad Khatib was not merely a 'descendant from a Padri kadi'; his mater-nal grandfather was none other than Tuanku Nan Rinceh. On his father's side he hailed from an aristocratic family who had traditionally held the office of *jaksa kepala* (chief of native legal officials) in Padang – the port city on Sumatra's west coast. His paternal grandfather Abdallah is thought to have been a Hijazi emigrant who became *imam* and 'state preacher' (*khatib negeri*) in Kota Gedang, whereas his father Abd al-Latif joined the Dutch colonial administration as district head of Empat Angkat. Thanks to this position, Abd al-Latif was able to send his son Ahmad to the Dutch primary school and the teachers' training school (*kweekschool*) in Bukittingi. However, more interested in religious studies, in 1881, Ahmad went to Mecca – accompanied by his grandfather and cousin Muhammad Tahir bin Jalal al-Din al-Azhari (1869–1956). Better known as Tahir Jalaluddin, the latter would go on to become a leading Islamic reformist in his own right. In Mecca, Ahmad Khatib attended the lectures of Ahmad Dahlan, but avoided Nawawi al-Bantini. This seems to suggest a possible division of the wider *jawi* community along ethnic lines, possibly exacerbated by different Sufi affiliations. Although Ahmad Khatib was an initiate of the Naqshbandiyya order, he was nevertheless hostile to the Qadiriyya branch operating in Banten. After concluding a strategic and advantageous marriage with the daughter of the Meccan bookseller Shaykh Muhammad Salih al-Kurdi, Ahmad Khatib was considered eligible for the office of *imam* of the Shafiʿi rite in the Grand Mosque. Appointed to the position by Sharif Awn al-Rafiq of Mecca, this gave Ahmad Khatib the right to convene his *halaqa*, or teaching circle, in the mosque rather than at his home – as even Nawawi al-Bantini had been obliged to do.

From this secure position, Ahmad Khatib felt confident enough to assert his authority vis-à-vis the leadership pretensions of Arab (in particular Egyptian and Hadhrami) *ulama*. He also used it to engage in polemic exchanges with Sayyid Uthman, the de facto *mufti* of Batavia, about the permissibility of accepting Dutch patronage for Islamic affairs in Indonesia. Given Ahmad Khatib's prestigious office and high profile at the time, it is somewhat surprising that his prolific writings have not enjoyed the same longevity as the output of Nawawi al-Bantini. One explanation for this may be the peculiar nature of Ahmad Khatib's *oeuvre*, which is dominated by texts on trigonometry and treatises attacking Minangkabau *adat*. Reminiscent of the hostility of Ahmad Khatib's Padri ancestors, this persistent animosity towards customary law was a result of continuing Dutch partisanship toward *adat* and their association with the matrilineal Minangkabau aristocracy. Consequently, to Ahmad Khatib, 'adat and colonialism implicitly represented a united opposition to the Islam that he wished to propagate' (Laffan 2003: 110). Starkly contrasting with the political quietism of older *ulama*, Ahmad Khatib's belligerence and alleged incitement to a *prang sabil* or *jihad* set off alarm bells in Batavia. Snouck Hurgronje instructed his chief 'spy' in the Hijaz, Raden Aboe Bakar Djajadiningrat (c. 1854–c. 1914), to keep a close eye on the wily Minangkabau scholar.[3]

In view of his vehement opposition to Minangkabau *adat* and his growing criticism of the 'absolutist practices' of the masters of Sufi orders, such as the Samaniyya, but later also the Naqshbandiyya-Khalidiyya; and considering the fact that he was familiar with and possibly not entirely unsympathetic to the ideas of the Egyptian reformist Muhammad Abduh (1849–1905), it is tempting to see Ahmad Khatib as a precursor of Cairene Reformism in Indonesia. However, Michael Laffan remains cautious:

> it is worth remembering that in Mecca in the 1890s, Jawi reformists and tradi-
> tionalists were not yet engaged in the vitriolic debates about tradition that would
> characterize the Islamic movement in the Indies in the 1910s and 1920s. [. . .]
> It seems rather that future members of both factions were united in the quest to
> regain their independence of action and reinstate Islam as the guiding philoso-
> phy in their own communities; whether quietly like Nawāwī, or aggressively like
> Ahmad Khatīb. (Laffan 2003: 112–13)

Laffan and Latif agree that, although Ahmad Khatib permitted his students to read the works of Muhammad Abduh, he probably allowed this mainly with the intention of better equipping them for refuting the Egyptian's ideas, and that he saw himself first and foremost as a religious scholar of the Meccan *ulama* establishment. The fact that the young Indonesian Muslims who were among his pupils would go on to take up positions in the last remaining sultanates of Sumatra, or ended up as rival traditionalist and reformist activists illustrates the very liminality of Ahmad Khatib's position.[4]

Making Islam modern in Cairo

Where Michael Laffan speaks of 'Cairene Reformism', Yudi Latif refers to the religious trend of which Ahmad Khatib was so sceptical as 'hybrid "Islamic reformism-modernism"'. It was a synthesis of the Islamic reformism, started by the *ulama* in the seventeenth century, and the 'Islamic modernism' embraced by a new generation of Western-influenced Muslims. Often the beneficiaries of both an Islamic religious and colonial state education, these modernist reform-ers had the ambition to adopt that new civilisation while at the same time trying to remain loyal to Islamic culture. In that sense, they can be considered occupy-ing an 'interstitial space between "Islamism" and "secularism"' (Latif 2003: 73).

Cairene reformism and Islamic reformism-modernism both refer to a new strand of Islamic thinking about religious renewal and revival triggered by the activities of the colourful intrigant Jamal al-Din al-Afghani, but developed into a more consistent discourse by Muhammad Abduh and Rashid Rida (1865–1935).[5] Recalling al-Afghani's advocacy of Pan-Islamism discussed in the previ-ous chapter, his involvement in journalism and politics rather than scholarship affirms that it is appropriate to qualify al-Afghani's attempt to make Islam relevant again for the modern Muslim world as 'revivalism' – in contrast to the more cerebral nature of Abduh's reformism. Equally defendable is Yudi Latif's hyphenated 'reformism-modernism', as Cairo had also become an important staging ground for a new Egyptian intelligentsia exposed to Western educational influences, set in motion in the 1840s by the Paris mission of Rifa'a Badawi Raf'i al-Tahtawi (1801–73) and the work of Ali Mubarak Pasha (1823–93) as

minister of schools and works. The advancement of a Western-oriented intelligentsia benefitted further from the introduction of a secular state-sponsored
schooling system that followed in the wake of the British occupation (1882) and
which paralleled in many ways the Dutch efforts in the Netherlands East Indies.
The combined effects of these developments resulted in 'a radical reorientation
of the Egyptian elite through the foundation of modern schools, journals, and
infrastructure' that was mirrored in comparable circles in the Indies (Laffan
2003: 116; Latif 2008: 73).[6]

Against the background of this intellectual onslaught that accompanied
European economic and political imperialism, al-Afghani and Abduh sent out
a clear and urgent message to Muslims worldwide, calling upon them to reunite
by drawing inspiration from the early community of Medina, known as the
salaf salih or 'pious ancestors'. It is important to stress that the initial reincarna-
tion of the *salaf salih* envisioned by this first *Salafiyya* movement was nothing like
that of the literalist Islamism advocated by later activists referred to as Salafis.
Instead, the slogan 'back to the Qur'an and Sunna' was coupled with a call for
the modernisation of education. In order to make Islam into a progressive religion again, Abduh urged Muslims to avail themselves of all knowledge, including Western scientific advances. What also distinguishes this religious discourse
is the role given to the individual:

> Empowered by free will, the individual is to enact the Sunna through a rational
> and personal investigation of the sources of Islam (*ijtihad*, the exponent of such
> being a *mujtahid*) and the application of all aspects of modernity not hostile to
> Islam. [. . .] This methodology forms the structure against which the Cairene
> reformists often define themselves. (Laffan 2003: 121)

Abduh's articulation of this epistemological distinctiveness stands in stark
contrast to the contradictions and inconsistencies in his writings on the envisaged ideal Muslim community. While clear in his rejection of ideologies based
on ethnicity (*al-jinsiyya*) or territorial affiliation (*al-wataniyya*) as materialist and
destructive to human solidarity, his proposed alternative religious sense of community captured in the term *umma* remained ambiguous, because this word 'can,
like the Malay *bangsa*, define a multiplicity of meanings spanning "generation"
to "nation"' (Laffan 2003: 119). Drawing on the Syrian-German social scientist
Bassam Tibi, Laffan adds that this vagueness can be attributed to the fact that,
historically, there never has been a harmonious, undivided Islamic *umma*.

At the same time, it is important to remain cognisant of the fact that Egypt had
not been completely turned into a centre of modernisation or religious reform.
In fact, Abduh's ideas met with a very hostile reception at the bastion of traditionalist Sunni learning: al-Azhar – to which many students from around the
Muslim world continued to flock. In this regard, it is also important to point out
the existence of a so-called *riwaq al-jawi* or '*jawi* hall' at al-Azhar, which catered

for students coming to this Islamic metropole from Southern Arabia, India and Southeast Asia. Michael Laffan's meticulous research of Arabic and *jawi* source materials has turned up one Isma'il al-Minankabawi as the shaykh of the *riwaq* during the 1880s. Educated in Mecca and active as a Naqshbandiyya recruiter in Singapore during the 1850s, his Minangkabau origins – together with the later presence in Cairo during the 1890s of yet another scholar from that same region, Shaykh Isma'il Abd al-Mutallib – may have motivated Ahmad Khatib's encouragement of his own pupils to pursue further studies in Cairo. One individual to take up that suggestion was his own cousin Tahir Jalaluddin, who came to Egypt after a fifteen-year tenure in Mecca. In fact, it was during his time at al-Azhar (1895–9) that Tahir Jalaluddin made contact with Muhammad Abduh and also established a relationship with Rashid Rida for future collaboration.

Taking Cairene reformism home: the *kaum muda* of Sumatra

The prominence of Muslim scholars from the Minangkabau in the early introduction of Islamic reformist ideas is further illustrated by the role played by returning students of Ahmad Khatib in the dissemination of this new Islamic discourse in Sumatra and in the profiling of its proponents as *kaum muda* or 'young generation'. According to Werner Kraus, this *kaum muda* activism can still not be completely divorced from the traditionalist discourse of the *kaum tua*, as he sees the Naqshbandiyya order as the predecessor and trailblazer for the modernist reformism coming from Cairo (Kraus 1984: 125).

Back in Sumatra, the *kaum muda* found their primary field of activity in educational reform. The first modern Islamic school was pioneered by Abdullah Ahmad (1878–1933), who had attended a Dutch-language primary school and studied with Ahmad Khatib in Mecca (1895–9), followed by a short visit to Cairo. Initially working at his father's *surau* in Padang Panjang, in 1909 he founded a *madrasa*; introducing graded classes, classroom teaching instead of the traditional *halaqa*, and non-religious subjects that were also taught at secular state schools. In terms of organisation and curriculum, the Indonesian *madrasa* (Javanese reformists were deploying similar initiatives) positioned itself between a *pesantren* or *pondok* and a secular state school. Naming a school *madrasa* indicated that the educators had the ambition of taking part in the emancipation project of *kemajuan* (*kemadjoean*), or 'progress', while remaining rooted in an Islamic worldview (Latif 2008: 83). In 1915, Abdullah Ahmad's school received Dutch recognition as the *Hollandsch-Inlandsche School* (HIS) *Adabijah*. This association with the colonial authorities was later reason for other Islamic modernists to disown Abdullah Ahmad's contributions.[7] Other former students of Ahmad Khatib, including Muhammad Djamil Djambek (1862–1947) and Muhammad Thaib Umar (1874–1920), were also involved in similar initiatives; but the most successful endeavour was a school founded by Abdul Karim Amrullah (1879–1945), alias Haji Rasul (Hadji Rasoel).

Haji Rasul was destined to become the most prominent exponent of his generation of *kaum muda*. The son of a local Naqshbandiyya shaykh, Haji Rasul spent seven years in Mecca before returning to Sumatra in 1906. First working as an itinerant teacher in the Padang and Bukittingi region, he then set himself to reform a traditional Islamic school that had been established in the late nineteenth century, *Surau Jembatan Besi*. Haji Rasul felt emboldened to take such a step because of the support he had managed to secure from the Dutch in an earlier confrontation with *penghulu* chiefs of the Lake Maninjau region in 1911. In this dispute the local colonial administrator had sided with Haji Rasul, affirming that – while *adat* fell within the jurisdiction of the *penghulu* – 'matters of religion were Rasoel's domain' (Laffan 2003: 173). Starting in 1912, he initially worked with the support of Abdullah Ahmad, following the latter's example of introducing classrooms and grades in 1916, but also infusing its teachings with a new internationalist Islam. Eventually, the school became part of a federation of reformed *surau* and gained fame under the name *Sumatra Thawalib*. Reassured by the earlier Dutch backing he had received, Haji Rasul also oversaw the building of a new mosque with Middle Eastern-style minarets to replace the old Kubu mosque at Lake Maninjau with its traditional Minangkabau architecture.

An even wider *madrasa* network called *Persatuan Guru-Guru Agama Islam* (PGAI) was set up in 1918 under the chairmanship of Zainuddin Labai al-Junusi. This project tried to also bring on board the traditionalist *ulama*. However, throughout the Indies, the latter preferred to develop their own initiatives. As early as 1906, Surakarta's Susuhanan Pakubuwono IX (r. 1893–1939) founded *Pesantren Mambaul Ulum*, while in the Minangkabau, one of Ahmad Khatib's former pupils on the traditionalist side of the spectrum, Sulaiman al-Rasuli (1871–1970), established the *Ittihadul Ulama* to rival the PGAI.[8]

The role played by the Naqshbandiyya 'purification agenda' vis-à-vis certain Sufi practices and the bridge function performed by transitional figures such as Ahmad Khatib, affirm the importance of being cognisant of both continuity and change when assessing religious reformism.[9] Naqshbandi involvement and interstitial *ulama* like Ahmad Khatib are illustrative of the blurred lines between Meccan and Cairene Reformism, between *kaum tua* and *kaum muda*. The distinctions between the two are ambiguous and only tend to turn into dichotomies or binary opposites when demarcations of respective spheres of influence and political power come into play.

At the same time, it cannot be denied that the introduction of a new Islamic education system open to Western and West Asian intellectual and cultural influences, or even mundane changes such as the adoption of Western dress, resulted in growing tensions between traditionalist and modernist Muslims. Laffan reports how the *kaum tua* branded the *kaum muda* not only as *zindiq* (heretics) and *mu'tazila* (a controversial rationalist theological school dating back to the ninth century), but also accused them of being *khawarij* (a rebellious sect first emerging in the seventh century), and – with the rise of a new Saudi state in Arabia – agents of Wahhabism. While the Sumatran reformists initially rejected such appellations, after becoming better acquainted with the writings of Ibn Taymiyya (1263–1328) and Ibn Qayyim al-Jawziya (d. 1350), they defiantly identified with this duo's opposition to local practices, which were considered *bid^c a* or unlawful innovations. Angered by this provocation, in 1916, the *kaum tua* representatives wrote to the Meccan *ulama*, who in response issued a *fatwa* in which Abdullah Ahmad, Haji Rasul, Djamil Djambek and Zainuddin Labai al-Junusi were declared 'apostates and liable to imprisonment by the Sharif should they journey to Mecca' (Laffan 2003: 172).

While by the early 1900s the battle-lines appear to have been drawn, it should also be clear that with their shared *santri* backgrounds, the differences between traditionalist and reformist-modernist Muslims tend to fade, in particular when compared with Sumatra's matrilineal Minangkabau culture or Java's *abangan*. Notwithstanding their shared preoccupation with *kemajuan*, there was also growing diversification among the *kaum muda* themselves. All this forms part of what Yudi Latif calls the 'polyphony' and 'polyvalence' of Indonesia's public sphere (Latif 2008: 129–30).

Print Islam

Aside from educational innovation, another important tool in the spread of reformist Islamic ideas was the introduction of the printing press and the establishment of new media, such as newspapers and other periodicals. For centuries, the Muslim world had held off introducing the printing press for a variety of reasons, including its traditional reliance on the oral transmission of knowledge and permission to teach from individual teachers to pupils. Additionally, there were objections by the copyist guilds because of the threat the new technology posed to their trade; rumours that presses were cleaned with brushes made of pig bristles; and associations with Western – colonial – influences (Larsson 2011: 194). Consequently, Ottoman *ulama* had issued *fatwas* against the use of the printing press and while – eventually – permission was granted in 1727, it was not until well into the nineteenth century that, on the back of other modernisation efforts, it became a more widespread medium throughout the Muslim world (Albin 2009: 171). The first identified presence and use of a printing press by Southeast Asian Muslims can be traced to Palembang in 1848. New presses followed suit in Surabaya and Riau. Between the 1850s and 1870s, these early publishing houses began turning out the first printed Qur'ans and editions of the writings of al-Raniri, al-Palimbani and al-Banjari. In Batavia, Sayyid Uthman had been running his own press since 1875 to turn out tracts against his Naqshbandiyya opponents. Interestingly, the latter were at the forefront of what Laffan calls 'Sufi Print'. Other *tarekat* were not to be outdone and refused to give in, and 'evidence from the 1890s suggests instead that competing local orders employed similar strategies' (Laffan 2011: 60–1).

Malay-language periodicals promoting Cairene reformism

Although Laffan questions whether copies of al-Afghani and Abduh's short-lived Parisian journal *Al-Urwa al-Wuthqa* (1884) ever reached a Southeast Asian Muslim audience, its format and that of the most important organ of Cairene Reformism, Rashid Rida's *Al-Manar* (established in 1898) did stimulate aspirations among Southeast Asian Muslim intellectuals to emulate these publications.[10] However, the gateway this created for Muhammad Abduh's ideas, and later for those of Rashid Rida as well, was not in the Minangkabau, Palembang or anywhere else in what is now Indonesia, but in Singapore.

The first such Malay-language periodical modelled on *Al-Urwa al-Wuthqa* and *Al-Manar* was *Al-Imam* (1906–8), set up in Singapore by Ahmad Khatib's cousin and now Azhar graduate, Tahir Jalaluddin, whom Yudi Latif identifies as one of the first so-called '*ulama-intelek* [religious scholars who were literate in modern scientific knowledge]' (Latif 2008: 18). After his studies in Mecca and Cairo, Tahir Jalaluddin's reservations against the Minangkabau's matrilineal culture and adherence to *adat* made him decide not to return home, accepting instead a position at the court of the Sultan of Perak, in British Malaya, before moving on to Singapore in 1905. The *Al-Imam* circle also included Ahmad al-Hadi (1862–1934), a Hadhrami who had been adopted by the half-brother of the Sultan of Riau and who had accompanied Tahir Jalaluddin on the latter's second pilgrimage to Mecca in 1902–3, where they met with Rashid Rida. Another associate, a Cirebon-born Acehnese Hadhrami by the name of Muhammad Salim al-Kalali, about whom little else is known, acted as the journal's managing director. Also involved was a son-in-law of Snouck Hurgronje's Batavia-based associate Sayyid Uthman: Shaykh Sayyid Muhammad bin Aqil bin Yahya (1863–1931). When he became the director of *Al-Imam* Printing Company after the venture's commercial reorganisation in 1908, this gave Rashid Rida reason to believe that Bin Aqil was also responsible for the circulation of his *Al-Manar* in Southeast Asia. In the same year, Tahir Jalaluddin was succeeded as editor by his fellow Minangkabau Haji Abbas bin Mohammad Taha (1885–1945), a Singapore-born intellectual who had been educated in Mecca and who worked as a translator of educational books from Syria and Egypt.[11] In terms of how *Al-Imam*'s content reflects the concerns of its reformist editors, Azyumardi Azra observes that:

> *Al-Imam*'s first concern was with religion and not directly with social, even less with political change. At the same time, such a tripartite division would have in some measure been foreign to the editors and writers of the journal, who shared the traditional Islamic concept of the undifferentiated umma in which spiritual,

social, and political well-being is subsumed under other criteria – the good and profitable life according to Divine Law. (Azra 2006: 149–50)

Although political quietists, *Al-Imam*'s editors did entertain one pet project: Pan-Islamism. Given its intellectual lineage and the fact that the periodical's brief existence (1906–8) coincided with the final years of Sultan Abd al-Hamid II's reign, this is not surprising. However, as a further survey of its issues shows, the contributors' most enduring concern and abiding interest was in the general state of affairs in Southeast Asian – in particular Malay – Muslim societies. Self-critical in its reflection, *Al-Imam* sought the root causes for its societal ills – backwardness, laziness, complacency and subjugation to foreigners – in Malay ignorance of the teachings of Islam. To escape from this lethargy, the writers urged their readers to use their God-given intellect and make use of all available knowledge. Rejecting the claims of their detractors that Islam is hostile to Western knowledge and progress, they insisted it is imperative for Muslims to educate themselves, albeit within the confines of the spirit of Divine Law. Consequently, it is also incumbent on rulers, traditional leaders and the *ulama* to stimulate education and economic development, while cleansing Islam of impurities brought about by incorporating local customs and beliefs derived from other religions than Islam. This means a return to *ijtihad* and refraining from *taqlid*, which modernist reformists qualify as 'blind imitation' (*taklid buta*).

Michael Laffan, meanwhile, has checked *Al-Imam*'s discourse for instances of the 'joining of religion with place and people' in order to analyse how Arabic and Malay terms for 'homeland', such as *watan* and *tanah air*, or 'people/nation' – *umma* or *umat* and *bangsa* – slipped into the vocabulary of the religious reformists, in spite of their warnings against attaching too much importance to ethnicity, at the expense of humankind's shared inner nature and knowledge of Islam. Another challenge facing *Al-Imam*'s editors was how to link *jawi* religion and culture to the historiography of the wider Muslim world. The end result of their efforts to balance or reconcile the different aspects impacting on Indonesian Muslim identity formation was a tendency to belittle their own traditions and regard Muslim Southeast Asia as peripheral to what are so persistently perceived to be the central lands of Islam in West Asia. In the final analysis, *Al-Imam*'s attempts to merge religion, territory, ethnicity and historical experience into a notion of Islamic nationhood were prone to the same ambiguities as Laffan signalled earlier in Muhammad Abduh's writings.

Another pioneering periodical in the same vein as *Al-Manar* and *Al-Imam* was *Al-Munir* (1911–15). Although it was primarily targeted at a Minangkabau audience, its readers too were 'bound to both Arabic- and Western-language metropoles', because 'more than anywhere in the Indies, reformism and the networks of the Ethici intersected in the Alam Minangkabau' (Laffan 2003: 172–3). Established in 1911, *Al-Munir* was managed by Ahmad Khatib's former student and founder of the *Adabijah* School, Abdullah Ahmad. It also included Haji Rasul among its correspondents. The latter was chiefly responsible for the publication's shift from a pro-Western to a more puritanical strand of reformism inspired by the thinking of Rashid Rida. The journal encouraged Indonesian Muslims to go study in Cairo and actively promoted the ideas expounded by Rashid Rida in *Al-Manar*. In 1913, it also set up a sister publication in Cairo called *Al-Ittihad*, with Abdullah Ahmad acting as its agent in the Indies. Although focussed on showcasing the inspirational ideas emanating from Cairo, *Al-Munir* remained supportive of *jawi* scholarship in Mecca, which now gravitated around the figure of Abdallah al-Zawawi (1850–1924). After a long exile in Pontianak (1893–1908), this scholar had returned to Mecca to take over Ahmad bin Zaini Dahlan's position as *mufti* of the Shafi°i school, thus becoming the *guru besar* (professor) and mentor of the Indonesian student community (Laffan 2003: 199). Like *Al-Imam*, the writers of *Al-Munir* also promoted Muslim self-improvement and vigilance against 'the decline of one's *bangsa* and homeland – now phrased [. . .] as the *tanah air*' (Laffan 2003: 174–5). *Al-Munir*'s editors attached equal importance to not appearing anti-Dutch: 'They were Minangkabau Muslims first and (Sumatran) Malays second – guarded by a benevolent Dutch government that spread its protection over the whole Indies' (Laffan 2003: 176). To underscore this sense of nationhood, *Al-Munir* ran a series of articles in which they celebrated love for the fatherland. The accompanying passive acceptance of colonial rule also echoed Muhammad Abduh's attitude towards the British in Egypt.

This ambition of mobilising a national movement, in which the self-identification as Muslim and an embryonic sense of 'Indonesianess' converged, also opened the way for *Al-Munir* editor Abdullah Ahmad to make overtures to H. O. S. Cokroaminoto (also Tjokroaminoto, 1882–1934), one of the founders of Indonesia's first Islamic mass organisation, the Sarekat Islam (SI). Together they founded yet another newspaper, *Al-Islam* (1916–17). It differed from other *jawi* periodicals in that it also included a final page in *rumi* (Latin) script – signalling a new nationwide focus, which also became clear from its 'significant subtitle: "organ for Indies Muslim nationalists" (*organaan voor Indisch-Mohammedaansche nationalisten*)' (Laffan 2003: 178). The periodical did not last very long, because the educated elites had begun looking for alternative ways of organising their activities. That also meant the use of Latin script in publications. As a result of this reorientation, *jawi* periodicals quickly went out of fashion, and *jawi* script only survived in book printing catering to the traditionalist Islamic – *kaum tua* – circles. This genre of books became known as *kitab kuning* or 'yellow books' – named for the tinted paper from the Middle East on which they were printed. The literature in Latin script used by the *kaum muda* was referred to as *kitab putih* or 'white books' (Bruinessen 1990: 227).

From the 1930s there also began to emerge an Islamic literature written by intellectuals from modernist-activists backgrounds such as Mas Mansur (1896–1946), the jurist Muhammad Hasbi Ash Shiddieqy (1906–75), the future politician Mohammad Natsir (1908–93) and Hamka (1908–81), a son of Haji Rasul who went on to become Indonesia's leading Muslim 'man of letters'. It was through his editorship of *Pedoman Masyarakat* (1936–43) that the latter established his reputation as the leading author on Islamic themes – through both fiction and non-fiction (Riddell 2001: 216–17). In addition, his Minangkabau background also kindled an interest in reconciling Islamic reformism with the sustained Sufi influences in his native region. This led to the publication of his articles about the subject from the 1930s in book form under the title *Tasauf Moderen* (1939), or 'Modern Sufism', which is still widely read in Indonesia today. His fellow Minangkabau, Mohammad Natsir, was also a prolific writer, using a number of pseudonyms to publish articles on Islamic civilisation and the renewal of Islam's teachings in *Pedoman Masyarakat*, *Pandji Islam* and other outlets. Many of these were later bundled into a massive two-volume collection published under the title *Capita Selecta* (1955–7). Natsir had a keen interest in the philosophers and theologians such as al-Farabi, Ibn Sina and al-Ghazali; the scientific contributions of the polymath Ibn al-Haytham; and in Ibn al-Miskawayh, a humanist thinker who is thought even to have influenced the thinking of the German philosopher Schopenhauer. In his study of twentieth-century Islamic theological discourse in Indonesia, Saleh notes that the writings of these Muslim intellectuals tended to keep doctrinal and textual arguments to a minimum, relying primarily on logic and reason, but adding the critical conclusion that it made them prone to 'gross oversimplifications' (Saleh 2001: 105).

Muslim emancipation: the rise of Indonesia's Islamic mass organisations

Aside from the printing press, another important innovation that has been crucial in shaping Indonesia's Islamic landscape is the establishment of Islamic mass organisations or *Ormas*. They are an institutional manifestation of a strategy employed by pious Muslims in the Indies to distance themselves from the coloniser, while becoming more self-assertive by working toward an – initially – non-political emancipation through their own education initiatives and *daʿwa* efforts. This particular focus on learning and teaching was stimulated not least by the more vigorous education efforts of the colonial state itself as part of its Ethical Policy.

Differentiated along 'modernist-reformist' and 'traditionalist' lines, the Islamic mass organisations have also been instrumental in articulating varying doctrinal and ideological positions; thus they have influenced the enduring categorisation of the Muslim segment of the Indonesian people. Since their foundation in the 1910s and 1920s, the mass organisations have grown into a phenomenon that is to be considered as the single most important contributing factor to the Islamisation process in twentieth-century Indonesian society, because they have been definitive for what Islam in Indonesia looks like today, in terms of both the religion's institutionalisation and its discursive formations. The activities of these organisations also generated a certain critical mass in terms of capacity-building. Their education systems and other emancipatory initiatives created a wider pool of human resources from which to draw, thus expanding the organisations' support bases in what is in effect a dialectical dynamic. As has become clear from the discussion so far, intellectual guidance, direction of activism, and political leadership for Indonesia's Muslim population was provided by a handful of individuals. That is not to say that such influential persons have ceased to exist. Turning Islamic mass organisations into effective social movements continued to require the inspiration of charismatic leadership figures.

From Muslim trade union to anti-communist party: Sarekat Islam (SI)

Although roughly one decade into its existence, it would evolve into a political party, at its foundation in 1912, the Sarekat Islam (SI, Islamic Union) started out as a trade union of Muslim merchants with the ambition of becoming a social movement for the sake of emancipating Indonesian Muslims. The first organisation of its kind, the establishment of the SI was the earliest instance of an attempt to fuse Islam and nationalism, thus offering the ingredients for a discourse that continues to recur in Indonesian politics. SI also acted as an incubator in which founders of other Islamic movements and political parties acquired their first organisational experiences. These include not only the founders of the Muhammadiyah, the Masyumi Party and renegade Darul Islam, but even future leaders of the Partai Komunis Indonesia (PKI, Indonesian Communist Party).

Notwithstanding the ambition to combine Islam and nationhood, the SI had 'initially a Javanese character' (Laffan 2003: 167). The union's origins are also a bit muddled. As early as 1905 a Javanese batik trader from Surakarta – originally named Sudarno Nadi, but better known as Haji Samanhudi (1868–1956) – established a self-help organisation for Muslim traders under the name Rekso Rumekso. In her history of the Hadhrami community in the early 1900s, Natalie Mobini-Kesheh notes that, four years later, a journalist and former medical student of *priyayi* origins, Raden Mas Tirto Adhi Suryo (also Tirtoadisurjo, 1878–1918), was involved in the establishment of a similar organisation in Buitenzorg (Bogor), known as Sarekat Dagang Islamiah (SDI, Islamic Commercial Union).[12] She notes that this was set up as a joint venture with members of the Bajunayd family of the local Hadhrami community (Mobini-Kesheh 1999: 42–4). While the first SDI became defunct in 1910, a year later,

Tirto teamed up with Haji Samanhudi to restart the trade union under the name Sarekat Dagang Islam Surakarta. In 1912, Tirto moved to Surabaya where he met the Dutch-educated nobleman-turned-civil servant, H. O. S. Cokroaminoto (Raden Mas Haji Oemar Said Tjokroaminoto in full). With its named shortened to Sarekat Islam, the SI was transformed into a more politicised body with the ambition to represent all Muslims in the Indies.[13] The more senior Haji Samanhudi stayed on as chairman until 1914, when Cokroaminoto took over.

In view of its self-proclaimed 'Islamic commonality and cooperativeness', even members of the Muslim establishment endorsed by the Dutch colonial establishment lent their approval to the SI, including Sayyid Uthman who even spoke at its first mass rally in 1913 (Laffan 2003: 168). With his captivating personality, Cokroaminoto was regarded by many people in the SI's rapidly expanding support base as the embodiment of a 'messianic figure in the mould of the Just King' – the *Ratu Adil* (Laffan 2003: 167). By 1919, SI claimed that its membership had passed the two million mark, although that number has been disputed and put at not more than half a million (Latif 2008: 122, 150). Aside from its Dutch-educated leaders and claims to represent a nationwide Islamic movement, the SI also displayed left-leaning tendencies, evinced by the early involvement in the SI of the two co-founders of the Indonesian Communist Party: Raden Darsono (1897–?) and its first chairman, Semaun (c. 1899–1971). The socialist orientation of the SI is further demonstrated by a 1924 publication from the hand of chairman Cokroaminoto, but with an important difference from Bolshevik ideology. Appearing under the title *Islam dan Sosialisme* ('Islam and Socialism'), it promoted a form of socialism that was at odds with the Marxist theory of historical materialism because it also advocated retaining a place for God. In the course of the 1920s, the socialist-communist presence became the most important factor in the fragmentation of the SI into a 'White SI' (*SI Putih*) and 'Red SI' (*SI Merah*), from which – in 1924 – evolved the political parties Partai Sarekat Islam (PSI) and Partai Komunis Indonesia (PKI) respectively.

An important figure in purging the SI's left wing was the Minangkabau Haji Agus Salim (Hadji Agoes Salim, 1884–1954), Cokroaminoto's successor as party chairman and a future minister of foreign affairs. Added to the pantheon of national heroes in 1961, the figure of Agus Salim is emblematic of the transformation of a bright young administrator and intellectual co-opted by the Dutch colonial authorities into an assertive activist for both Indonesian nationalist and Islamic causes. He was born as Masjhoedoelhak in Kota Gedang, and his father and grandfather had served as *jaksa kepala* of Riau and Padang respectively. He adopted the nickname 'Agus' – given to him by his Javanese nanny – as his official name, which the Dutch then styled into 'August'.[14] Agus Salim's father – who also worked as correspondent for *Al-Imam* and *Al-Munir* –

insisted that his son receive a Dutch-language education. Graduating with the highest honours, Agus Salim's ambitions to become a physician were waylaid by Snouck Hurgronje, who arranged for his admittance to the Colonial Service. In 1904, Agus Salim was '*gelijkgesteld*, that is, elevated to the official rank of a European' (Laffan 2003: 182). Considered a rare honour, he quickly found out that – in practice – this meant very little as he continued to face both discrimination and suspicion. Two years later, Snouck Hurgronje recommended Agus Salim for the post of 'trainee dragoman' (interpreter) at the Dutch consulate in Jeddah. While the Dutch authorities in Minangkabau were concerned about the possibility of Agus Salim falling under the influence of his relative Ahmad Khatib, in Muslim circles questions were actually raised about his commitment to Islam and whether he could be even considered a Muslim at all. This scepticism was eventually dispelled by responses from the editors of *Al-Imam*, who even appointed him as their agent in Jeddah.

Agus Salim's years in Arabia (1906–11) became a transformative experience. Feeling unappreciated by his Dutch superiors, who – in turn – considered him undisciplined and arrogant, he found consolation in visiting Mecca and meeting with Ahmad Khatib:

> Here, then, is the source of Salim's apparent volte-face from emancipated Indiër to committed Muslim [. . .] It is in the Hijaz then that his homeward vision would have been founded, to lie ready for his later role as the leader of an organization which claimed to represent all the Muslims in the Netherlands Indies. Moreover, being a Minangkabau with experience in the wider Indies, his vision of an Islamic homeland would have been broad and inclusive. Yet he was connected to two opposing metropoles – Mecca and Batavia – and his later (nationalist) activities symbolize the coming together of the reformist and secular strands of the national movement. (Laffan 2003: 185)

Back in the Indies, Agus Salim first worked at the central administration in Batavia, before returning home to Minangkabau to establish a *Hollandsch-Inlandsche School* (native Dutch school), only to transfer back again to Batavia to work as a translator for *Balai Poestaka*, the publishing arm of the Office of Native Affairs. For a while, he retained the interstitial or liminal position shared by many members of the emerging indigenous intellectual class – not just in Indonesia but also in other colonies. In his history of Indonesia's Muslim intelligentsia, Yudi Latif invokes Stuart Hall to illustrate that for the *bangsawan pikiran* or intellectual elite, 'Islamic identity was not a fixed condition' and that this 'hybrid intelligentsia [. . .] would later lead to the formation of the so-called "*intelek-ulama*" [modern intellectuals/intelligentsia who were literate in religious knowledge]' – a category different from the earlier identified *ulama-intelek* (Latif 2008: 64, 66). Although *Ethici*, like Snouck Hurgronje and his protégés in the Office of Native Affairs, were sympathetic to both Islamic modernism and even moderate forms of nationalism, they also intended to render these tendencies harmless by manipulating Indonesia's Muslims into continued association with the Netherlands.[15] In 1915, Agus Salim was sent to attend his first meeting of the SI as a police informant. However, his meeting with Cokroaminoto brought about a definitive conversion to the Indonesian cause on grounds of a commitment to both modernism and Pan-Islamism, a step that was 'not so much an experience on the road to Damascus, but rather the confluence of several influences on his life' (Laffan 2003: 185).

Soon Agus Salim began carving out a place for himself on the Indonesian political stage. First presiding over the foundation of the Jong Sumatranen Bond (JSB, League of Young Sumatrans) in 1917, he then took up a post as adviser to the broader Jong Islamieten Bond (JIB, League of Young Muslims), which was formed in 1925 as a joint initiative of the SI and the Muhammadiyah. With his campaigning for an independent Indonesia brought together under the banner of Islam, Agus Salim continued in the footsteps of Abdullah Ahmad and Cokroaminoto.[16] However, he also began to press his own stamp on the SI: Agus Salim was instrumental in ending the declarations of loyalty to the Dutch government that had been issued at the organisation's national congresses since 1918. He also became one of the chief critics of perceived Dutch favouritism towards non-indigenous Muslims – the largest segment among the *Vreemde Oosterlingen* (Foreign Orientals) – which was further enforced by his personal annoyance over the patronising attitude of Arab expatriates. What kept Agus Salim's relationship with the Dutch intact was the opposition he orchestrated against the SI's left.

As a demonstration of the Muslims' ability to act in their own right, Agus Salim began preparing for the expulsion of the communists, whose materialism was at odds with the SI's vision of socialism. In 1921, Agus Salim managed to impose Islam as the single foundation of the SI. In order to consolidate this strategy, the SI promoted solidarity with the wider Muslim world, exemplified by its engagement with Pan-Islamism in its international affairs and the establishment of yet another short-lived newspaper, *Doenia Islam* ('World of Islam', 1922–3), which Agus Salim edited himself. While Muslim solidarity was one of the main pillars of the SI, in order to exercise control over its members, Agus Salim directed that affiliations with other Muslim organisations – with the exception of its modernist sister organisation, the Muhammadiyah – had to be renounced (Laffan 2003: 189–91). The combined effect of these moves was the loss of the SI's support base among the Indonesian left, as well as increased competition on the reformist and modernist side of the Islamic spectrum.

Introducing modern Islamic reformism: the Muhammadiyah

The Muhammadiyah was not only established in the same year as the SI, in the beginning it also shared its Javanese orientation. The founder, K.H. Ahmad Dahlan (also spelled Achmad Dachlan, 1868–1923) – not be confused with the

Meccan ʿalim Ahmad bin Zaini Dahlan – was born with the name Muhammad Darwis in the Kauman district of Yogyakarta, the son of the khatib of the sultan's mosque (Laffan 2003: 168). Ahmad Dahlan had been a student of the Minangkabau Ahmad Khatib during his first study tour in Mecca (1890–1), when he deepened his knowledge of Islam and astronomy (Ahmad Khatib's specialist field); while during his second sojourn to Mecca (1903–5), the ideas of Muhammad Abduh had begun to gain greater popularity in the Hijaz. However, upon his return to his native Yogyakarta, he became involved in Budi Utomo, an association for aspiring Javanese intellectuals.[17] As a batik merchant by trade, he also joined the SI; even serving on its central committee, until his preoccupation with the Muhammadiyah became too time-consuming. After coming back from Arabia for the first time, Dahlan caused great unrest by insisting that the qibla (direction of prayer) in the sultan's mosque be adjusted based on his new astronomical calculations. Following his definitive return in 1905, he set up an experimental madrasa along similar lines as the kaum muda schools in Minangkabau. This was followed by the establishment of a reformist Islamic primary school in the Yogyakarta kraton. These modest educational initiatives formed the starting point of the Muhammadiyah, which Dahlan founded in 1912 and formally registered with the authorities in Batavia in order to obtain official state recognition.[18]

In contrast to the SI's preoccupation with economics and politics, the Muhammadiyah concentrates on education and social welfare. Using the groupings of activities proposed by the California-based Indonesian scholar of Islam, Muhamad Ali, for categorising the ways in which reformist Muslims became modern, the Muhammadiyah can be said to concentrate on the revitalisation of daʿwa or proselytisation and strengthening the umma through education rather than politics, although it did have a vivid interest in accommodating religious law. Fauzan Saleh notes that 'the main factors which led to the establishment of the Muhammadiyah were the perceived impurity of religious life, the inefficiency of religious education, the activities of Christian missionaries, and the indifferent attitude of the intelligentsia' to Islam (Saleh 2001: 83). Contrasting him with Muhammad Abduh as 'a man of the pen', Muhamad Ali describes Ahmad Dahlan as 'more a man of action [. . .] who hardly recorded his thoughts in writing' (Ali 2016: 38).[19]

Eager to ensure that Islam remained meaningful for Muslims of the Indies, and taking their cue from both Christian missionaries and the colonial state, Dahlan and his initially small but dedicated group began setting up charitable institutions, such as schools, hospitals and orphanages. The early Muhammadiyah activists made sure to both operate within state-imposed constraints and adopt procedural and institutional conventions from Dutch administrative practices. However, Muhammadiyah leaders were at the same time critical of conversions to Christianity and resentful of the financial support the missionaries received from the state. It was this competition that motivated them to establish their own alternative Islamic charitable networks and use these as platforms for *da^cwa* activities. This still does not mean that relations between the Christian clergy and the Muhammadiyah can be solely seen in antagonistic terms; on a personal level, Dahlan maintained good relations with priests, pastors, Christian doctors and even theosophists. The point raised earlier, not to exaggerate the differences between traditional and reformist Muslims, is mirrored in Muhamad Ali's observation that in modernising Indonesia, 'Islamic reform and European colonialism worked often in different spheres but did not fundamentally serve as contradictory forces' (Ali 2016: 2). Ahmad Dahlan's progressive outlook is further evinced by his attention to the role of women, setting up units within the Muhammadiyah for both women and girls, called Aisyiyah and Nasyi'atul Aisyiyah – named after the Prophet's wife Aisha.

Until Ahmad Dahlan's death in 1923, the organisation's activities remained confined to Java and only following a link-up with Haji Rasul's Thawalib movement on Sumatra did it begin to expand across the other islands. In 1926, another Muhammadiyah branch was set up in South Sulawesi involving, among others, former SI members who were more interested in education and *da^cwa* than politics. Between 1932 and 1934, Haji Rasul's son Hamka played an important role in consolidating the Muhammadiyah's position in South Sulawesi. Since then it has grown into the second-largest Islamic mass organisation of Indonesia – presently claiming to have thirty million adherents. Such numbers must not be regarded as paid-up and card-carrying members, because as the Muhammadiyah expanded, 'it became increasingly not merely an association (I. *persyarikatan*), but a movement (*gerakan*)' – that is, not so much an institutionalised as a dynamic phenomenon that unites people and motivates them into joint action (Ali 2016: 49).

The following statement by Ahmad Dahlan underscores the primacy he attached to education: 'keep going to school, seek knowledge everywhere. Be a teacher and come back to the Muhammadiyah. Be a doctor and come back to the Muhammadiyah. Be an engineer, and come back to the Muhammadiyah' (quoted in Ali 2016: 228). This type of non-religious knowledge was presented under a variety of names: worldly knowledge (*ilmu dunya*), general knowledge (*ilmu umum*), modern knowledge (*ilmu moderen*), as well as perhaps a bit more negatively, foreign knowledge (*ilmu asing*) and Western knowledge (*ilmu-ilmu barat*). Aside from this concern for benefitting from scientific advances, the Muhammadiyah also promotes a holistic view of education; the acquisition of skills for the job market must be balanced with an integrated spiritual and physical development, a sense of nationhood should not come at the expense of religious obligations. While promoting these complementarities, from the Muhammadiyah's primary schools to its universities, priority continues nevertheless to be attached to 'knowledge about the "seeds of religion" (I. *benih agama*)' (Ali 2016: 229).

It has been suggested that the Muhammadiyah's educational initiatives in Yogyakarta met with a more welcoming reception than, for example, Abdullah Ahmad's *Adabijah* School because of the organisation's urban location, where there was already a greater openness to modernisation. While this may apply to its starting point, the fact that – already in the first decade of its existence – the Muhammadiyah had founded close to 300 schools may also have something to do with the population density on Java as compared with the Minangkabau. What the Muhammadiyah shared with the *kaum muda* initiatives on Sumatra was its willingness to work with the colonial authorities. Indicative of this is the adoption of Dutch designations for state-subsidised Muhammadiyah schools, while the unsubsidised schools had to be distinguished by using Arabic alternatives (*madrasa*) or Indonesian adaptations of the original Dutch (*sekolah*). How important financial support from the colonial government was becomes clear from the number of schools run by the Muhammadiyah in 1923: 207 Westernised schools as opposed to eighty-eight *madrasa*.

Although giving primacy to education and being less politicised than the SI, the Muhammadiyah does display an interest in the place of Islamic law in Indonesian society. Rather than relying on *ijma^c* or the consensus of scholars, the Muhammadiyah favours *ijtihad* – more specifically *qiyas*, or individual reasoning by analogy – in dealing with the so-called *mu^camalat*, that is, those issues that do not form part of religious doctrine or acts of worship and for which there are no explicit stipulations in either the Qur'an or Traditions of the Prophet. Ahmad Dahlan regarded reason (*aql*) as an educational tool, but this did not extend to 'comprehending the divine' or to *ibadat* – acts of worship (Ali 2016: 40–1). To that end, the organisation has established an internal body that is charged with the production of legal opinions or *fatwas*. Coming into existence in 1927, this *Majlis Tarjih* or 'Assembly for Deliberation' is envisaged to maintain unity and coherence in the positions taken by the Muhammadiyah.[20] For that purpose the members of this body are expected to reach an agreement on the matters under consideration by deliberating the 'various opinions in dispute and to decide on the most acceptable solution (A. *marjuh*) according to their interpretations of the Qur'an and the hadith' (Ali 2016: 167). The role of the *Majlis Tarjih* is consultative, so its decisions are not binding on judges of religious courts. In line with its loyalist attitude towards the colonial regime, the Muhammadiyah also tended to respect the applicable Dutch laws in the Netherlands Indies, but it was critical of *adat* or customary law and the tendency of the Dutch legal administration to accommodate non-Islamic indigenous legal systems. The Muhammadiyah's hands-on initiatives to resolve social problems were underpinned by the inspiration derived from Abduh's advocacy of *talfiq*, the prevalence of best practice in legal reasoning, over adherence to a particular school (*madhhab*) and its consequential imitation (*taqlid*).

There is a persistent tendency to associate the foundation of the

Muhammadiyah with the first introduction of Muhammad Abduh's ideas in Indonesia, but the previous sections have already made clear that the story is not so straightforward. First of all, Abduh's ideas had already affected students of Ahmad Khatib and entered into the Indonesian public space through periodicals such as *Al-Imam* and *Al-Munir*. Secondly, while Abduh may have influenced the Muhammadiyah regarding educational organisation and a call for returning to the original sources of Islam, when it comes to elaborating religious teachings and beliefs, both Michael Laffan and Fauzan Saleh submit that Muhammadiyah theologians 'were more amenable to conservative Ashᶜārī doctrine which Rashīd Ridā, and not Muhammad ᶜAbduh offered' (Laffan 2003: 170). Consequently, Fauzan Saleh's detailed study of Muhammadiyah theologians shows that – in terms of doctrine – there is more that unites *santri* Muslims from traditionalist and modernist backgrounds than separates them; the differences are more a matter of accent than of kind.

The Muhammadiyah is adamant that its doctrinal positions are firmly embedded within Islamic orthodoxy, even though it does not explicitly self-identify as belonging to the *Ahl al-Sunnah wa'l-Jamaᶜah* ('People of the Tradition and Community') – except when it comes to decisions promulgated by the *Majlis Tarjih* which 'are to be based on the precepts of the Ahl-Haqq wa'l-Sunnah' (Saleh 2001: 68). The Muhammadiyah rejects criticism by its detractors that by its promotion of *tajdid* (renewal) as a necessity it has placed itself outside of this community. This view of *tajdid* is twofold. First of all, it envisages restoring the teaching of Islam to the pure and original form in which it is laid down in the Scriptures, that is, the Qur'an and Hadith. Secondly, 'since Islam encompasses at the same time universal values, the *tajdīd* of the Muhammadiyah also refers to the implementation of Islamic teachings in accordance with the demands of the developments of the modern age' (Saleh 2001: 82). Leading Muhammadiyah figures such as Munawar Chalil (1908–61) and Jarnawi Hadikusama (1920–93) have persistently argued that because, in both its social and religious activism (*amal wa ibadah*), the Muhammadiyah bases itself on the Qur'an and the Traditions of the Prophet, the organisation must be considered as adhering to Sunni orthodoxy. It could even be argued that, since the Muhammadiyah does not explicitly state that it represents the *Ahl al-Sunnah wa'l-Jamaᶜah*, it can 'claim fairly that it is a "non-sectarian" movement' (Saleh 2001: 81).

Moreover, given the Muhammadiyah's orientation towards the practical implementation of Islamic teachings, its preoccupations are different from classical theological schools in that:

> The Muhammadiyah [. . .] will not involve itself, for instance, in debating the nature of God or the number of His attributes as the Ashᶜarites or Māturidites delighted in doing, nor will it be distracted by controversy over the *qadā'* and the *qadar*, or the validity of the five principles of Muᶜtazilism (*usūl al-khamsah*). (Saleh 2001: 89)

Instead, in regards to purifying Islam, the Muhammadiyah is very much concerned with weeding out instances of *bid^c a* (unlawful innovations) and *khurafat* (superstitions). Together with *takhayyul* – heretical phantasms – they form the three central terms in the movement's theological vocabulary, or what Fauzan Saleh has dubbed 'Muhammadiyah phraseology' (Saleh 2001: 107). The persistence of this concern is demonstrated by the resurfacing of these terms in more recent polemical exchanges, where the Indonesianised versions, *takhayyul*, *bid^c a*, *churafat* have been disparagingly abbreviated to 'TBC', so as to imply a pathological condition on the part of those who do not subscribe to the positions held by the Muhammadiyah's puritan wing. The importance of combatting undesirable accretions and innovations was triggered by the success of the Ahmadiyyah Movement among the Indonesian Muslims, since its arrival in the country in the 1920s.[21] It was this immediate concern that had led to the establishment of a 'Consultative Gathering of Ulama' (*Perkumpulan Musyawaratul Ulama*) in 1927. As the predecessor of the *Majlis Tarjih*, it was tasked with the production of a number of doctrinal tracts or treatises, in which the fundamental beliefs – to which Muhammadiyah members must adhere – were laid down.

Eventually these texts have become part of a collection called the *Himpunan Putusan Tarjih* or 'Compilation of Tarjih Decisions' (Saleh 2001: 109).[22] While this text collection represents the official Muhammadiyah position on doctrinal matters, that is not automatically the case with the views held by the various Muhammadiyah thinkers mentioned in this section and other later writers, such as Hamka. One should also not lose sight of the fact that this early text compilation dates to the late 1920s, and that the Muhammadiyah's doctrinal positions have continued to evolve. An instance of this is Hamka's exploration of the issue of predestination, captured in the adage of *qada' wa'l-qadr*, which he began in the 1950s. Although the theological intricacies of this question are beyond the scope of this book, it points to a shift from unquestioned adherence to the adage in the *Himpunan Putusan Tarjih* to the less fatalistic propositions of Hamka, which are informed by reliance on the use of reason and a resulting qualified acceptance of human free will in terms of an ability to judge one's actions as good or evil.

According to Fauzan Saleh, such a diversification of positions 'may be considered a token of the existing "internal pluralism" within the Muhammadiyah' (Saleh 2001: 79). That, in the course of its 100-year existence, the Muhammadiyah has developed into a 'broad church' also becomes clear from the various factions that have been identified within the movement by one of its leading historians, Abdul Munir Mulkhan. First of all, there is the moderately puritan mainstream Dahlan Group, named after the organisation's founder; then there is the more reactionary *ikhlas* group, which takes the most uncompromising stance toward *takhayyul*, *bid^c a* and *khurafat*. More progressively minded Muhammadiyah members are united in nationalist and proletarian strands, known as *Muhammadiyah Nasionalis*

(*Munas* for short) and *Marhaenis Muhammadiyah* (*Marmuh*) respectively. Finally, and indicative of the relativity of the differences between Islamic modernists and traditionalists, there is a bloc of Muhammadiyah members from traditionalist backgrounds, referred to as *Muhammadiyah NU* (*Munu*).[23]

An Arab initiative: Al-Irshad

The 1910s also saw the establishment of a smaller organisation, which had its roots in the Hadhrami community. It was set up by Ahmad Muhammad Surkati (1872–1943), a Sudanese scholar trained in the Haramayn (1896–1908), who was recruited to run a school for the Jamᶜiyat al-Khayr. This charitable organisation catering to the Arab community in Batavia drew its inspiration from the Egyptian nationalist party leader Mustafa Kamil and from the Ottoman Committee for Union and Progress.[24] It was during his tenure with the Jamᶜiyat al-Khayr (1908–13) that Surkati established contact with other Muslim reformists in the Indies, who shared his interest in the ideas of Abduh and Rida. Because of these relationships, Surkati got caught up in the intra-Hadhrami rivalry between the traditionalists, gravitating around the *Alawiyun Sada*, usually referred to as *sayyids* (descendants of the Prophet), and the reformists who were generally not of such noble descent.[25] In 1914, Surkati was forced to leave the Jamᶜiyat al-Khayr, because of his criticism of the obligatory hand-kissing of the *sayyids* and his suggestion that men of non-*sayyid* descent should be allowed to marry women of aristocratic birth.

At the request of other reformist activists, including Cokroaminoto, Dahlan and Salim, Surkati remained in the Indies and founded another *madrasa*, which in turn led to the establishment of the Arab Association for Reform and Guidance (Jamᶜiyat al-Islah wa'l-Irshad al-ᶜArabiya).[26] Although open to all Muslims, the Irshad movement – as it became known – was primarily geared towards 'the propagation of Arabic and Arab norms among locally born Arabs (*al-muwalladūn*) first and their Jawi coreligionists second' (Laffan 2003: 191). Because of its Hadhrami background, the Irshad movement remained much smaller than the SI and the Muhammadiyah. The influence it was able to exercise beyond the numbers of its membership or the community it represented was due to Surkati's cordial relations with the leadership of other Muslim mass organisations and the excellent reputation of its education system.[27]

The puritan Islamic revivalism of Persatuan Islam (Persis)

Compared with the Muhammadiyah or the traditionalist Nahdlatul Ulama, the Persatuan Islam (Persis, Islamic Union) was also a much smaller organisation. Nevertheless, it too occupies an important place on the spectrum of Islamic organisations in Indonesia; not least because it produced one of the leading Muslim politicians of the early postcolonial period: Mohammad Natsir, who not only served as prime minister and leader of the largest and most successful

Islamic party after independence, but in later life continued to play a prominent role in Islamic activism in Indonesia.

Persis too was founded on Java. But where central and east Java were the epicentres of the Muhammadiyah and NU respectively, Persis's activities are associated with Bandung. Apart from its location in the Sundanese heartland, Bandung was also the intellectual capital of the Netherlands Indies, as well as the starting point of a secular nationalist independence movement. Here Persis was founded in September 1923 by merchants descended from traders who had migrated two generations earlier from Palembang, but who now considered themselves Sundanese. It grew out of a Muslim reading group dedicated to the study of articles from *Al-Manar* and *Al-Munir*. Another abiding interest of the members was the ongoing debate between Al-Irshad and Jam'iyat al-Khayr about the status of Arab and non-Arab Muslims. Originally its number of members did not exceed twenty and the only requirement for joining was an interest in Islam.

It was not until 1926 that Persis began to espouse modernist principles, and it was only then that the individual who become the organisation's leading figure in its early existence began attending its sessions. Ahmad Hassan (1887–1958) – later nicknamed 'Ahmad Bandung' – was a Singapore-born Tamil, who had moved to Java to set up a textile business. Although not a scholar or an academic in either the traditional Islamic or modern Western sense of the word, he had received considerable training in the Islamic sciences and would become Persis's chief ideologue (Federspiel 2001: 121). His arrival also led to a split in the original study group, with traditionalist Muslims setting up their own group called the Permufakatan Islam (Islamic Association), which was eventually absorbed by the Nahdlatul Ulama. During the first few years, Sundanese and Minangkabau activists dominated Persis membership, but there were also other foreign-born Muslims like Ahmad Hassan and a number of members of Arab origin. In comparison with other Islamic mass organisations, Persis remained very modest in size until World War II. The reason for this was that expansion of its membership was not a priority for its leaders. Instead, the organisation focussed on creating a 'small, loose-knit organization' that cultivated 'an *esprit de corps*' (Federspiel 2001: 88–9). Leading activists were also involved with other Muslim organisations, with Sabirin holding a prominent position in the Sarekat Islam and Mohammad Natsir serving as one of the leaders of the JIB. Women's and youth wings were also added, but it was not until the 1936 Persis Conference that this constellation was integrated into a more structured organisation.

In its founding statutes, Persis explicitly takes the Qur'an and Traditions of the Prophet as the basis for its propagation and instruction of Islam. Focussing primarily on expounding the correct Islamic positions vis-à-vis contemporary issues, its leaders 'came to regard themselves as a new brand of religious scholars whose efforts were designed to cleanse religion of unauthorized innovation'

(Federspiel 2001: 87). While these objectives are very similar to those of the Muhammadiyah, Persis activists were more confrontational in their approach to purifying Islam of undesirable additions. An example of Persis's assertiveness turning into a form of vigilantism was the formation of so-called Islamic Defence Committees (*komité pembela Islam*). In 1933 and 1934, the committees in Pekalongan and in Bandung launched campaigns against visits to the tomb of the Hadhrami Saint Sayyid Ahmad bin Abdullah al-Attas and against the Ahmadiyya Movement respectively.

The preferred format of Persis for combatting *bidᶜa*, *takhayyul* and *khurafat* was debate. Exchanges with opponents took place in writing as well as in face-to-face encounters, both in private and publicly. Most of the publicly staged debates dealt with challenging traditionalist Muslims, the Ahmadiyya, Christian groups that were perceived to be hostile to Islam, and atheists. In these encounters, Persis was generally represented by Ahmad Hassan, who built up a reputation as an astute debater and who used these exchanges to compose his thoughts for later publication. As for debates in written form, particularly famous was the initially private correspondence between Ahmad Hassan and the future President Sukarno (1901–70) during the latter's exile on the eastern island of Flores. While Hassan's letters have been lost, Sukarno's replies were published later and became known as *Letters on Islam from Endeh*. Hassan also wrote criticisms of Haji Rasul's position on female Muslim attire and of his son Hamka's novels.

In contrast to the Muhammadiyah, Persis did not develop its own organisation-driven education system; these initiatives were generally left in the hands of individual activists. An exception was the *Pendidikan Islam* ('Islamic Education Association'), which in 1932 came under the leadership of Mohammad Natsir, who had given up a scholarship for studying law in the Netherlands in order to become a teacher. 'Taken aback by the lack of religious knowledge of his secondary school classmates', he had already written a number of textbooks in Dutch on religious practices and obligations (Madinier 2015: 289). Partly state-funded, partly fee-charging, the association ran a Dutch-language primary school (*Hollandsch-Inlandsche School*) and a junior high school (*Meer Uitgebreid Lager Onderwijs*, MULO). Later Natsir added a teachers' training school (*kweekschool*) in Bandung and, by 1938, the association was running schools in five other Javanese locations. In 1936, Persis introduced a different educational format under the name *pesantren*, which focussed primarily on teaching religious subjects. This school was directed by Ahmad Hassan, with Mohammad Natsir as the principal teacher.

Like other Islamic organisations, Persis too recognised the importance of print media in getting its message across and for presenting the arguments made in the debates to wider audiences. Closely associated – but never formally acknowledged – to the above-mentioned Islamic Defence Committees was the organ *Pembela Islam* (1929–35). Circulating in wider modernist Islamic circles, it was distributed not only in Java but also in Minangkabau, Kalimantan, South Sulawesi and even southern Thailand. After six years the Dutch withdrew its publishing licence on account of a fiery rebuttal to criticisms of Islam by Christian writers. Another Persis periodical was *Al-Fatwa* (1931–3), which dealt with legal issues and was printed in *jawi* script. *Al-Lisan*, founded in 1935 as the successor to both *Pembela Islam* and *Al-Fatwa*, continued to appear until the Japanese occupation of 1942. Between 1937 and 1941, the Bandung branch of Persis ran a Sundanese-language periodical called *Al-Taqwa*, consisting mainly of translated reprints of earlier articles from *Pembela Islam* and *Al-Fatwa*, with a particular focus on those dealing with the need to cleanse Indonesian Muslim life of Hindu and pagan influences. Aside from editing and contributing to periodicals, Persis writers also published their ideas and thoughts in book form. Those texts dealt with doctrinal issues, law and jurisprudence, the Qur'an, Islamic history, the Persis organisation and its objectives, but also politics – in particular Islam and nationalism.

The interests of Persis leaders induced Federspiel to draw a parallel with 'the Afghānī-Abduh-Ridā' [sic] exposition of Islamic modernism' (Federspiel 2001: 186). To my mind, more than anything else, Persis's attitude is a reflection of the rigidity displayed by the later Rashid Rida, rather than the pragmatism and intellectual flexibility of his predecessors, al-Afghani and Abduh. That image is further reinforced by Federspiel's more accurate identification of an affinity between the positions held by Persis and the ideas of the Pakistani Islamist ideologue and leader of Jamaat-e-Islami, Syed Abul A'la Maududi (1903–79), as well as those of the founder of Egypt's Muslim Brotherhood, Hasan al-Banna (1906–49). This is much more in line with Persis's tendency to regard those holding different positions as real adversaries. It also corresponds to Federspiel's characterisation of its members as first and foremost ideologues.

In comparison with other Islamic reformist-modernists, Persis was much less open to moderation or reconsideration of its position. Ahmad Hassan's writings exude learning combined with a firm conviction in the correctness of his own position, regardless of whether he was writing about theological issues, prophethood, sacred texts, law or nationalism. Persis's concern with the purification of Islam is also illustrated by Ahmad Hassan's preoccupation with *tawassul* – the question of the use of intercession in soliciting divine favours. A widespread practice among Muslim traditionalists, who trace its permissibility to the works of the *Wali Songo*, in Ahmad Hassan's view this harboured the danger of '*shirk*, or polytheism, especially when it is directed towards the spirits of the dead' (Saleh 2001: 147). Whereas one would expect this uncompromising rectitude to translate into a very restrictive definition of who can be considered a Muslim, Fauzan Saleh suggests that Ahmad Hassan actually took a very minimalist position, because he was satisfied with just the pronouncement of *shahadah* or creed – although fulfilment of the other obligations determine the sincerity of that belief. As an explanation for such a relatively relaxed attitude, Saleh suggests that such '[t]olerance is born out of a desire for solidarity which reflects the worldview held by the association Hassan represented, Persatuan Islam, or the "union of Islam". This association sought to bring Muslims together into a single social union' (Saleh 2001: 153). On the other hand, Saleh also notes that Ahmad Hassan qualified 'religious statements or decisions made by teachers or *^culamā*' which are not approved by the Qur^cān and the Sunnah as *shirk*' (Saleh 2001: 148).

Consequently, Persis proposed a stark purification agenda to rid Indonesian Islam of its syncretic elements and superstitions. In line with the erasure of cultural accretions that had no part in what Persis considered the standard Islamic practices and teachings of Islam, Persis ideology held that:

> Within Islam all believers were equal in status before God, so there could be no race, people, family or individual who could claim superiority. The only legitimate completion among Muslims was to be achieved in piety. Consequently, claims of Arab superiority over other races, claims of descent from the prophet giving special status, or the use of titles indicating academic attainment or previous performance of pilgrimage were not valid in the functioning of the Islamic community. Ancillary to this principle was the corollary that all languages were appropriate for carrying the Islamic message. (Federspiel 2001: 184)

This emphasis on piety should not just guide Muslims in their personal conduct, but should also inform family and communal life. Consequently, religious affiliation should have primacy over nationalist feelings of attachment to the country and its people. The only validity of Indonesia as a political entity was to consolidate Islamic identity. Combining this commitment to Islam with the imperative of dismantling colonialism suggests an allegiance to the Pan-Islamist agendas of politicised Muslim activists.

The traditionalists respond: the founding of the Nahdlatul Ulama (NU)

The 1926 establishment of the Nahdlatul Ulama (NU) by traditionalist religious scholars was not simply a reaction to the formation of reformist-modernist Islamic organisations in Indonesia and their challenges of what the latter considered un-Islamic practices, but which the former regarded as part and parcel of acculturated orthodoxy. The NU's founding was also connected with developments in the Hijaz and the so-called Caliphate Question arising after the 1924 abolition of the Ottoman Caliphate by Mustafa Kemal Atatürk (1881–1938).

In the run-up to this dramatic event, as the leaders of the *kaum tua*, the traditional religious scholarly community – among them the future NU's co-founder and first chairman Kyai Hasyim Asy^cari (1875–1947) – had been rallying around Sharif Husayn of Mecca (1853–1931). In him they found an ally for making common cause against attempts by their *kaum muda* opponents to gain influence in the Haramayn and the wider Hijaz region. While Sharif Husayn helped the *jawi* scholars in keeping Mecca as their enclave by convening a meeting of Javanese, Malay, Minangkabau and Palembangese residents of Mecca to warn them against emulating Egyptian *kaum muda* practices, the local congregation of scholars from Southeast Asia were also a welcome support base for the sharif against the advancing Wahhabi movement, again led by the Al Saud dynasty from Central Arabia. A contributing factor to the growing *kaum tua–kaum muda* antagonism was the latter's shift 'from the open and eclectic attitude of Muhammad ᶜAbduh and Achmad Dachlan to the rigidity of Rashīd Ridā and Hadji Rasoel' (Laffan 2003: 203).

In the confusion caused by the Saudi conquest of Taif and Mecca in October 1924, during which several *jawi ulama* had died alongside Mufti Abdallah Zawawi, most of the surviving scholars returned home on vessels chartered by the Dutch colonial authorities for the evacuation of the Indies community from the Hijaz. Arriving back home, the repatriated scholars became caught up in a whirlwind of activity around a recently formed Caliphate Committee, which – in turn – had been set up within the context of a series of so-called Al-Islam congresses, organised by the SI with the purpose of bringing the broadest possible spectrum of Indonesian Muslims together in order to coordinate their activities. Pushed onto the defensive by in particular Agus Salim's enthusiasm for the Saudi ruler Abd al-Aziz ibn Saud as a prospective caliph, in August 1925, traditionalist scholars from central and east Java formed a spinoff *Komité Hijaz* (Hijaz Committee). Meeting again 'in Surabaya in January 1926, the Hijaz committee decided to reconstitute itself as a permanent organization, choosing the name *Nahdlatul Ulama*' (NU) or 'Renaissance of the scholars' (Bruinessen 2015: 110).

The driving forces behind the newly formed NU were its first *rais akbar* or 'Supreme President', Hasyim Asyᶜari, and his former pupil Wahab Chasbullah (c. 1883–1971), who took the position of secretary (*katib*) to the Consultative Council. The senior *kyai*'s prestige was closely attached to the successful *pesantren* he had set up in 1899 at Tebuireng, in the Jombang district – the very heartland of east Java's '*pesantren* world'. Wahab Chasbullah's reputation rested on his erudition and abilities for sharp argumentation. Aside from these qualities, Michael Laffan points up other similarities between Wahab Chasbullah and the Minangkabau *kaum muda* leader Haji Rasul: both were former students of Ahmad Khatib in Mecca, strong advocates of educational reform and proponents of the need for *ijtihad* to ensure jurisprudence remained in line with social conditions. Although Wahab Chasbullah's conventional *pesantren* background and resolute leadership had gained him a loyal following, these other affinities explain why he was at the same time a controversial figure – not to mention his fondness for fast cars and motorcycles. Consequently:

The more devoted of his supporters regarded him as a *wali* (saint), an *ulama besar* (eminent religious scholar) and *bapak rohani* (spiritual father). For his detractors he epitomised some of the worst aspects of traditional ulama-hood; he was seen as authoritarian, self-serving, casuistical, politically naïve and corrupt. [. . .] he nonetheless had a profound impact on traditional Islam from the late 1910s and, to a lesser extent, on national politics in the 1950s and early 1960s. (Fealy 1996: 2–3)

From his return from Mecca in 1915 and well into the 1920s, Wahab Chasbullah maintained close relations with the SI, with Indonesian communists and with a very young Sukarno, thus becoming a fixture in Surabayan politics too. In partnership with the future Muhammadiyah scholar Mas Mansur, he established the *Madrasah Nahdlatul Wathan* (Revival of the Homeland School). At the same time, he remained active within traditionalist circles. Apart from setting up a commercial cooperative for Muslim traders in Jombang called *Nahdlatul Tujar* (Revival of the Traders), of which he was the treasurer with Hasyim Asyᶜari serving as chairman, he also took the initiative for a discussion group called *Tashwirul Afkar*.²⁸ Against the background of the earlier mentioned growing antagonism between Meccan and Cairene reformists, in which Chasbullah profiled himself as the chief spokesperson for the traditionalist bloc, his own once cordial debates with figures such as Ahmad Dahlan and Ahmad Surkati also became more acrimonious, while his business relationship with Mas Mansur broke down in 1922. At the Al-Islam congresses held between 1922 and 1924, the modernists accused the traditionalists of *shirk*, while the latter retorted by branding the modernists as unbelievers (*kuffar*) – a serious allegation by any Islamic standard. As a sharp-witted debater, Wahab Chasbullah played a prominent role in these heated exchanges. In the highly charged atmosphere of the interwar period '[h]ostility between the traditionalist and reformist groups in Indonesian Islam peaked during the late 1920s and early 1930s' (Fealy 1996: 14). In contrast to the ideological animosity, the NU adopted some of the modernist-reformists' institutional and organisational practices, establishing journals and opening branches in different regions of the archipelago. It must be said that – in comparison with the Muhammadiyah – the NU has remained more focussed on Java and Madura, while institutionally it has also remained more chaotic than its modernist counterpart.²⁹

It is in this antagonistic climate that the fifteen *ulama* who formulated the so-called *Khittah 1926* – the organisation's constitution of 1926 – entered an explicit declaration of subscribing to 'the doctrines of the Ahl al-Sunnah wa'l-Jamāᶜah as far as their religious beliefs and practices are concerned' (Saleh 2001: 67). As explained earlier, this is one of the key doctrinal differences from the Muhammadiyah, which – while not denying such adherence – does not go beyond an implicit recognition of such principles. Aside from this claim of representing Sunni orthodoxy in its Shafiᶜi legalist manifestation, Ashᶜari or Maturidi theology, and the Sufism of al-Junayd and al-Ghazali, the NU is also cognisant of the cultural dimensions of traditionalist Indonesian Islam. To illustrate this difference, Fauzan Saleh cites the two divergent approaches propagated by the *Wali Songo*, according to which Sunan Ampel and Sunan Giri advocated an undiluted Islam whereby 'indigenous customs would not be tolerated', whereas Sunan Kalijaga displayed a 'broad tolerance of local customs [. . .] trying to accommodate or revive local culture' (Saleh 2001: 69–70).

Outside Java: the establishment of the Persatuan Ulama Seluruh Aceh (PUSA)

Not all initiatives for Islamic mass organisations originated on Java. At the end of the 1930s, reform-minded Acehnese *ulama* formed an organisation of their own, the Persatuan Ulama Seluruh Aceh (PUSA, All-Aceh Association of Ulama). While James Siegel says they had the same goals as nineteenth-century reformist *ulama*, Edward Aspinall characterises them as modernist, because they established *madrasa* with curricula that fused religious instruction with secular learning (Siegel 2000: 97; Aspinall 2009: 28). Whereas mass organisations introduced from the outside had little success in Aceh, by the early 1940s, PUSA claimed to have more than 40,000 members, with another 100,000 in its youth wing. Although PUSA may be regarded as a local organisation because it was exclusively Acehnese in composition, Aspinall stresses that it 'did not exemplify localism' (Aspinall 2009: 28). Its ambition was to unite all Muslims through its religious law with Aceh acting as a source of inspiration and example of Islamic unity. PUSA's concern with Aceh's former glory, when Javanese, Minangkabau and others flocked there to learn about Islam, was expressed in broad Islamic terms and presented within an Indonesian framework – because 'the new signifier, *Indonesia*' had also arrived in Aceh (Aspinall 2009: 30).

James Siegel's close reading of the ideas espoused by PUSA (POESA in his spelling) shows an affinity with the purification of religion from localised cultural accretions advocated by earlier reformists of the nineteenth century, the difference now being 'the willingness of the villagers to understand them' (Siegel 2000: 97). Another important feature is its view of the human person, in which great importance is attached to restraining its instinctive nature, called *hawa nafsu*, by the use of reason (*ʿaql* or *akal*) in achieving obedience to God's commands. According to Siegel, the scholars of PUSA even went so far as to state that '[r]eligion is a guide to *akal* and by means of *akal* we know religion' (Siegel 2000: 104). This dialectic between Islam and reason is generated through the medium of prayer, which is not to be understood as communication with God (an impossibility due to divine transcendence), but as a technique of self-control. Involving ritual purification and a fixed set of ritualised actions, its sacredness consists in its performative character. While this may seem like a denial of the use of reason, it is the 'very arbitrary character of prayer that expresses the self-control of the believer' – a sacred enactment of what is required of a social actor in secular life (Siegel 2000: 114–15).

The connection between the acts of worship – which are more expansive than only prayer – and Acehnese society is also the subject of a series of articles in the organisation's periodical *Penjoeloeh*, where one of the authors draws not only on Islamic Scripture, but also on wider learning and philosophy, even citing the writings of Dutch historians. Interpreting Acehnese history as a cyclical sequence of periods of rationality and irrationality, they conclude that the *ibadat* do not prescribe a particular form of social organisation. However, one particular period is singled out for emulation: 'there is one era which we cannot forget – the era of Al Raniri and Fansoeri [. . .] the time of the flying of the flag of Islam in the land of Atjeh' (Siegel 2000: 121). In contrast with the glorious reign of Sultan Iskandar Muda, the authors regard Aceh during their own time of writing as having regressed into a dormant state from which it needs to be awakened through a proper understanding of Islam. While it may have been a mighty sultanate, Aceh's reputation did not rest on its political prowess, but rather on its 'religious significance as "the doorway to Mecca"' (Siegel 2000: 125). Since their conclusion was that there is no fixed shape for Islamic societies:

> POESA writers offer no suggestions about the shape of a unified society. There is in their writings nothing like the Western conception of a just society. [. . .] One looks to history not for an image of social organization but for an expression of a state of being. (Siegel 2000: 126–7)

This condition has been captured by one of the *Penjoeloeh* writers in a Qur'anic image, which Siegel has borrowed for the title of his book: 'Men want to bind themselves together with the rope of God, the rope which neither rots in the rain nor cracks in the sun' (Siegel 2000: 124).[30]

Modernist-reformist and traditionalist organisations from a comparative perspective

An examination of the differences emerging from the mutual criticisms by traditionalist and modernist Muslims offers valuable insights into the practices of common believers in Indonesia, because earlier historical sources tell very little about this due to their focus on scholarship or court culture. It is only from these disputations and – even more recently – thanks to the work done by anthropologists that it becomes possible to make some tentative historicised extrapolations as to what Islam meant to the Muslim community at large.

Many of these differences are on the level of the so-called *furuᶜ al-ibadat* – the practices of worship. For instance, whereas NU members make twenty-two *rakᶜa* (a sequence of bows and prostrations) for the supplementary evening prayers (*tarawih*) during the month of Ramadan, the Muhammadiyah limit that to eight. The NU holds its prayers at the end of the fasting and the completion of the hajj in mosques, while the Muhammadiyah insist they must take place in the open (Saleh 2001: 76). As part of its campaign against *takhayyul, bidʿa, khurafat*, modernist reformers criticise the celebration of the *laylat al-qadr* or the Prophet's birthday; the recitation of Prophetic panegyrics; and the use of music as developed in the *pesantren*. They also reject the claims of NU scholars that the practices of *tahlilan* (repeated recitation of the first part of the creed), *tawassul* (intercession by dead saints) and *slametan* or *kenduri* (communal charitable meal) are divinely vindicated (Saleh 2001: 75–6, 86–8). Based on her examination of the NU periodical *Berita Nahdlatoel Ulama* (BNO, 'News of the Nahdlatul Ulama'), which appeared during the 1930s, Andrée Feillard has demonstrated the toleration by the NU of certain forms of martial arts and supernatural medicinal and healing practices, on grounds that this formed part of *kebudayaan* – local culture (Feillard 2011: 64–5).[31]

Muhammad Ali has noted that Ahmad Dahlan was not opposed to *tasawwuf* per se – a point picked up later by the leading Muhammadiyah propagator in Sumatra, Haji Rasul, and his son Hamka – both of whom published articles and books on modernised variants of Sufism (Ali 2016: 41; Riddell 2001: 218–20). He also mentions that while Muhammadiyah leaders were often critical of *adat* as part of their mission to purify Islam, on other occasions they also recognised that they had to adopt a more tolerant attitude if they wished to achieve the unification of diverse Muslim groups (Ali 2016: 43, 50). These observations are also in line with Greg Fealy's contention that by the late 1930s, relations between the NU and Muhammadiyah had improved. He suggests that this was due to a shared concern over the growing influence of Christian missionaries and new colonial legislation, which was regarded as increasingly anti-Islamic (Fealy 1996).

The emergence of Islamic political parties in late colonial Indonesia

Chiara Formichi has rightly criticised the downplaying of the 'Islam factor' in earlier studies of late colonial politics in Indonesia during the 1920s and 1930s. By 'bringing religion back into the analysis', she wants to make a case for taking the ideological foundations of such movements seriously (Formichi 2012: 6). An explanation for such reductive views may be found in the scaling back of the influence of organisations such as the SI after the expulsion of its left wing, and in the parallel rise to prominence of figures such as Sukarno and Dr Soetomo (1888–1938),[32] as well as Mohammad Hatta and Sutan Sjahrir (1909–66), all of whom – despite their (nominal) Muslim backgrounds – decided to opt for a secular rather than religiously inspired form of nationalism. The lack of appeal of Islam as a political ideology was further exacerbated by the shift from the eclectic openness found in the earlier Cairene reformism of Abduh and Dahlan toward the more rigid interpretation of Rashid Rida and Haji Rasul, which inhibited the kind of inclusiveness required to rally a multi-ethnic and multi-religious society like Indonesia's behind the independence struggle. Finally, the early attempts to politicise Islam took place against the background of the earlier mentioned Caliphate Question. While the rivalry between different claimants eroded Pan-Islamist unity, the parallel rise of Atatürk after the notorious abolition of the caliphate in 1924 also had great appeal outside the newly established Turkish republic, including giving inspiration to Indonesians such as Sukarno and Hatta. Together with Muslim divisiveness as a result of factional rivalries and ideological infighting, this may help explain why politicised Islam lost much of its earlier lustre, and why it was eventually pushed out of the limelight by the secular nationalists.

In the early 1920s, Islamic political assertiveness had been on the rise. Both Michael Laffan and Rémy Madinier talk explicitly of a 'political hijra' instituted by the Sarekat Islam as a watershed event in the politicisation of Islam (Laffan 2003: 188; Madinier 2015: 39). With Laffan putting that moment in 1919 and Madinier opting for 1923, both agree that the resulting declaration of non-cooperation with the Dutch further weakened the SI. In spite of these tribulations, they also present the total of twelve Al-Islam Conferences convened between 1922 and 1941 as a red thread running through the pre-war trajectory of political Islam. So while this politicisation of religion in its early evolutionary stage was livelier than acknowledged in later historiography, it was already marred by internal divisions. The previous section already pointed at a link between the Caliphate Question and the founding of the NU. Events in the Hijaz, Turkey and – tangentially – also Egypt during 1910s and 1920s remained relevant to Indonesian political Islam in the final decades of Dutch colonial rule. This development must be seen against the background of continuing loyalty of the *kaum tua*, guided by their patrons in the Haramayn, to Sharif Husayn of Mecca and the opposition of *kaum muda* to the latter's inability or unwillingness to protect pilgrims against disrespect, lack of support and outright abuse. Already susceptible to the ideas of Rashid Rida, after the Saudi conquest of the Hijaz in 1926, the *kaum muda* followed the *Al-Manar* editor in his preference for Abd al-Aziz bin Saud as a possible new caliph over the Egyptian King Fu'ad, who had replaced the now totally discredited Sharif Husayn as an alternative contestant for the caliphate.

From Islamic Union to Indonesian Islamic Union Party

The transformation, in 1923, of the Sarekat Islam (SI) into the Partai Sarekat Islam-Hindia Timur (PSI) can be considered 'as marking the beginning of its existence as an explicitly Islamic party', which no longer had as its objective the emancipation of Muslims within the colonial context, but which was intent on achieving genuine self-determination by pursuing Indonesian independence (Formichi 2012: 23). It was on the back of this sea change that, in the course of the 1920s, individuals who would turn into leading Muslim politicians of the post-war period became closely associated with the PSI: the future leader of the Darul Islam (DI), Sekarmaji Marjan Kartosuwiryo (1905–62) joined the party when he was a medical student in Surabaya; then four years later, the future Masyumi leader Mohammad Natsir also became involved in the PSI.

The Dutch-educated scion of an impoverished *priyayi* family, Kartosowiryo became a more or less full-time political activist after his expulsion from medical school in 1927. Chiara Formichi surmises that, in that very same year, he may already have served as General Secretary of the twelfth PSI congress which was held in Pekalongan.[33] At the congress, differences became apparent between the religious, political Islamic and nationalist concerns of Agus Salim and Cokroaminoto's preoccupation with the economic conditions of the indigenous population. However, the duo continued to work together in establishing a 'Council of Religious Scholars' (*majelis ulama*) as a representative body of the so-called *ulil amri* – a term used in the scholarly Islamic literature for Muslim religious leaders who are expected to provide the wider community with guidance. In the wake of this conference, Kartosuwiryo began publishing articles in *Fadjar Asia* that created an impression on the Dutch authorities of having to do with anti-European religious fanaticism. When Agus Salim travelled to Geneva to attend the International Labour Conference hosted by the League of Nations, Kartosuwiryo took over the editorship of *Fadjar Asia*. Aside from his journalistic activities, in 1928, he represented the PSI as a delegate to a large congress bringing together all Indonesian youth organisations, held in Weltevreden and, later, at the JIB congress in Bandung. Kartosuwiryo also pioneered a new way of fundraising, by establishing the PSI's *Komité Zakat-Fitrah*, which was responsible for collecting the mandatory charitable tax. He was also present as executive secretary at the congress where the party's name was changed to Partai Sarekat Islam Indonesia (PSII), signalling its nationalist stance and vision for the future.

The congress also had a broader significance, because it was attended by wide array of Islamic organisations, as well as by the Lahori Ahmadiyya of Yogyakarta, the drivers' union, and even Sukarno and his PNI Bandung branch representative. Sukarno's presence was surprising given the conflict that had arisen between him and the PSI over his 1926 pamphlet *Islam, Nasionalisme dan Marxisme*, and the subsequent establishment of the Permufakatan Perhimpunan Politik Kebangsaan Indonesia (PPPKI, 'Agreement of the Indonesia's People's Political Associations). Originally a joint initiative of Sukarno, Cokroaminoto and Agus Salim, by 1929 the PSI's federative interpretation of the PPPKI came under pressure as a result of differences of opinion over cooperation with the colonial authorities and the PNI's drive towards a merger of nationalist, religious and socialist organisations into a unified front under the PPPKI aegis. In the meantime, another rift had occurred between Cokroaminoto and the Muhammadiyah intellectual Mas Mansur over the former's work on a

Malay version of an English-language Ahmadi translation and commentary of the Qur'an. This was also the reason for the noticeable absence of the Muhammadiyah from the PSII's 1929 congress.

By this time, Kartosuwiryo also began entertaining his own ideas about the kind of unity that the PSII provided for Indonesia's Muslims. He not only framed this in terms of bringing together Islamic groups on a national level, but also added a transnational or Pan-Islamic component. Consequently:

> for Kartosuwiryo and the PSII, *kebangsaan* [nationhood] was not to be linked to worldly desires nor was it limited by any territorial boundary. It was wide and broad, and connected only to the religious affiliation and the unity of Islam: Islamic nationalism was solely committed to the prosperity of God. (Formichi 2012: 44)

Although Kartosuwiryo left the editorial board of *Fadjar Asia* after barely a year, as a protégé of Cokroaminoto he remained a key player in the PSII. It was not until after the death of Cokroaminoto in 1934 and a falling out with Agus Salim over the *hijra* policy of non-cooperation in 1936 that things came to a head within the PSII.

Natsir, meanwhile, had arrived in Bandung in 1927 from the Minangkabau to complete his high school education at the AMS (*Algemene Middelbare School*) – the same year when Sukarno founded the Partai Nasional Indonesia (PNI, Indonesian National Party), an event that turned Bandung into a hotbed of anticolonial activism. Natsir was already close to the PSI through his activities in the JIB, of which PSI leader Agus Salim was one of the founders. At the time, the party's internal politics became very acrimonious, resulting in the further fragmentation of the Muslim camp, when Cokroaminoto declared that party members could no longer belong to the Muhammadiyah, because the latter had objected to working against the colonial administration. According to Audrey Kahin, Natsir never formally joined the PSII, but Howard Federspiel claims that he had been a member until the 1932 purge of Persis members (Kahin 2012: 15; Federspiel 2001: 90).

Islamic or secular nationalism?
While Islamic politics in the 1920s can be said to be characterised by internal dissent and fragmentation, the 1930s were shaped by two other developments: first of all, the confrontation between politics based on Muslim solidarity and secular nationalism became more pronounced. On the one side stood PSII leaders Cokroaminoto, Agus Salim and Kartosuwiryo, as well as Ahmad Hassan and Mohammad Natsir from Persis; on the other side were Sukarno, Soetomo, Hatta and Sutan Sjahrir. Secondly, as a result of this polarisation and the increased profiling of Sukarno as *the* face of the Indonesian independence struggle, the various Muslim parties, factions and mass organisations were

pushed to bury their differences and unite in the Majelis Islam A'laa Indonesia (MIAI, Supreme Council of Indonesian Muslims).

While the PNI was not only in danger of getting crushed under heavy-handed repression on the part of the colonial authorities, but also susceptible to internal divisions over cooperation or non-cooperation with the Dutch, the PSII too became increasingly isolated and further divided because of its persistent rejection of any form of cooperation with the Dutch and its emphatic insistence on couching nationalist politics in Islamic terms. In 1930, this resulted in the PSII's withdrawal from the PPPKI. As part of its alternative Islamo-socialist programme grounded in the unity of the *umma*, the party began to revive the Al-Islam congresses through a permanent Al-Islam Committee initiated by Cokroaminoto. Persistent disagreements on the principle of non-cooperation led to further purges and breakaways from the PSII. In 1933, some expelled party members founded an alternative, cooperationist, party called Partij Politiek Islam Indonesia. Five years later, after managing to recruit several Muhammadiyah members, it renamed itself Partai Islam Indonesia (PII, Islamic Party of Indonesia). Within the PSII itself, remaining leaders such Agus Salim and Kartosuwiryo struggled to fill the void left by the demise of Cokroaminoto.

In 1936, disagreements between the two over the *hijra* policy erupted into open confrontation. Agus Salim's disagreement with an uncompromising continuation of the *hijra* policy formulated by Kartosuwiryo in a document known as the *Brosoer Sikap Hidjra PSII* ('Pamphlet on the PSII's Non-Cooperation Policy') resulted in the ousting of Agus Salim and a victory for the hardliners around Kartosuwiryo. In her analysis of the ideas contained in the pamphlet, Chiara Formichi notes that:

> the *hijrah* to Medina-Indonesia – and hence to an Islamic state – is marked by three steps: *jihad, iman* (faith) and *tauhid* (unity). This path is well trodden, as it places Kartosuwiryo in an intellectual and strategic tradition that connects al-Ghazali (1058–1111), Ibn Taymiyyah (1263–1328), Hasan al-Banna (1906–1949), Abu 'Ala Maududi (1903–1979), Sayyid Qutb (1906–1966) and contemporary Islamist militants. (Formichi 2012: 63)

Kartosuwiryo now became the party's new vice-president. In this new role, he 'declared that the PSII was neither communist nor fascist and inspired by neither Arabism nor "Indonesianess", as its foundation was only Islam' (Formichi 2012: 61). However, other members of the party leadership regarded Kartosuwiryo's ideas as 'mystical' and a step in the direction of founding a 'Sufi *tarekat*' (Formichi 2012: 67). Consequently, in 1939 it was his own turn to be expelled from the PSII. With both Agus Salim and Kartosuwiryo gone, the PSII effectively splintered into three factions. As a result of this constant infighting, the PSII's membership base dwindled from hundreds of thousands to 40,000 in 1937. While a dramatic loss, it still compared favourably to the membership base of Hatta and Sjahrir's PNI Baru or 'new PNI', which had barely a thousand members, and other secular nationalist parties, such as the erstwhile Partai Indonesia (Partindo) or Partai Indonesia Raya (Perindra, Greater Indonesia Party) which hovered between 3,000 and 20,000 throughout the 1930s (Formichi 2015: 58: Kahin 2012: 19).

With Sukarno trying to capitalise on the near-martyr status he had attained as a result of repeated imprisonment and internal exile during the 1930s to keep together a nationalist camp that was equally marred by divisions as a result of disagreements over cooperation or non-cooperation like the PSII, Persis became one of the most important voices opposing the secular nationalists. In the course of the 1930s, Mohammad Natsir rose to prominence as one of the most articulate critics of secular nationalism, alongside the ever eloquent Ahmad Hassan. The previous section alluded already to the Hassan–Sukarno correspondence during the latter's exile in Endeh. Sukarno was later transferred to Bengkulu in south Sumatra. Hatta and Sutan Sjahrir were also arrested and detained at Boven-Digul in New Guinea, but Natsir and Hassan remained free and therefore able to expound their viewpoints more or less uninhibited – although closely watched by an ever vigilant colonial security apparatus.

Aside from being a skilful debater and fiery orator, Ahmad Hassan also wielded a sharp pen dipped in vitriol. In response to a claim by Dr Soetomo, who was both a proponent of Javanese culture and fervent nationalist, that Islam was a moribund religion and that the Kaaba was just an idolatrous Arab shrine, making Mecca less significant for Indonesian patriots than the penal colony of Boven-Digul, Hassan wrote:

> Believers should mark anyone who speaks of [going to prison camp at Boven] Digul as being better than going to Makkah! Anyone who orders the moving of the direction of prayer to [the earlier Islamic kingdom of] Demak [in central Java!] Anyone who abuses the Prophet Muhammad and refers to him as the old fellow of the people of . . . [the desert]! Anyone who holds the law of polygamy revealed by God as wrong . . .! Watch out! (Federspiel 2001: 176)

Natsir shared Ahmad Hassan's indignation over the denigration of the pilgrimage by the secular nationalists as a loss of income to Indonesia. Although insisting that hajj was an 'invisible asset' of tremendous value, Natsir did not attach the same importance to international Muslim solidarity as the Tamil expatriate from Singapore.[34] While Natsir acknowledged the influence of Rashid Rida, he had never warmed to the latter's idea of the caliphate or Pan-Islamism. Since he did not see any realistic opportunity for uniting with colonised Muslims elsewhere, he focussed instead on the Netherlands East Indies. Already in 1932, Natsir had written a series of articles in *Pembela Islam* in which he defended Persis against allegations that it was undermining and effectively splitting the nationalist movement. He retorted that – since Indonesia lacked any other criteria or means to create a sense of *kebangsaan*, such as ethnicity or language – Islam remained the unifying tie and Muslim organisations could therefore claim credit for having been at the forefront of raising and forging a sense of national consciousness and solidarity. In contrast with the antagonism and polemical tone radiating from Ahmad Hassan's correspondence with Sukarno, Natsir actually shared many of the latter's views on democracy and he also agreed with the importance of independent thinking. However, using Sukarno's vivid interest in Mustafa Kemal's Turkey and the way religion's place had been defined there, Natsir wrote two articles in *Pandji Islam* (using the pseudonym A. Moechlis) in which he objected to the reduction of religion to an 'extra', and in which he also cautioned against unbridled 'freethinking' (Kahin 2012: 20–1).[35] While these articles demonstrate Natsir's interest in politics, until the end of the 1930s, his other main activity besides writing had been education. However, in 1938 he decided to join the PII, which had just been established by Wiwoho Purbohadidjojo – like Natsir, a former member of the JIB.

Concluding remarks

Faced with continuing challenge and competition from the secular national- ist camp, Muslim politicians and activists were increasingly pushed to find a common ground. In 1937, this resulted in the establishment of MIAI. Initially set up in protest against a new Dutch marriage ordinance envisaging the con- clusion and dissolution of marriage contracts through civil courts, as well as the prohibition of polygamy, it was then reconceived as 'an Indonesian parlia- ment based on Islamic legislation' (Formichi 2012: 59; see also Kahin 2012: 32). Aside from trying to resolve the differences between cooperationist and non-cooperationist parties, the MIAI also constituted a reconciliation between reformist-modernists and traditionalists. The organisation's central body included not only NU's Wahab Chasbullah (later replaced by the son of Hasyim Asy°ari and Mahfudz Shiddieq) and Mas Mansur from the Muhammadiyah, but also Ahmad Hassan as Persis representative, and the PSII's Kartosuwiryo as treasurer.[36] The formation of MIAI indicates that, during the interbellum, religion had become increasingly politicised for traditionalist and modernist Muslims, political quietists and activists alike. However, the political mobilisa- tion of Islam by Indonesia's Muslim leaders for their own purposes was cut short by the Japanese occupation that lasted from 1942 until 1945.

CHAPTER 5

An Indonesian Islam?

Moving toward the second half of the twentieth century, the Islamisation process in Indonesia was forced onto new trajectories. The confrontations with Dutch colonialism during the preceding 100 years, in the form of the Cultivation System and Ethical Policy, were replaced by the need for a very sudden and rapid adjustment to the accelerated pace on the way to independence brought about by the Japanese occupation during World War II. In the ensuing decades, Muslim activists were not just required to adapt to drastically changing circumstances; in the face of increasingly repressive governments, between the late 1950s and the end of the century, they were effectively forced to reinvent themselves in order to be able to continue their Islamisation efforts under such restrictive conditions. Then on the eve of the new millennium, regime change brought a new opportunity for democratisation.

The political history of postcolonial Indonesia can therefore be divided into three periods, each dominated by a different regime with its own characteristic ways of governance, presenting different contexts within which the Islamisation process has continued to evolve over the last seventy years.

The first two decades of independence coincided with the presidency of Sukarno, in which the elections of 1955 form a kind of caesura. The period began with a decade of continuing nation-building, when the young republic was first engaged in armed conflict with the Dutch (1946–9) and then able briefly to experiment with liberal democracy, an experience in which Islamic political parties played an important role. This was followed by a briefer period during which Sukarno basically ignored the outcome of the 1955 elections and shifted toward what he called 'Guided Democracy' (1957–66) – effectively a presidential system that increased his personal power, although he came to depend on support from the left in the form of an ever more confident communist party. During the same twenty-year period, the unity of Indonesia was also challenged by an Islamic state in west Java proclaimed by Kartosuwiryo; the emergence of other Islam-inspired rebellions in South Sulawesi and Aceh during the 1950s; and eventually by the establishment of a renegade counter-government in south Sumatra when Sukarno's authoritarianism reached its high at the end of that decade. Faced with exclusion from the political process, some leaders of the main Islamic political party, Masyumi, felt compelled to side with the rebels in south Sumatra, which then led to the party's dissolution.

These threats to Indonesia's political and territorial integrity increased the influence and power of the military, which eventually managed to suppress these uprisings in the early 1960s.

Sukarno's rule effectively came to an end with a military intervention in response to a bloodbath in which a number of senior generals perished on 30 September 1965. Allegedly thwarting an imminent communist take-over, the coup resulted in large-scale massacres of suspected communists and their sympathisers. The murky circumstances under which these crimes were perpetrated have never been properly investigated, but the estimated numbers of casualties run into at least the hundreds of thousands. For the next three decades, Indonesian politics would be dominated by the military *Orde Baru* (New Order Regime) of coup leader General Suharto (1921–2008). While keeping political Islam under very tight control and occasionally manipulating it for its own purposes, in the course of the 1970s, the New Order Regime did make some allowances for Muslim participation in governance. This was done in order to mobilise popular support for its energetic development policies – urgently needed to repair an economy left in tatters by Sukarno's disastrous Guided Democracy. In the second half of his rule, Suharto had to walk a tightrope, balancing reduced reliance on the military with the reintroduction of Pancasila as the 'sole foundation' (*asas tunggal*) for all social and political actors, while also making overtures to the Muslim segment of the Indonesian population as an alternative political powerbase.

By the late 1990s, it became clear that these concessions had proved too little, too late. After the dramatic regime change on the eve of the new millennium, the democratisation process that started in 1999 saw an unprecedented opening-up of the public sphere. This sea change in Indonesia's political climate offered new opportunities for socio-political activism across the Islamic spectrum, but also presented a new set of challenges for the world's largest Muslim nation state. Islamic mass organisations, newly formed political parties, NGOs, think tanks and other platforms began presenting a range of competing Islamic discourses. Subscribing to a variety of interpretations and proposing diverging political agendas, they may envisage very different futures for Islam in Indonesia, but at the same time they also appear increasingly assertive and self-confident in articulating an Islam that is distinctly geared towards Indonesia's particular circumstances.

Political Islam during the Japanese occupation

In contrast to the Dutch, after invading and occupying the Netherlands East Indies, the Japanese wartime administration considered political Islam a useful vehicle for what in present-day jargon of military interventions is called 'winning the people's hearts and minds'. Although the PSII and PII were abolished in

1942 and the MIAI disbanded in 1943, the Japanese were more inclined 'to make concessions to Islamic, rather than nationalist, let alone *priyayi*, demands' (Boland 1971: 8). As a substitute for the Dutch Office of Native Affairs, they set up an Office for Religious Affairs (*Shûmubu* in Japanese, *Kantor Urusan Agama* in Indonesian), initially under the direction of a Japanese military officer. In October 1943, Hoesein Djajadiningrat (1886–1960) – a nephew of Snouck Hurgronje's confidant in the Hijaz, the late Aboe Bakar Djajadiningrat, and the first Indonesian to obtain a PhD – took over, but within a year, he was replaced by NU leader Hasyim Asy^cari. Because of his advanced age, the *kyai* preferred remaining at his *pesantren* in Tebuireng – leaving his Muhammadiyah deputy Abdul Kahar Muzakir (1907–73), and his own son Wahid Hasyim (1914–53) in charge of the Office for Religious Affairs.

More important for the future of political Islam in Indonesia was the establishment of the Majelis Syuro Muslimin Indonesia (Consultative Council of Indonesian Muslims; better known under its acronym Masyumi, at the time spelled as Masjoemi). While its predecessor, the MIAI, had primarily focussed on religious activities, Masyumi was destined to become a political institution, thus also enhancing the influence of its members – in particular the NU and the Muhammadiyah. Again, Hasyim Asy^cari was made chairman, with his son acting as his deputy and another Muhammadiyah leader, Mas Mansur, serving as one of its vice-chairmen. Closely linked to Masyumi was the Hizbullah (Party of God); an Islamic youth organisation *cum* militia set up in late 1944. Commanded by NU youth wing leader and future deputy prime minister Zainul Arifin, its top echelons also included the Muhammadiyah activist and future minister Mohammad Roem (1908–83), and several former PSII leaders.[1] After the Japanese capitulation in August 1945, Hizbullah remained not only important for the armed struggle against the Dutch, but also because many of its members eventually merged into the regular armed forces, thus becoming part of the national army of Indonesia (Tentara Nasional Indonesia, TNI).

In the final year of the war, Muslim activists became involved in a series of initiatives deployed in preparation for independence which now seemed imminent – although no longer on the basis of early Japanese promises to that effect, but due to a dramatic the turn of events in the Pacific and Southeast Asian theatres of war that was making a Japanese defeat inevitable. One such body was the Committee of 62, in which Masyumi representatives took part 'to prepare Muslims for the liberation of their country and their religion' (Boland 1971: 16). This addition is important, because for Muslim politicians, Indonesian independence remained closely bound up with the formation of an Islamic state, even though secular nationalists (which also included politicians from Muslim backgrounds) campaigned for a unitary nation state in which religion was kept out of the political process. Whereas the secular nationalists often took their cue from developments in Turkey, while at the same time pointing at the cultural and demographic differences between the Arab world and Indonesia, Muslim leaders drew inspiration from developments in British India and the eventual emergence of Pakistan. Therefore, Sukarno's soon infamous 'Pancasila Speech' did not bode well for Islamist aspirations in Indonesia.

Toward independence: the Pancasila Speech and the Jakarta Charter
In this landmark address, Sukarno laid out his 'Doctrine of Five Principles'. Using the Sanskrit term *Panca Sila* rather than an Arabic expression with Islamic connotations, it consisted of nationalism (*kebangsaan*), humanitarianism (*peri-kemanusiaan*), mutual deliberation (*musyawaratan*) or democracy, social welfare (*kesejahteraan*) and the belief in one God (*ketuhanan yang maha esa*). While studiously avoiding the name Allah, Sukarno tried placating the Muslims by assuring them that the third principle of democracy offered sufficient safeguards:

> For Muslims this is the best place to promote religion [. . .] And this Islamic heart of 'Bung Karno' wants to defend Islam by mutual agreement, achieved by deliberation, namely in Parliament . . . That is the place to promote the demands of Islam [. . .] If we take it that Parliament has 100 members, then let us work, work as hard as possible, so that 60, 70, 80 or 90 of the representatives sitting in Parliament will be Muslims, Islamic leaders. Then, the laws which Parliament promulgates will naturally be Islamic laws. (Boland 1971: 22–3)

This did not convince Masyumi. Consequently, as part of their involvement in a smaller committee charged with drafting a constitution, Masyumi delegates such as the NU's Wahid Hasyim and the new Muhammadiyah leader Ki Bagus Hadikusomo (1890–1954) campaigned hard for an explicit recognition of Islam and Islamic law within the framework of an independent Indonesian state.[2] Eventually, in June 1945, this resulted in a 'gentlemen's agreement' about a preamble to the constitution that became known as the 'Jakarta Charter'. The nine signatories to this document consisted of four secular nationalists and five Muslim politicians. Given the high profile of the participants in these delicate negotiations, it is not surprising that 'in retrospect it can be considered that later discussions on the relationship of State and Islam in Indonesia were to a large extent determined by some words of this Djakarta Charter' (Boland 1971: 25).

A hard-fought addition to the fifth principle of the Pancasila Doctrine, whereby the belief in one God came 'with the obligation for the adherents of Islam to practice Islamic law', the Jakarta Charter became also known as the 'Seven Words', because in Indonesian the phrase read '*dengan kewadjiban meng-djalankan Sjari'at Islam bagi pemuluk-pemeluknja*'.[3] Throughout Indonesia's seventy-year history as an independent state with a majority Muslim population, the Jakarta Charter has remained a bone of contention because, at the last minute, it was dropped from the formal declaration of independence by Sukarno and

Hatta on 17 August 1945. Consequently, what was considered by Muslim politicians as the most crucial phrase in the whole document had simply disappeared and was also not mentioned in the subsequent Provisional Constitution. Overtaken by the fevered pace of events in August 1945, Boland concludes that 'the new Indonesia came into being neither as an Islamic State according to orthodox Islamic conceptions, nor as a secular state which would consider religion merely a private matter' (Boland 1971: 38), whereas Madinier suggests that, for a while at least, the prospect of an 'Islamisable state' offered in Sukarno's Pancasila Speech remained alive (Madinier 2015: 66).

However, at the time there was no opportunity to dwell on this matter, because the newly proclaimed independent *Republik Indonesia* (RI) was almost immediately confronted with the appearance of a Netherlands Indies Civil Administration (NICA). Helped by pro-Dutch Indonesian politicians and supported by the people in certain reoccupied areas (especially those with large Christian populations), the NICA sought to reimpose Dutch colonial rule by moving swiftly with the formation of a number of so-called federal states. This inaugurated almost four years of 'physical revolution' – an armed struggle in which the young republic had to fend off two military attempts to restore Dutch authority by force in July 1947 and December 1948 (in Dutch still euphemistically referred to as '*politionele acties*'). As a result, the RI found itself increasingly isolated and confined to Java and parts of Sumatra, eventually forcing the government to retreat from Jakarta and make Yogyakarta its temporary capital. Aside from the threat of an imminent Dutch take-over, it also had to contend with a fragmented political scene: in the wake of the declaration of independence no fewer than forty parties were established, sixteen of which were represented in the so-called Komité Nasional Indonesia Pusat (KNIP, Central Indonesian National Committee), the provisional parliament appointed by President Sukarno.

Islamic party politics and governance in early postcolonial Indonesia

Initially, members of the wartime Masyumi were reluctant to form a political party because they were worried about the effects of an explicitly Islamic party on the national unity that was considered vital for the survival of the infant Republic and its embryonic government. Only later, once independence was ascertained, and confronted with a decline in its influence following internal splits, regional secession attempts and the disappointing outcome of the 1955 elections, did Masyumi shift towards a more assertive Islamist line, adopting a more intransigent stance in the face of the political manoeuvring by President Sukarno as he attempted to take Indonesia from a parliamentary system modelled on Western democracies toward Guided Democracy in which he could rule by decree.

Taking over only the acronym of its wartime parent organisation, Masyumi's founding congress of November 1945 'added the subtitle, Partai Politik Oemmat Islam Indonesia (the Political Party of the Indonesian Muslim Community), to its name' (Madinier 2015: 75). The organisational structure, made up of a Leadership Council (*Dewan Pimpian*) and Consultative Council (*Majelis Syuro*), was envisaged to be inclusive, but the composition of both bodies was skewed in favour of members of the former PSII and PII. While the Islamic mass organisations were also represented – with the Muhammadiyah supplying eight members as opposed to the NU who had only four – their chairmen were not part of the executive, but served only on the Consultative Council. Formally, the NU's Hasyim Asyᶜari was in charge of this council, assisted by his son Wahid Hasyim, and with Agus Salim, Ki Bagus Hadikusomo and the octogenarian Sumatran reformist Djamil Djambek acting as vice-chairmen. The distinction between executive and consultative positions also reflected a division between political and religious roles, which had been discernible before the war. However, it became increasingly pronounced as the first two party presidents, Sukiman Wiryosanjoyo (1898–1974) and Mohammed Natsir, as well as another future minister, Sjafruddin Prawiranegara (1911–89), began to distinguish themselves as increasingly pragmatic and consummate politicians. For them, religion provided 'a set of general principles whose application could be adapted to the present day', in contrast to the functionaries in the consultative council, who regarded it as 'an inherent truth which must remain immutable' (Madinier 2015: 295).

Open to individual as well as institutional membership, in the beginning, Masyumi's primary focus was on the formation of the Gerakan Pemuda Islam Indonesia (GPII, Movement of Young Indonesian Muslims), which was to be used in the struggle against the Dutch. For the rest, Masyumi's earliest political vision remained community-based. Using the designation *Keluarga Masyumi* or 'Masyumi Family', Madinier opines that the 'vagueness of its programmes' was compensated by its 'direct control over the various organisations charged with providing social infra-structure to the Muslim community' (Madinier 2015: 348). Presiding over a vast network, Masyumi oversaw social care organisations, retained control of the Hizbullah militia and established a civil defence organisation called Barisan Sabilillah. The latter two remained of crucial importance during the 'physical revolution' between 1945 and 1950. Legal backup and inspirational support for this armed struggle was provided by the Masyumi Party Congress and a *fatwa* from Hasyim Asyᶜari, encouraging Muslims to 'fight [more accurately, to expend effort] in the way of God (*berjihad fisabilillah*)', and instructing them that under these adverse circumstances this *perang sabil* was also a *fard al-ᶜayn*; a duty imposed on individual Muslims (Boland 1971: 43; Formichi 2012: 85). Although the Masyumi executive, dominated by pragmatic modernists, was reluctant to endorse the NU leader's *fatwa*, they felt compelled to reiterate its dedication to the establishment of an Islamic state. While adopting the same terminology used by Hasyim Asy^{c}ari in his *fatwa* – that the RI's territory constituted a *Darul Islam* – the congress also vowed to do so through parliamentary consultation, thus expressing its adherence to the Pancasila.

The difference in attitude between Masyumi's political realists and its religious idealists is reflected by the fact that 'in the case of Masyumi, the notion of the Islamic state was by turns, and sometimes, simultaneously, a slogan, a myth, a programme and a reality'; a confusion further exacerbated by the ambiguity of the Indonesian term *negara*, which 'can be understood to refer to a state, a country, or, in certain cases, a nation' (Madinier 2015: 285–6). Consequently, the evolution of Masyumi's political ideology proceeded in a chaotic and sometimes even contradictory fashion. Together with the political infighting of the formative years of Islamic political organisations during the 1920s and 1930s which carried over into the postcolonial era, these internal ideological differences resulted in the 1947 breakaway from Masyumi of a re-established PSII, the secession of Kartosuwiryo's Darul Islam Movement in 1948, and the departure of the NU four years later. As noted earlier, the Japanese preference for rural *ulama* had already undermined the position of outward-looking Islamic modernists, who were often also of Sumatran origin. The first years of the party's existence were therefore a chaotic affair. With individual members joining cabinets of the early independence years in their personal capacity rather than as official party representatives, Masyumi was effectively split between idealists striving for an Islamic state, who preferred a role in the opposition, and realists who considered participation in governance more constructive, even if that meant making compromises. Madinier attributes this 'political schizophrenia' to the different geographical origins, social backgrounds and political affinities of the Masyumi leaders (Madinier 2015: 61).

Two developments during the independence struggle were important for Masyumi's maturing as a party and the formation of its political identity. The first one was a communist rebellion, which was rapidly put down by the Siliwangi Division of the Republican Army in September 1948 and which became known as the 'Madiun Affair'. That incident put the army and Masyumi at odds with the PKI. Ricklefs draws a parallel between the PKI–Masyumi confrontation and the *abangan–santri* divide, and agrees with Madinier that the execution of numerous Masyumi members by the rebels was the starting point of the party's virulent anti-communist attitude and the origin of the reverse massacre of alleged leftists in the mid-sixties (Ricklefs 2012: 71–8; Madinier 2015: 147–54). The other development was the secession of Kartosurwiryo's DI early in 1948, and subsequent proclamation of the Islamic State of Indonesia (Negara Islam Indonesia, NII) in August 1949. This development will be discussed in more detail in the next section; what is relevant here is that Darul Islam's simplistic Islamist radicalism pushed Masyumi towards the political middle ground.

While this enabled the party to participate in coalition governments of varying make-ups, it also posed a challenge in terms of presenting a clear and distinct Islamic image.

Capitalising on the growing nationalist sentiments and international sympathy for the cause of Indonesian independence as a result of Dutch brutality during its military campaigns in 1947–8, dramatic events in the final phase of that struggle provided three Masyumi leaders with opportunities to profile themselves as future statesmen: after the capture of the Sukarno–Hatta cabinet during the Dutch invasion of Yogyakarta, the only escapee, Finance Minister Sjafruddin Prawiranegara, proclaimed an Emergency Government of Indonesia (Pemerintah Darurat Republik Indonesia, PDRI) in Bukittinggi, the republican capital in Sumatra's Minangkabau region. Thus keeping the revolutionary ideal alive, his actions added enormously to Masyumi's prestige. Meanwhile, after his release, Interior Minister Mohammad Roem negotiated the final Dutch–Indonesian agreement for the transfer of sovereignty to the Republic. Finally, Mohammad Natsir distinguished himself by convincing Prawiranegara to accept the Roem–van Royen Agreement, which Prawiranegara had criticised as making too many concessions to the Dutch, and return executive power from the PDRI to the reinstated Sukarno–Hatta government. These actions raised this trio from being relatively low-key advocates of realist policies to political prominence, putting them in an advantageous position for taking power within Masyumi on the eve of the formal Dutch recognition of independence for the United States of Indonesia on 27 December 1949. This political constellation of the Java- and Sumatra-based RI and a number of federal states inherited from the NICA soon turned out to be untenable. Within a few months it had collapsed and was replaced by a unitary state. Still led by Sukarno as president and Hatta as vice-president, the new chairman of Masyumi's executive board, Mohammad Natsir, became the first prime minister of what was now once again called the *Republik Indonesia*.

Although the years from 1950 to 1957 are regarded as Indonesia's first experiment with parliamentary democracy, elections were not held until 1955. At the same time, it was also a period of great instability, during which the country had six governments. Even though Masyumi was the main government party in five of these cabinets (providing the prime minister for three), the notoriously unstable and ineffective coalitions with the PNI followed each other in rapid succession due to 'policy differences, disagreements over ministerial appointments and the role played by party factions', which were disproportionately influential because of the absence of an elected parliament accountable to voters (Madinier 2015: 134).

In April 1952, intra-party squabbling within Masyumi led to the departure of the NU. The split occurred over the disdain with which the Islamic modernists treated the traditionalists. When Hasyim Asyᶜari's successor as the NU's *Rais*

Aam (General President), Abdul Wahab Chasbullah, claimed the posts of foreign affairs (Abu Hanifah), defence (former Hizbullah leader Zainul Arifin) and religious affairs (Wahid Hasyim) for NU, this move was criticised and arrogantly dismissed by the senior Muhammadiyah leader Hamka. The NU's national congress reacted by voting in favour of leaving Masyumi altogether and turning the NU into an independent political party. Used to holding a virtual monopoly on the political representation of Indonesia's Muslims, Masyumi's haughtiness backfired completely in 1953, when the League of Indonesian Muslims (Liga Muslimin Indonesia), consisting of the NU, PSII and the tiny Persatuan Tarbiyah Islam (Perti), managed to bring down the PNI–Masyumi coalition and relegate the latter for the next two years to the opposition.[4] By then Sukarno was becoming personally involved. He used another speech – given in Amuntai in South Kalimantan – to speak out unambiguously in favour of a national state because a state based on Islam would lead to the breakaway of areas such as Bali, parts of Sulawesi, the Moluccas and a string of other eastern islands. This then constituted a 'definite break' between the president and Masyumi (Boland 1971: 48). Another consequence – at face value seemingly a minor issue but with a long-lasting effect – was Masyumi's loss of the Ministry of Religion, which remained under NU control from 1953 until 1971.

According to Madinier, Masyumi's miscalculations can be attributed to the disconnect between what he calls – with a nod to Herbert Feith – the Dutch-educated party elite of 'administrators' and 'solidarity makers'; popular figures with grassroots-level support but no government responsibility (Madinier 2015: 127). This problem had already been noted by Masyumi executive Kasman Singodimejo during his years in the JIB: not only were the urban and European-influenced lifestyles of most Masyumi cadres at odds with those of the rural peasantry, but because of their Dutch education they also lacked the linguistic abilities and cultural frame of reference to communicate effectively with ordinary people. Making a similar acknowledgement, Boland notes that, as 'wielders of symbols, both traditional and nationalistic', the NU was much better suited to this solidarity-making role, but that – ironically – the developments of 1952 and 1953 turned NU into 'a typically government-minded party' (Boland 1971: 51). In contrast to Masyumi, the NU toned down the anti-communist rhetoric that had dominated the Muslim political discourse since the Madiun Affair. In 1954, Religious Affairs Minister K.H. Masykur convened a congress of *ulama* who were closely associated with the NU. They issued a *fatwa* in which Sukarno was recognised as belonging to the so-called *ulil-amri* ('those who are in command'), thereby giving him legitimacy as the ruler of a Muslim country. From then on, the NU was often accused of opportunism because of its willingness to join any cabinet to stay in power. Thus, the NU became part of an informal alliance gravitating around the figure of Sukarno, which also included the PNI, PSII and PKI, and which outmanoeuvred Masyumi and its leader

Natsir, who could only count on support from Sutan Sjahrir's PSI and two Christian parties.

The effects of the collapse of the PNI–Masyumi coalition and the NU break-away also had repercussions from the first and only free national elections until 1999. With only 43.5 per cent of the votes, overall results for the Islamic parties in the 1955 elections were disappointing. Although Masyumi itself came in second after the PNI with 20.9 per cent against 22.3 per cent of the votes, it remained barely ahead of the NU's 18.4 per cent – now the third-largest party before the PKI. Even the oratory abilities of Isa Anshary (1916–69), a native of the former Padri stronghold of Maninjau in the Minangkabau's Agam Valley, fell short as an electioneering device. Referred to as 'the little Napoleon of Masyumi', he was one of the few who was able to develop a rapport with his constituency in west Java, but it made no difference to the overall outcome of the 1955 elections (Madinier 2015: 204). Meanwhile, the NU's electoral success was attributed to the 'aroma of orthodoxy' exuding from what many voters considered 'emo-tionally the truly Islamic party' (Boland 1971: 50). Still predominantly a rural country, to Indonesia's Muslim peasantry, the urban-oriented Masyumi seemed distant and its centralised campaigning could not replace the personalised *guru–murid* relationships in which the otherwise rather disorganised NU excelled.[5] As 'an "extra-Javanese" party representing the periphery of the country', Masyumi managed to command 40 per cent of the votes in its strongholds of Sumatra and South Sulawesi, while barely making the 10 per cent mark in the densely popu-lated NU heartlands of central and east Java (Madinier 2015: 211).

Aside from a disconnect between the Masyumi cadres and its envisaged grassroots-level electoral support base, another reason for the party's dismal performance was its decision to change its overall campaign rhetoric. In order to avoid alienating non-Muslims and also in response to the language used by Sukarno, Masyumi refrained from using religious idiom or making refer-ences to Islam. Instead it employed an abstract political vocabulary appealing to generic democratic values that failed to convince a significant part of the Muslim electorate:

> As the elections approached, the timidity of Masyumi's claims was even more obvious. The party's press made no bones about playing the Muslim card, but the party itself seemed to want to hush up its Islamic identity as well as any demands which were of a religious nature. (Madinier 2015: 302)

Although after the elections Masyumi returned to government, there was no denying the fact that it had gone from 'foremost political party' to being 'simply one of four large political parties which could legitimately aspire to a role in government' (Madinier 2015: 203). On the back of this relative marginalisation, relations with Sukarno deteriorated further as the president began exhibiting an increasingly soloist attitude. In the wake of the Asia–Africa Conference, which he had hosted in Bandung, Sukarno moved closer to the third-worldism and leftist inclinations of his new-found friends, President Nasser of Egypt and the Indian Prime Minister Nehru. In 1957, Sukarno announced plans to do away with parliamentary democracy and opt for Guided Democracy. Invoking the traditional Javanese village system of mutual assistance, known as *gotong royong*, he foresaw people's representation through 'functional groups' (*golong fungsional*) rather than political parties. He also abolished the office of vice-president, thereby ending the Sukarno–Hatta power sharing arrangement (*dwitunggal*) that had been in place since 1945. Natsir had always emphasised Masyumi's commitment to democratic consultation and – because of its anti-communism – displayed a leaning towards pro-American foreign policies. Having secured not only support from PNI and PKI, but – because of an increasingly precarious security situation as a result of various secessionist rebellions and a failed assassination attempt on Sukarno's life – also from the army, Masyumi found itself alone in opposing the president's move towards authoritarianism.

Masyumi became even further isolated when party leader Natsir and Bank of Indonesia President Sjafruddin Prawiranegara criticised Sukarno for his rash decision to nationalise Dutch companies and expel tens of thousands of Dutch citizens over the question of West New Guinea. This led not just to economic chaos, but also to jeopardised relations with Western democracies, 'moving Indonesia closer to the Russian bloc' (Madinier 2015: 247).[6] When in early 1958 political pressure turned to personal intimidation, the Masyumi leadership found itself forced into a *hijra* to Sumatra and reluctantly teaming up with the renegade Pemerintah Revolusioner Republik Indonesia (PRRI, Revolutionary Government of the Republic of Indonesia) centred on Natsir's native Minangkabau area. The individuals going into internal exile included some of those who had evolved into Indonesia's leading statesmen during the challenging immediate post-war years. Now Mohammed Natsir, Sjafruddin Prawiranegara and another former prime minister, Burhanuddin Harahap (1917–87), found themselves in the political wilderness and, as the tide turned against the PRRI, soon also in the actual jungle of Sumatra.[7] It was a bitter irony that for the sake of preserving the integrity and unity of Indonesia, these political pragmatists found themselves in the company of secessionist rebels.

In the final years of its existence, Masyumi found itself performing a balancing act that ultimately proved impossible to maintain. Natsir and Sjafruddin's dramatic turn from political realism to what was in effect an act of sedition stood in stark contrast to their earlier commitment to democracy and insistence on the rule of law. The remaining party leadership found itself emitting ambiguous signals. Led by a Natsir protégé, Prawoto Mangkusasmito (1910–70), as acting party president, Masyumi had to disavow support for the PRRI while avoiding a total breakdown of the party which would almost certainly have occurred if figures such as Natsir and Prawiranegara were unequivocally condemned. On the other hand, Masyumi had to act against Sukarno's attempts to abolish the party-based system of parliamentary democracy and concentrate power in his own hands. Eventually, it failed at both. Within two years of its proclamation the PRRI had collapsed; incapable of responding to the military campaign launched by the army which had remained loyal to the government in Jakarta, the USA withdrew its initial support for what it had regarded as a potential ally in stemming the growing influence of communism in Southeast Asia. While by 1961 the PRRI's military officers, led by the Aceh-born Colonel Zulkifli Lubis (1923–93), had managed to negotiate a deal that not only enabled them to avoid being court-martialled but even to return to the regular armed forces, the Masyumi leaders faced many years in prison.[8]

Masyumi was unable to capitalise on two aspects of Sukarno's strategy to impose his Guided Democracy. When the president proposed to restore the 1945 Constitution at the expense of the Provisional Constitution negotiated and drafted in 1950, Masyumi regarded this as an opportunity to offset Sukarno's power grab by reintroducing the former *duatunggal* with Hatta. More significantly even, with the original constitution back on the table, 'once again the Djakarta Charter became one of the most important issues on which some Islamic leaders brought discussion to a head' (Boland 1971: 94). However, unable to rally a united Islamic bloc behind these two points, Masyumi not only stood alone but was also internally divided. Although critical of the dismissal of the Jakarta Charter as a 'historical document', NU leader Wahab Chasbullah was fearful of a military putsch, whereas former Masyumi minister Jusuf Wibisono (1909–82) had been voicing his dissenting opinion in favour of Guided Democracy since 1957. In a last-ditch attempt to save his party and reunite the Islamic bloc, after his formal election as Masyumi president in what was to be the party's last congress, Prawoto Mangkusasmito gave in. However, this consent came too late.

Sukarno's speech on the occasion of Independence Day in 1959, which became known as the 'Political Manifesto' (*Manifest Politik*, abbreviated to Manipol) and in which he outlined his ideas for Indonesia's political future, was also the prelude to the final demise of Masyumi as Indonesia's leading Islamic political party. Manipol consisted primarily of two propaganda slogans: USDEK, an abbreviation composed of the initial letters of the Indonesian terms for the 1945 Constitution, Indonesian-style Socialism, Guided Democracy, Guided Economy and Indonesian Identity; and NASAKOM, an acronym for a state ideology proclaiming 'the doctrine of unity of the three component parts of Indonesian society, the Nationalists (*NASionalis*), the religious groups (*Agama* = religion) and the Communists (*KOMunis*)' (Boland 1971: 102). These terms became the shorthand for *Aliranisasi*; the Indonesian translation of a Dutch phenomenon called *verzuiling* or pillarisation – the division of a society into segmented silos representing different religious and political affiliations (Kersten 2015: 4). Masyumi tried to curb Sukarno's power grab by forging a new alliance called the 'Democratic League', but with only the PSI and PSII joining, while the NU remained loyal to Sukarno, these efforts came to naught. Confronted with a series of presidential decrees in early 1960, which further undermined parliamentary democracy and the existence of political parties, and failing in 'rekindling the "Natsirian" spirit to condemn Sukarno's manoeuvre' (Madinier 2015: 275), Prawoto Mangkusasmito and his colleagues in the executive dissolved the party. According to Madinier, Masyumi's insistence that its dissolution had been voluntary 'is indicative of the extent to which the party was traumatised by the participation of Natsir and his close supporters in the PRRI rebellion' (Madinier 2015: 284).

However, even this step did not absolve Masyumi from the continuing wrath of Sukarno, whose treatment of the Masyumi leadership in the early 1960s began to resemble that of Nasser's persecution of the Egyptian Muslim Brotherhood. After the dissolution of Masyumi and the arrest of Natsir, Prawiranegara and Harahap, the party was unofficially held together by Mohammad Roem and Prawoto Mangkusasmito. Jakarta's al-Azhar mosque became a rallying point for the Masyumi constituency. Its *imam* was the former Masyumi deputy and leading Muhammadiyah intellectual Hamka, who turned his magazine *Pandji Masjarakat* into a Masyumi mouthpiece and leading organ for criticising Sukarno's Guided Democracy. Thanks to his cordial relations with former Vice-President Hatta and senior military officers such as Generals Nasution and Sudirman, Hamka enjoyed a degree of protection. Eventually, however, he too – together with the rest of the Masyumi leadership – was declared guilty by association and rounded up by the army which had thrown in its lot with Sukarno. On the back of the defeat of the PRRI and the loyalist army's suppression of other regional rebellions, Chief of Staff Nasution had managed to achieve a power-sharing agreement with Sukarno. By 1963, the whole Masyumi leadership was imprisoned.

Darul Islam (DI) and regional secessionist movements

Aside from being a result of the party's opposition to Guided Democracy and involvement in the PRRI rebellion, the dismantling of Masyumi was also a consequence of persistent suspicions as to Masyumi's attitude toward the DI uprising led by Kartosuwiryo, which lasted from 1948 until 1962. This rebellion formed part of no fewer than five regional insurgencies claiming to be inspired by Islamic political ideology with which Indonesia had to contend from the late 1940s onward. In the course of the 1950s two rebel groups operating in South Sulawesi and Kalimantan respectively began collaborating with Kartosuwiryo's DI. In 1953, troubles also arose in Aceh, but its PUSA-led resistance movement against the central government in Jakarta did not enter into a formal alliance with Kartosuwiryo. Finally, there were three separate guerrilla movements active in central Java, which claimed to support Kartosuwiryo's DI but failed to form a united front.

Kartosuwiryo had separated from Masyumi in 1948 because of disagreements over how to achieve the establishment of an Islamic state in Indonesia. Already in pamphlets written during his time in the pre-war PSII, namely the *Brosoer sikap hidjrah PSII* (1936) and *Daftar oesaha hidjrah* (1940), Kartosuwiryo had spelled out that the 'PSII was neither communist nor fascist and inspired by neither Arabism or "Indonesianism", as its foundation was only Islam' (Formichi 2012: 61). Although such a stance is reminiscent of figures such as Maududi, Al-Banna and Qutb, in her landmark study of Kartosuwiryo, Chiara Formichi nevertheless insists on seeing his 'radicalization as a development strictly correlated with domestic political and social dynamics' (Formichi 2015: 63).

It is difficult to trace Kartosuwiryo's activities during the war years, but it appears that the PSII splinter faction he led continued to exist until 1942 and that his 'Suffa Institute' (*Institut Supah*, also spelled *Soeffah*), an educational initiative which initially provided religious-cadre education but then switched to guerrilla training for the Hizbullah and Sabilillah, operated until 1948.[9] At the founding of Masyumi as a political party, Kartosuwiryo became a member of its executive board and a delegate to the provisional parliament, the KNIP. Things changed with the Dutch invasion of 1947, which turned Kartosuwiryo's west Javanese stronghold of the Priangan into a theatre of war, isolating it from the territories of the republic and thus laying 'the foundations for the region's divergent political path to independence' (Formichi 2012: 103). Invoking a 1946 speech known as the *Haloean Politik Islam*, Kartosuwiryo felt obliged to abandon Masyumi policy of achieving an Islamic state through democratic means, opting instead for *perang sabil* ('war on the path [of God]') or *perang suci* ('purifying' or 'holy war'). Although now committed to armed struggle, it must be pointed out that Kartosuwiryo had always objected to confining the meaning of *jihad* to Western understandings as only signifying 'warfare':

> To Kartosuwiryo, both the national and social revolutions – now explicitly defined as *al-jihad al-ashgar* [lesser *jihad*, CK] and *al-jihad al-akbar* [greater *jihad*, CK] – were necessary to eradicate colonialism by acting on external (state and government) and internal (citizens' souls) objects of foreign domination. (Formichi 2012: 91)

This interpretation constituted the founding principle or groundwork for what, between November 1947 and May 1948, evolved from a west Javanese Islamic resistance movement into an Indonesian Islamic Army (Tentara Islam Indonesia, TII) and a *de facto* Islamic state. Given the exceptional circumstances governing west Java during the Dutch hostilities, Masyumi leaders had agreed to suspend conventional party activities and 'Kartosuwiryo was nominated *imam* of the Islamic community in West Java' (Formichi 2012: 115). By April 1948, Kartosurwiryo's military successes in terms of expanding territory and the vigour with which his followers implemented governance in accordance with Islamic law caused concern to both the Dutch occupying forces and the Republican security apparatus. These worries were vindicated by the subsequent proclamation of a parallel government and the release of a *Kanun Asasy*; an alternative constitution in August of the same year (Boland 1971: 59)

A second Dutch military invasion in late 1948 and the subsequent capture of the Indonesian cabinet, enabled Kartosuwiryo to charge further ahead with what he now called a total war against the Dutch waged by his TII alone, because Sukarno's nationalist army was in a state of collapse. It is important to note here that, at this stage, 'Kartosuwiryo was placing the Darul Islam's struggle on the same plane as Soekarno's, rather than in opposition to it' and that 'Republic forces were not identified as the enemy' (Formichi 2012: 128). This all changed in early 1949, when Kartosuwiryo – true to his lifelong commitment to non-cooperation – accused PSI leader Sjahrir of selling out to the Dutch at the Conference of Linggadjati and also criticised Sukarno for his willingness to strike a bargain by opting for the path of diplomacy.

Even when relations soured further as the differences between the Republican government and DI came into even sharper relief after the conclusion of the Roem–van Royen Agreement and the occurrence of armed clashes between the TNI and TII, Masyumi stood by Kartosuwiryo because it saw the confrontation as playing into the hands of the Dutch and their continuing divide-and-rule politics. That spectre became reality when Kartosuwiryo formally proclaimed the Islamic State of Indonesia (Negara Islam Indonesia, NII) in August 1949:

> The Negara Islam was rooted in the law of God and had its base in 'Medina'. As had been anticipated in the *Brosoer sikap hidjrah PSII* and in *Haloean politik Islam*, this choice of toponym pointed to the city's status as the destination of the *hijrah*, as a physical migration and a metaphorical transformation. Either way, Kartosuwiryo referred to the beginning of a new life for the *ummah*, one in full conformity with Islam. (Formichi 2012: 134)

Having succeeded in turning theory into political reality, DI's ambition of further territorial expansion was complimented by efforts to develop the state's legal infrastructure and set up its own administrative entity. One of the first actions was the promulgation of a criminal code or *hukum pidana*, which contained not only the conventional *fiqh* distinctions between different categories of crime and their appropriate punishments, but also an Islamic version of martial law. Under the latter's terms, there were only two communities: the Muslim *umma* and that of the infidel colonisers. Consequently, *jihad* was declared an obligation imposed on individual Muslims (*fard al-ʿayn*). The code further stipulated that failure to contribute financial surplus to the treasury was to be treated as an act of rebellion, while those maintaining good relations with enemies of the state were declared *munafiqun* or hypocrites. In Chiara Formichi's estimation, this document and the earlier mentioned constitution can be considered 'one of very few attempts to formally structure an Islamic state in the Sunni Muslim world in the twentieth century' (Formichi 2012: 124).

The Republic's initial response was conciliatory and at the behest of Vice-President Hatta, Mohammad Natsir was sent to Bandung to try to make contact with Kartosuwiryo. Using his Persis friend Ahmad Hassan as intermediary, Natsir reported back with neither a condemnation nor an endorsement of DI. Later he also headed a commission which recommended that no military action be taken against DI as this would only benefit the Dutch. During his brief term in office as prime minister in 1950–1, Natsir opened official negotiations on behalf of the newly formed unitary state to reintegrate the guerrilla forces which were operating not only in west Java, but also elsewhere in the archipelago, in civil society. Without any concrete results to show for these efforts, Natsir's successor Sukiman shifted from finding a political solution to the military option. By now, the Republic had to contend not only with DI, which at its peak was able to mobilise no fewer than 13,000 men; it also faced rebelling guerrilla forces in central Java, South Sulawesi, the Kalimantan region of Borneo and Aceh. The three movements in central Java could not muster the same numbers as DI, and while two of them – the Amir Fatah faction and elements from the army's Diponegoro Division – originated in the Masyumi-linked Hizbullah militia, the Angkatan Umat Islam had no such connections.

Far more serious was the Kasuatan Gerilya Sulawesi Selatan (KGCC, Union of South Sulawesi Guerrillas) led by Kahar Muzakkar (1920–65),[10] a member of the Buginese aristocracy of the state of Luwu and educated at a Muhammadiyah school in Surakarta. After returning to Sulawesi with a Javanese wife, Muzakkar was ostracised (*ripaoppa-ngi-tana*) (Boland 1971: 62–3). When refused integration of his forces into the Republic's army in 1950, Muzakkar put his troops at the disposal of Kartosuwiryo and was made TII commander of South Sulawesi in 1952. A year later, Muzakkar proclaimed South Sulawesi part of the Islamic Republican State of Indonesia (its name slightly deviating from Kartosuwiryo's NII), and was made Kartosuwiryo's deputy minister of defence in 1955. Although Muzakkar's initial motive for rebelling against the central government was the frustrated ambition of becoming a military strongman, Boland claims that after being 'converted', Muzakkar became a 'radical revolutionary' set on enforcing what is called the 'Makalua Charter' (Boland 1971: 85). In this document, the PNI and PKI are condemned as hypocritical and godless, whereas Masyumi, NU and PSII are rejected as counter-revolutionary. The charter also contains stipulations which make opposition to polygamy a criminal offence, and which impose a strict regulation of capital goods, valuables and luxury articles – reminiscent of the fiscal policies of Kartosuwiryo's *hukum pidana*. Boland further records instances of corporal punishment, as well as acts of banditry and murder by Muzakkar's forces. He also claims to have received information about the persecution of Christians.

The rebellious forces on Borneo led by former marine corps officer Kyai Ibnu Hadjar did not team up with DI until 1954. As his grievances were due to the political take-over of his domain in Kalimantan by the unitary government, Ibnu Hadjar's involvement was only symbolic: Islamising his political rhetoric and assuming the title *Ulil Amri*. Like Boland and Madinier, Formichi also makes a distinction between the 'original spark' of DI and the uprisings in Sulawesi and Kalimantan:

> these regional rebellions were framed in Islamic terms, in more or less detail, only after having become involved in Kartosuwiryo's Islamic state project. In West-Java the process was reversed, as the platform for an Islamic state had first been developed and implemented when there was no unitary national government to challenge. (Formichi 2012: 167)

The 1953 insurgence in Aceh was also inspired by the lack of autonomy for the region under a centralised administration. Shaped by Aceh's specific political, religious and social circumstances, the Acehnese rebels pursued a regionalist agenda revolving around what Edward Aspinall refers to as the 'four myths' of Acehnese history: the golden age of the seventeenth-century sultanate, the struggle for self-preservation, Aceh as the mainstay of Indonesian national liberation and the so-called 'broken promise' (Aspinall 2009: 31–4). Both Aspinall and Formichi stress that it was not until Sukarno reneged on his promise to establish Islamic law in Aceh that PUSA founder and former military governor Teungku Daud Beureu'eh (1899–1987) decided to 'join Kartosuwiryo's DI-TII [and] declare Aceh a "federal state" within the NII in 1955' (Formichi 2012: 159). The alliance between Beureu'eh and Kartosuwiryo must therefore be considered as motivated by strategic considerations rather than ideological agreements, notwithstanding the underlying religious motivations of the Acehnese ambitions.

While the army began its operations to rout these various rebellious forces, Masyumi politicians continued to advocate an 'alternative path' (*jalan lain*) over 'this "military-centred" (*Tentara-centrische*) approach' to what Natsir considered to be a political and sociological problem (Madinier 2015: 173, 175). While Isa Anshary, the head of Masyumi in west Java made every effort to resist DI infiltration attempts, Natsir's efforts to find a political solution were hampered by the fall of his cabinet, the willingness of his successor to go along with a tougher line against DI, and the break with the NU. Although Masyumi had specified its differences with DI as to how to achieve an Islamic state by taking a clear stance in favour of parliamentary democracy, rejecting any form of populism and warning against the danger of the conflict exploding into a full-fledged politico-religious war, it kept certain lines of communication with DI open. The ambiguity of these contacts became clear in 1953, when two leaders of the Masyumi youth wing GPII, Afandi Ridhwan and Achmad Buchari, were charged and convicted for passing on messages between Kartosuwiryo's aides, assistants of Prawoto Mangkusasmito, and Kahar Muzakkar in Sulawesi. Given the long-standing relations between senior Masyumi and DI leaders, suspicions of support and allegations of complicity between the party and the rebels persisted throughout the decade-and-a-half-long confrontation between the Republic and Kartosuwiryo. While 'the involvement of certain Masyumi members in rebellions is indisputable', Rémy Madinier reckons that this does not make the party 'collectively responsible'. However, 'on the side of the army and the justice system, but also on the side of Darul Islam, there were many who had an interest in maintaining this belief in a collaboration' (Madinier 2015: 179).

The groundwork for DI's defeat was laid between 1953 and 1955, when the NU took Masyumi's place in government and Sukarno's position grew stronger through his personal friendship with NU leader Wahab Chasbullah, who – in defiance of his own organisation – supported the president's plans for Guided Democracy: From then on, 'Kartosuwiryo and his Darul Islam were defined as "enemies of the state"' (Formichi 2012: 160). However, that did not prevent some Masyumi and NU leaders from voicing their dissenting opinions:

> Mohammad Roem argued that the DI, TII and Daud Beureu'eh were the party's allies in the fight for an Islamic state in Indonesia. In the mid-1950s, Isa Anshary declared that the 'Ummat Islam should not support a government which is not the NII', and K.H. Chalid Hasjim of the Nahdlatul Ulama proclaimed that Muslims who did not strive for the NII were hypocrites who lived in ignorance (*jahiliah*). (Formichi 2012: 163)

After Sukarno outlined Guided Democracy, the declaration of a state of emergency and imposition of martial law, the stage was set for 'Operation Annihilate' (*Operasi Penumpasan*), a campaign pursued with even more urgency and vigour after the *hijra* of Natsir, Prawiranegara and Harahap to PRRI territory in Sumatra (Formichi 2012: 168). Meanwhile in Aceh, a deal was struck to establish a 'special administrative district' (*daerah istimewa*) under another PUSA leader, Prof. Dr Ali Hasjmy. By 1962, the army had not just quelled the PRRI uprising and rounded up the Masyumi leadership, while Daud Beureu'eh was granted amnesty but kept under house arrest, it had also managed to capture Kartosuwiryo. The latter was summarily tried, executed and buried at an unknown location. Only Kahar Muzakkar managed to escape and evade TNI troops until 1965, when he was shot near Lawali in Southeast Sulawesi.

Intellectual developments toward an Indonesian Islam

There can be little argument then over the failing of political Islam in Indonesia during the first two decades of independence. In contrast to these setbacks, however, important achievements were realised in the intellectual domain; in fields such as Islamic education and the theorising of Islamic law. It is these developments, rather than Islamic party politics, that continue to have an enduring effect on what Indonesian Islam looks like today. The institutional and administrative framework for these activities is provided by the Ministry of Religion.

Establishing a Ministry of Religion and building Islamic higher education

The decision to avoid any reference in the constitution to Islamic law – or Islam for that matter – did not mean the banning of religion from the public sphere. The principle requiring every Indonesian citizen to believe in one Supreme Being is rather an indication of the contrary. While the establishment of a Ministry of Religion is often interpreted as a concession to Indonesia's Muslim population, an attempt to placate their disappointment over the dismissal of the Jakarta Charter, I suggest an alternative reading by looking at the parallel with the Turkish Republic (I have already referred to Sukarno's interest in developments in Turkey). In both instances, the establishment of the Presidency for Religious Affairs (*Diyanet*) in Turkey and Indonesia's Ministry of Religion (*Kementerian Agama*, Kemenag) represent the same desire to bring religion under state control. After initial hesitation about turning the war-time Office of Religious Affairs into a government agency, in January 1946, steps were taken by Prime Minister Sutan Sjahrir's second cabinet to establish a ministry that would take over administrative responsibility for the infrastructure and institutions developed during the Japanese occupation. After briefly considering naming this department the Ministry of Islam, in view of the substantial presence of other religious traditions it was instead decided to call it the Ministry of Religion. The ministry was composed of four sections: one each for Muslims, Protestants, Catholics and Hindu-Buddhists (formally called Hindu-Balinese religion). The new department took over from the Ministry of Interior responsibility for marriage registration and family affairs, mosque administration and the organisation of hajj; it relieved the Ministry of Justice of the care of religious courts and the Ministry of Education and Culture of the coordination of religious education. While Boland disagrees with Clifford Geertz's qualification of the department as 'a *santri* affair from top to bottom', he does admit that 'this Ministry was primarily set up on behalf of Islam' (Boland 1971: 106).

A young intellectual by the name of Mohammad Rasjidi (1915–2006), who was already serving as minister without portfolio, was appointed as the first minister of religion in March 1946. Born as Saridi in Kota Gede (near Yogyakarta) into what he called an *abangan* family, he received his early education from the Muhammadiyah and then attended the Hadhrami-sponsored Al-Irsyad school where received the name Mohammad Rasjidi from Ahmad Surkati himself. Between 1931 and 1938, Rasjidi studied at Cairo University. Presumably at

the advice of Abdul Kahar Muzakir, one of the later signatories of the Jakarta
Charter on behalf of the Muhammadiyah, Rasjidi took classes in philosophy
from a pupil of Muhammad Abduh: Mustafa ʿAbd al-Raziq. Muzakir also
introduced Rasjidi to the future Muslim Brotherhood ideologue Sayyid Qutb.
According to Rasjidi's biographer, Azyumardi Azra, this exposure to Sayyid
Qutb's Salafi ideas shaped Rasjidi's abiding 'revivalist or even fundamentalist
spirit', because the 'education and intellectual milieu in Cairo completed his
religio-intellectual journey' (Azra 1994: 95–6). This is a noteworthy conclusion, because throughout his subsequent scholarly career Rasjidi came into
contact with an array of very different ideas, which apparently did not leave
the same impression. Returning to Indonesia before the eruption of World
War II, his activities in a number of Muslim organisations positioned him well
for important functions in the religious establishment. After serving as minister
until November 1946, Rasjidi went on to pursue a diplomatic and academic
career, remaining one of the key contributors to Indonesia's postcolonial Islamic
discourse.

Because of the urgent need for qualified candidates to staff the young republic's religious courts, provide religious instruction in its state schools and run
the ministry's own burgeoning bureaucracy, religious education was one of the
ministry's primary concerns.[11] As an educationist by profession, Mohammad
Natsir was one of the driving forces behind the development of an Islamic
system of higher education. Together with Vice President-designate Hatta and
the NU's Wahid Hasyim, he had launched the initiative for *Sekolah Tinggi Islam*
(STI, Higher Islam School). First operating in Jakarta, in 1948 STI was transferred to Yogyakarta along with the Republican government. Its programmes of
study in theology and social sciences were modelled after the 1936 curriculum
of al-Azhar, and gradually expanded into law and other secular subjects such as
education, economics and technology.

From 1945 until 1960, this institution was led by the earlier mentioned Abdul
Kahar Muzakir, who had spent more than twelve years in Egypt and the wider
Middle East. Aside from studying at al-Azhar, he had also frequented both
secular and Islamist circles around the Wafd party and Sayyid Qutb. Following
the elevation of Yogyakarta's Gadjah Mada University to state university level
in 1950, STI merged with another Islamic university founded by a number of
religious scholars in Solo to form the Universitas Islam Indonesia (UII). A year
later, the government decided to split off the theology faculty from Yogyakarta's
UII and continue it as the Perguruan Tinggi Agama Islam Negeri (PTAIN).

Jakarta also got a new tertiary Islamic education institute called Perguruan
Tinggi Islam Jakarta (PTID), later renamed Universitas Islam Djakarta (UID).
Six years later, in Jakarta, the Ministry of Religion founded the Akademi Dinas
Ilmu Agama (ADIA, State Academy for Religious Officials). In 1960, ADIA was
merged with PTAIN into the Institut Agama Islam Negeri (IAIN, State Institute

for Islamic Studies). With initially two campuses in Jakarta and Yogyakarta, the IAINs had four faculties offering three- and two-year undergraduate and post-graduate courses in religious studies (*Usuluddin*, including theology and *da'wa*), law (*syariah*), education (*tarbiyah*) and humanities (*adab*). Since the 1970s, IAIN campuses have proliferated in all major Indonesian cities.

Developing an Indonesian *fiqh* or a national school of Islamic law

Although with dropping the Jakarta Charter, there has never been any explicit reference to Islamic law in the Indonesian constitution, *fiqh* or jurisprudence is nevertheless considered a core field of Islamic learning. Thinking through the relevance and foundations of Islamic law in the Indonesian context, not only in terms of *usul al-fiqh* as a 'toolbox' for jurists, but also in regards to the *maqasid al-shariʿa* or the 'higher objectives of Islamic law', was initiated by two scholars of very different backgrounds: Hasbi Ash Shiddieqy (1904–75) and Hazairin, also known as Gelar Pangeran Alamsyah Harahap (1906–75).[12]

Hasbi Ash Shiddieqy's family belonged to Aceh's religious scholarly elite. Aside from a traditional Islamic upbringing at his father's *pondok*, he also attended the Al-Irshad school in Surabaya. Although associated with the Muhammadiyah as well as the even more puritan Persatuan Islam (Persis), and serving briefly as a Masyumi politician in the Constituent Assembly (1956–9), Ash Shiddieqy's main occupation in independent Indonesia was in academia. Eventually rising to the post of Dean of the Faculty of Shari'a at IAIN Sunan Kalijaga in Yogyakarta in 1960, he also served as a professor and guest lecturer at other Islamic universities in Aceh, Semarang and Surakarta. Unlike Ash Shiddieqy, Hazairin never received any formal Islamic religious training and was for that reason not recognised by traditional *ulama* as 'fulfilling the technical requirements of a *mujtahid*' (Feener 2002: 107). Born in Bengkulu of a father of Persian descent and a Minangkabau mother, Hazairin received a Dutch state education and – having decided on a legal career – then opted for advanced training at colonial law schools where he specialised in *adat* or Indonesian systems of customary law. Both as a juridical practice and as a field of academic inquiry, the systematic study of *adat* was the brainchild of Cornelis van Vollenhoven (1874–1933), and Hazairin studied under his pupil Barend ter Haar (1892–1941), eventually receiving a doctorate from the School of Law in Batavia (Jakarta).[13] After working in the colonial court system, when Indonesia gained its independence, Hazairin first served in the provincial administration of south Sumatra before deciding on an academic career. Except for a brief stint as minister of home affairs (1953–4), he lectured in law at the secular Universitas Indonesia and ended his career as rector of the IAIN Syarif Hidayatullah in Jakarta.

The greatest intellectual influence on Hasbi Ash Shiddieqy's thinking about Islam as a religion in general and Islamic law in particular came from the Egyptian Azhar Shaykh Mahmud Shaltut (1893–1963), with whom he shared an interest in demystifying Islam in order to make it more accessible to Muslims without a background in traditional Islamic learning. It also led him to the conviction that the Muslim tradition could only be properly appreciated through the study of its historical development, so that its doctrinal and legal positions could be contextualised and reinterpreted in the light of contemporary circumstances. In theorising Islamic law in the Indonesian context, Ash Shiddieqy considered it imperative to first disentangle a conflation of three terms that was obscuring its proper understanding. Legal scholars from faculties of law at secular universities generally use the term *Hukum Islam* for Islamic law, whereas their colleagues at Islamic state universities tended to fall into a rather cavalier mixing-up of *shari'a* and *fiqh*, leading them to 'suggest that both are universal, absolute and everlasting' (Wahyudi 2007: 78). Ash Shiddieqy insisted, however, that only *shari'a* can be considered as universal and eternal, whereas *fiqh* deals with specifics and is therefore subject to change.

As a puritan Islamic reformist from the Persis mould, Ash Shiddieqy considered his intellectual labours on Islamic law as a contribution to the purification of Islam, but with the understanding that a 'return to the Qur'an and Sunna' formed the starting point for the transformation of a generic understanding of *fiqh* into an interpretation which would take the Indonesian context into account. The legislative intentions of the Qur'an are not meant to complicate things, but to provide Muslims with clear rules for the acts of worship (*ibadat*) and general guidelines for human interaction (*mu'amalat*), whereas the Sunna of the Prophet, captured in the authoritative hadith collections, provide detailed elaborations of these Qur'anic provisions. Notwithstanding this seemingly scripturalist orientation, Ash Shiddieqy remained always open to writings of different legal traditions and schools of thought: the practice known as *talfiq*, which had also been pursued by Abduh and Shaltut. His aim was 'not only to transcend established *madhhab* boundaries, but also to construct a new system of distinctively "Indonesian fiqh", or *Fikih Indonesia*', which was to be 'determined according to Indonesian personality and characteristics' (Feener 2002: 98). Such an interpretative endeavour is no longer to be executed by individual scholars but through a collaborative effort called 'collective ijtihad'. This also meant a revision of the notion of *ijma'*, or consensus of scholars. To that end, Ash Shiddieqy proposed composing a body of scholars trained at the IAINs and appointing them as what in the tradition is called the *ahl al-hall wa'l-'aqd* – or 'people who can loosen and bind' (those holding authority).[14] He also stressed that their competence and authority in developing an Indonesian *fiqh* should be restricted to the *mu'amalat* and would not concern *ibadat*. This way doctrinal purification could be reconciled with a discursive Indonesianisation of the Islamic legal tradition. His introduction of the term 'Indonesian fiqh' also sought to offer a compromise between Indonesian nationalism and Muslim reformism.

Hazairin had a similar interest in promoting a distinctly Indonesian version of Islamic law. Although largely an autodidact, Hazairin was nevertheless a perceptive student of Islam with a keen ability for reflective thinking about religion. In his view, students at the IAINs and similar institutions of higher Islamic learning should concentrate on acquiring knowledge of Islam by combining the study of traditional Islamic subjects with modern sciences. Sharing Ash Shiddieqy's ambition 'to see a new generation of scholars working within the context of a modern and distinctly Indonesian national *madhhab*', Hazairin's introduction of this term reflected the same 'nationalistic orientation' that underlay Ash Shiddieqy's promotion of an 'Indonesian fiqh' (Feener 2002: 109).

However, on account of Hazairin's specialist training in *adat*, his approach had a different accent from Ash Shiddieqy's, emphasising the role of indigenous customs because of their potential to offset the alien Arabian facets of Islamic law with more acceptable local cultural features. With this, Hazairin sought to turn legal precepts inherited from the Middle East into a living legal practice that would better suit the Indonesian situation. Whereas Ash Shiddieqy drew inspiration from Islamic religious scholars such as Mahmud Shaltut, Hazairin turned to cultural anthropology to aid Qur'anic exegesis in line with the requirements and challenges faced by Indonesian Muslims. Guided by Islamic ethical and legal principles, as well as a nationalist ideology, Hazairin insisted that 'religion was to be the measure of the validity of *adat* and not vice versa' (Feener 2002: 112). This was diametrically opposed to van Vollenhoven's privileging of customary over Islamic law. Rejecting the position of the guru of his specialist field constituted Hazairin's first step in the 'Indonesianization of fiqh' (Wahyudi 2007: 33).

Hasbi Ash Shiddieqy's conceptualisation of an 'Indonesian fiqh', through his immersion in both classical Arabic texts and the writings of latter-day reformists from the Middle East, and Hazairin's stress on the particular cultural circumstances that had shaped the Islamic content of Indonesian law foreshadowed comparable initiatives by Indonesian scholars of Islamic law in the 1980s and 1990s and the decision of the New Order Regime in 1991 to accommodate Hazairin's earlier call for the compilation and codification of Islamic legal materials through a Presidential Decree on the Islamic Law Compilation (*Kompilasi Hukum Islam*, KHI-Inpres).

Islam and the military: finding a *modus vivendi* under Indonesia's New Order

After successfully quelling the regional uprisings in west Java, Sumatra, Sulawesi and Kalimantan, by the mid-1960s, the military's reputation was at a high. Rumours of an impending communist take-over and the assassination of a number of very senior officers under very murky circumstances, offered General Suharto, a hitherto obscure logistics officer, the desired pretext for taking action.

In 1965 the army committed effectively a coup d'état (*kudeta*) against Sukarno, inaugurating a period of military rule that lasted for more than thirty years and which became known under the name *Orde Baru* (New Order Regime). Before long, the military intervention derailed into a pogrom against alleged communists and their sympathisers, resulting in the massacre of hundreds of thousands; not only at the hands of the country's official armed forces, though: the perpetrators also included irregulars and militias associated with Islamic mass organisations and Muslim student unions. Aside from the anti-communist scare fed by the military usurpers, the violence was also motivated by the sharpened *santri–abangan* divisions resulting from the *Aliran* politics of the 1950s. The NU's Ansor (youth wing) was particularly motivated to collaborate with the government, because the PKI had been its most fervent competitor for the loyalty of Java's rural populations since the Madiun Affair and 1955 elections.[15] The exact circumstances of the coup and the ensuing atrocities remain the subject of much speculation, as there have never been any official investigations with publicly shared findings.[16]

By 1966, the military was politically more firmly in the saddle than ever before and able to transform General Nasution's 'Middle Way' role of Indonesia's armed forces in the 1950s into what under Suharto became known as its 'dual function' (*dwifungsi*) – a comprehensive role, extending from conventional national security tasks to direct military involvement in government and business. Under these circumstances, the hopes of former Masyumi leaders to return to the political scene were quickly dashed. Not only were they kept imprisoned or under house arrest until 1967, when political parties were again tolerated in the late 1960s, it also became clear that the Suharto government would not permit any leading roles for erstwhile Masyumi or other *Orde Lama*, or 'Old Order', politicians. Thus ex-Vice-President Hatta was prevented from reconstituting his Partai Demokrasi Islam Indonesia (PDII) and former Masyumi politicians Natsir, Roem and Prawoto were disqualified as leaders of a newly established Islamic party, Partai Muslimin Indonesia (PMI, also known as Parmusi). Instead the regime first approved the son of former Muhammadiyah leader Bagus Hadikusomo, Jarnawi Hadikusomo (also spelled Djarnawi Hadikusama, 1920–93), as the chairman of Parmusi. However, when the latter began reaching out to former Masyumi leaders, he was replaced with another – more pliable – Muhammadiyah figure, Muhammad Syafa'at Mintaredja (1921–84). Just before the carefully orchestrated elections of 1971, Mintaredja was traded for what was in effect a New Order straw man: Djaelani (John) Naro (1929–2000). Not surprisingly, with only 6 per cent of the votes, Parmusi came out fourth – far behind the government party Golkar (Golongan Karya), the Sukarnoist PNI, and the NU. Two years later, the New Order Regime tried to establish an even tighter control over party politics, by forcing the four permitted Islamic parties, Parmusi, NU, PSII and Perti to unite under a single umbrella: the Partai Persatuan Pembangunan (PPP, United Development Party).[17]

The main reason for this move was to neutralise the NU, which had given the strongest performance of all Islamic parties in the 1971 elections by securing more than 18 per cent of the votes. Ironically, this inaugurated a reversal in the political fortunes of the NU under New Order. Thanks to close personal ties between senior NU leaders and Sukarno, as well as on account of its continuing loyalty toward his Guided Democracy plans, the traditionalist NU had done well under the Old Order, despite the fact that – as a political party – it was poorly organised. For decades, the organisation had largely depended on the authority of an NU aristocracy of 'blue-blooded' *ulama*, centring on the family networks of figures such as Hasyim Asy°ari and Wahab Chasbullah, who saw themselves as heirs to the *Wali Songo* – the 'model bridgers of cultural boundaries' (Ricklefs 2012: 87). By the early 1970s, the NU had made huge advances in restructuring its activities and modernising its outlook. The NU's influence was not just widespread among Java's vast rural population; it also went down to the grassroots level. This did not suit the New Order Regime and the envisaged *dwifungsi* of its military support base:

> Indeed, NU had shown itself nearly impervious to control by any regime. Its foundation was a network of personal and familial relations among *kyais* and its institutional base was its *pesantrens*, which operated as independent educational institutions teaching the classic works of Traditionalist Islam – the so-called 'yellow books' (*kitab kuning*) – with funding from students, their families, business activities of the *kyais* and endowments. It was not easy for any government to take control of such a network, so the New Order decided instead to compete. (Ricklefs 2012: 150)

Capitalising on the lingering distrust among large sections of the *abangan* because of the involvement of NU's Ansor in the 1965–6 atrocities, the regime turned the government party Golkar into a voting machine for canvassing support among the *abangan* and thus creating a 'bulwark against Islam' (Ricklefs 2012: 151). To meet this challenge, the NU adopted a confrontational strategy, but found itself paying a dear price for its defiance. In 1971, it not only lost the prized office of minister of religion and its status as an autonomous political party by its forced absorption into the PPP two years later, but many of its individual members holding public office lost their positions as well. While this eventually enabled the NU to grow into the main opposition force against New Order, in the course of the late 1960s and early 1970s, Indonesia's intra-Islamic power relations evinced a reversal in fortunes.[18]

Between Islamism and accommodationism

The year 1968 can be considered a watershed year for this role reversal between modernist and traditionalist Muslims. The importance of youth activism in this changing of the guard conjures up associations with trends elsewhere in the world during that fateful year. However, in contrast to the student protests against the established order in Western Europe and North America, Indonesia's Muslim youth activism had its own dynamics and it moved in two different directions. One strand kept a distance from the regime, focussing instead on propagation (*dakwah*) and religious training (*tarbiyah*) grounded in interpretations of Islam that belong on the puritan side of the modernist-reformist spectrum. The other strand adopted a more constructive stance in terms of engaging and cooperating with the New Order Regime – a reason for its detractors to refer to its proponents as 'accommodationists' (Hassan 1980). In both instances, these Muslim youths were mentored by intellectuals and leaders from the older generation.

Identifying this key moment in the Islamisation process under New Order comes with a caveat: its subsequent development between the late 1960s and early 1980s unfolds against the background of religious affiliations in the top echelons of the New Order government. Not only were Christians disproportionately well represented in the senior ranks of both the military and the police, but what Ricklefs calls 'Suharto spirituality' was a 'long way from Islamic orthodoxy' (Ricklefs 2012: 118). Although there were resonances with some aspects of Sufi practices among traditionalist *santri*, Suharto's orientation was much closer to the *abangan*. And yet, in spite of this affinity, because of their earlier communist associations, the regime remained suspicious of the *abangan*'s unregulated religious practices. While the taxonomy of Indonesian religiosity became more sophisticated with the introduction of alternative terms for the *abangan*'s 'non-standard Islam', such as *kebatinan* ('mystical cults of "interiority"') and *kejawen* (Javanism), these were not legally recognised sets of religious beliefs and practices (Hefner 2011: 73; Ricklefs 2012: 269). Collectively referred to as *kepercayaan*, these were not administered as institutionalised religions (*agama*) by the Ministry of Religion, but fell under the responsibility of the Ministry of Culture. In addition, they were closely monitored by a special unit from the Attorney General's Office known as PAKEM – short for Peninjauan Aliran Kepercayaan Masyarakat (Observation of People's Belief Streams) (Ricklefs 2012: 137).

Once they realised that a return to Indonesia's political stage was not on the cards, the former Masyumi leadership opted for an alternative route towards influencing Indonesian society. Since his early days as an educator, Natsir had been concerned with the lack of knowledge of Islam among his peers. In the 1920s, this had been his main reason for becoming a teacher instead of pursuing a legal career. Analysing the situation in which Indonesia's Muslims found themselves almost forty years later, he came to the conclusion that their condition was still very much the same and that Masyumi's earlier political failures and the inability of its former leaders to canvass sufficient support for a return to politics and governance was still a result of these intellectual shortcomings. Working together with Roem, Rasjidi and Haryono, in 1967, Natsir was able to get government approval for the establishment of the Dewan Dakwah Islamiyah Indonesia (DDII, Indonesian Islamic Propagation Council):

> A majority of these reformists belonged to what was often called the Keluarga [or Keluarga Besar] Bulan Bintang (Family [or Large Family] of the Crescent Star), which saw Mohammed Natsir as its political and spiritual leader. Ties among its members were unusually close, involving long-standing friendships and family relationships, and also 'solidarity based on the spirit of Islamic reformism and the years of shared suffering during the period of Sukarno's Guided Democracy.' Most members of the 'family' remained distinct from the fundamentalists who saw the struggle of the Muslim community (*perjuangan ummat Islam*) as one aimed at establishment [sic] of an Islamic state. Natsir and his fellows, rather, 'interpret *perjuangan* [struggle] in a religio-political sense, as a striving to achieve an Islamic society (though not necessarily an Islamic state) and an influential role for Islamic parties.' (Kahin 2012: 163, quoting Samson 1978)

Aside from wanting to improve Islamic religious instruction along the puritan lines which he had embraced during his Persis years but had largely abandoned as Masyumi party leader, another motivation behind Natsir's founding of the DDII was his concern with growing trends among the *abangan* to convert to Christianity, and his indignation at the government's failure to put a halt to this and curtail Christian missionary activity in general.

The DDII's activities benefitted greatly from Natsir's network of international contacts, which he had been building since his days as Indonesia's most senior Muslim politician in the 1950s. Natsir was an appreciated figure in neighbouring Malaysia, but also in Pakistan and Saudi Arabia. He was a founding member and vice-president of the Karachi-based World Muslim Congress and involved in the establishment of the Muslim World League (MWL), a globally working organisation initiated by Saudi King Faysal (1906–75), of which Natsir became chairman in 1969. In particular, Natsir's relations with Saudi Arabia and other Gulf States provided the DDII with access to generous financial support, which became especially beneficial for its youth activities when the DDII expanded its influence to Indonesia's university student population. To this end, 'the Dewan Dawᶜah had initiated a campus-based program under the name of *Bina Masjid Kampus* (Campus Mosque Building)' (Kahin 2012: 178). One of its most successful exponents was the 'preacher combatant' training programme (*Latihan Mujahid Dakwah*, LMD) at the Salman Mosque on the campus of the Institute of Technology in Bandung (ITB). This initiative was coordinated by one of Natsir's personal protégés, Imaduddin Abdulrahim (1931–2008), and Endang Saefudin Anshari (1938–96) – the son of Isa Anshary. Such initiatives were an important tool in mobilising Indonesia's Muslim population for Islamic causes, such as protests against the new marriage law proposal of 1973 or the growing influence of foreign investors in Indonesia. In the face of subsequent government crackdowns in January 1974, after the so-called Malari incident (*Malapetaka Limabelas Januari*) in which students rioted against a visit by Japan's Prime Minister Kakuei Tanaka, and again in 1978, during the army campaign for the 'Normalisation of Campus Life' (*Normalisasi Kidupan Kampus*, NKK), Bandung's LMD was transformed into the 'Communication Forum of the Indonesian Mosque Youth' (*Badan Komunikasi Pemuda Masjid Indonesia*, BKPMI). From there, the same formula spread to other university campuses across Indonesia, creating a kind of underground refuge for Muslim activists once the government's NKK campaign got under way.

One of the side effects of DDII's networking with activists elsewhere in the Muslim world was the growing influence of foreign governments and Islamic organisations. As a result of this trend, 'Imaduddin Abdulrahim's Indonesian approach was thus replaced by a distinctly internationalist and increasingly re-politicized Islamic discourse' (Kersten 2015: 77). This shift created a tension with the DDII's own rhetoric, in which it cautioned against the dangers of a *ghazwul fikri* or 'intellectual invasion' from the outside. Introduced by Hamka in a speech at the 1969 Muhammadiyah congress, it is clear that this warning only applied to Western ideas and did not extend to Islamic influences of Middle Eastern provenance.[19] Although by the late 1960s, Natsir had shifted away from political pragmatism, Kahin maintains that – in terms of political ideology – Natsir remained closer to the Pakistani Jamaat-e Islami leader Maududi than the Egyptian Muslim Brotherhood ideologue Sayyid Qutb.

However, in 1970 Natsir recruited two GPII members of Yemeni descent, Abdullah Sungkar (1937–99) and Abu Bakar Baʿasyir (b. 1938), to become DDII activists in the Surakarta or Solo area. Two years later, the duo founded their own Islamic school called *Al-Mukmin* ('The Believer') in the city's Ngruki district. Because of their militant revivalism and unabashedly Islamist agenda for the restoration of the caliphate, the school gained notoriety under the name *Pondok Ngruki*. It appears that, in 1976, Sungkar and Baʿasyir were also inducted into the underground remnants of the DI and that they later founded a separate organisation called Jemaah Islamiyah (JI). When Sungkar and Baʿasyir were arrested in 1979 and imprisoned for three years, it is claimed that other JI members were responsible for the subsequent assassination of the vice-rector of Surakarta's Universitas Sebelas Maret, an attack in which they were allegedly assisted by another shadowy organisation known as Komando Jihad (supposedly a front for covert operations coordinated by military intelligence chief Ali Murtopo). Thus, 'by the mid-1970s Surakarta was already becoming what it has remained – a city known for active Islamic proselytisation and even Islamic extremism, along with high levels of Christianity' (Ricklefs 2012: 185). When they were in danger of being rearrested in 1985, Sungkar and Baʿasyir were helped by Natsir to escape to Malaysia, setting them on a course of international and violent Islamist activism that was reimported into Indonesia upon their return after the fall of the New Order Regime.[20]

Meanwhile, on the other side of the Islamic modernist-reformist spectrum, another Muslim youth activist had been on the rise: Nurcholish Madjid (1939–2005). Born in the NU heartland of east Java during the 1950s, Madjid's family were outcasts because of their Sarekat Islam and Masyumi connections.[21] For that reason, he left the area to attend the famous *Pesantren Pondok Modern Gontor* (where, ironically Abu Bakar Ba'asyir was also educated), which offered modernised Islamic education in Arabic and English. Like Imaduddin Abdulrahim, he began his activist career in the Himpunan Mahasiswa Islam (HMI, Association of Muslim Students) – a student union which was not affiliated with either the Muhammadiyah or NU, but which nevertheless had strong connections with the 'Masyumi Family'. Although he did not share Abdulrahim's politico-religious outlook, Madjid also advocated the further development of an Indonesian Islam, as became clear when his writings from the late 1960s until the mid-1980s were first published in book form, appearing under the title *Islam Kemodernan Keindonesiaan* ('A Modern Indonesian Islam', 1987).

When Madjid became HMI chairman in 1967, he was hailed as a 'Young Natsir' (*Natsir Muda*). In an article published a year later, he demonstrated sharing Natsir's view that modernisation should not be equated with Westernisation, but two years later the honeymoon ended when Madjid disavowed political Islam and the need for an Islamic state in a speech that became famous and notorious for the slogan 'Islam Yes; Islamic Party No!' (Kersten 2011: 56). Even more upsetting to the former Masyumi establishment was Madjid's proposal for a radical renewal of Islamic thinking, in which he pleaded for the 'secularisation' and 'desacralisation of politics'. Although he made a careful distinction between secularisation as a process and secularism as an ideology, his argumentation was dismissed as 'sophistry' in the very polemical responses written by Endang Anshari and Mohammad Rasjidi (Kersten 2011: 57).[22] According to the latter, in contrast to the genuine *mujaddidun* or Islamic renewers, Madjid had gone from being the anointed successor of Natsir to becoming the 'ummat's *enfant terrible*' (Kersten 2011: 63). In spite of this opposition, Madjid's ideas caught on, becoming the starting point of what became known as the *Gerakan Pembaruan Pemikiran Islam* or 'Movement for the Renewal of Islamic Thinking'. It received the backing of two other senior Muslim intellectuals, Harun Nasution (1919–98) and Abdul Mukti Ali (1923–2004).[23] This duo shared the young activists' advocacy of using advances made in the study of religion by the Western humanities and social sciences.

Born as Boedjono, Mukti Ali had received both a secular Dutch-language and Islamic education at east Java's *Pesantren Termas* and at Yogyakarta's *Sekolah Tinggi Islam*.[24] After performing hajj in 1950, Mukti Ali left for Pakistan to study Islamic history at the Faculty of Arabic Literature in Karachi and then moved on to the Institute of Islamic Studies (IIS) which had just been established by the Canadian scholar of religion, Wilfred Cantwell Smith, at McGill University in

Montreal. There he became excited by the holistic fashion in which the study of Islam was presented. It was designed to enable Muslim students to become appreciative of modern discourses on such issues as intellectual freedom, the concept of the state, women's rights and interfaith dialogue. Back in Indonesia, Mukti Ali was put in charge of the first comparative religious programmes introduced at the recently established IAINs, which formed the foundations for his 1972 initiative for a Forum for Inter-Religious Consultation (*Musyawarah Antar-Umat-Beragama*). Just like the emergence of the Islamic literature of the 1930s and the DDII's *dakwah* activities, this undertaking was a reaction to the spectacular growth in conversions to Christianity during the 1950s and 1960s, but offered a more positive response to that phenomenon.[25]

By 1968, when Suharto had replaced Sukarno as president and with Natsir and Rasjidi increasingly side-lined, Mukti Ali's star was soon on the rise. New Order's first priority was to improve Indonesia's economic situation, which was in a terrible state as a result of the disastrous economic policies under Sukarno. Muslim intellectuals such as Mukti Ali were inclined towards a degree of cooperation, since the regime appeared to allow a space for the development of what became known as a 'civil' or 'cultural Islam' (*Islam Sipil* or *Kultural*), for which there was a place in Indonesian public life. When appointed minister of religion in 1971, Mukti Ali began defining what Karel Steenbrink has characterised as a 'Weberian' religious policy grounded in his earlier academic work in comparative religious studies and his involvement in interfaith dialogue (Steenbrink 1999: 285).[26] It was against this background that Mukti Ali began facilitating a set of reforms targeting all levels of Islamic education that would provide the necessary preconditions for the emergence of a new Muslim intellectual capable of elaborating this concept of cultural Islam in the context of the government's development policy. As part of his overhaul of Islamic education, Mukti Ali proposed a rejuvenation of the values of the traditional Islamic education system so that the *pesantren* too could become catalysts of community development and agents of change in Indonesia and facilitate community development. This revamping of *pesantrens* was enthusiastically received by the NU leader Abdurrahman Wahid (1940–2009). Affectionately known to Indonesians as Gus Dur, he was the grandson of NU founder Hasyim Asy'ari and already an influential figure in the organisation.

The hands-on reform of the IAINs fell to the new rector of IAIN Syarif Hidayatullah in Jakarta (1973–84), Harun Nasution. Born into a northern Sumatran *penghulu* family, Nasution studied at the Dutch Islamic Teachers' College (*Kweekschool met de Koran*). After an unhappy stint in Saudi Arabia, his father permitted him to move to Cairo, where he attended the American University, because he lacked the Arabic-language skills to gain access to al-Azhar. Cut off from Indonesia by the war, Nasution married an Egyptian woman and then joined Indonesia's embryonic diplomatic service as a consul working under Mohammad Rasjidi at the embassy in Cairo. At the height of the Guided Democracy period, Nasution was forced to resign: according to some, this was because of his strong anti-communist views, while others have suggested that his Sumatran origins had become a liability because of the activities of the renegade PRRI. On Rasjidi's recommendation, Nasution was admitted to McGill University. Like Mukti Ali, Nasution too was stimulated by the intellectual climate at McGill, first obtaining an MA degree with a dissertation on the Masyumi party and then, in 1968, receiving a doctorate on the basis of a thesis on Muhammad Abduh, in which he offered a positive argumentation for Mu'tazili influences on the thinking of the Egyptian reformist.[27] As rector, he oversaw the introduction of an innovative study programme and new curriculum, designed to equip students with an understanding of Islam as a civilisation. It encompassed the study of various legal and theological schools, alongside philosophy and Sufism, including the 'deviant' works of the Mu'tazila and Ibn al-ʿArabi, as well as the writings of Western scholars of Islam. These reforms did not go unchallenged and his former mentor Mohammed Rasjidi became one of his fiercest critics, objecting in particular to Nasution's openness to the scholarship of Western and Westernised scholars of Islam.

Thanks to the support from the New Order Regime, Mukti Ali's religious policies and the educational reforms of Harun Nasution were instrumental in shaping Indonesia's ongoing Islamisation process during the 1970s and 1980s. Helped by the financial windfall from which Indonesia profited as an oil-exporting country since the oil boom of 1974, the infrastructure of Islamic tertiary education was expanded massively, and increasing numbers of talented students were sent overseas for postgraduate studies, not only to the Muslim world, but – following the example of their mentors – also to universities in Australia, Europe and North America. The effects of this became very noticeable in the 1980s and 1990s, triggering developments that eventually escaped from the regime's control.

The 'greening' of Indonesian society

The next key moment in the relationship between New Order and Indonesia's Muslims came in 1983–4. First of all, it saw the reaffirmation of Pancasila as state doctrine. New Order went even further when – in contrast to the early independence years and the *Aliran* politics of the 1950s – Pancasila was declared the *asas tunggal*, or 'sole foundation', for all socio-political actors. However, this decision occurred alongside the introduction of the 'reactualisation agenda' (1983–93) by Minister of Religion Munawir Sjadzali (1925–2004); and the NU's decision to leave party politics altogether. Presented under the slogan *Kembali ke Khittah 1926* or 'Return to the 1926 Founding Document', this proved a strategically important decision for the NU. On the one hand, it enabled the traditional *ulama* establishment within the NU, led by General

President Achmad Siddiq (1926–91), to focus on their role as educators and recalibrate the organisation's course into a depoliticised 'Middle Path' or '*tawassut wa al-iᶜtidal*' (Kersten 2015: 88). On the other hand, it propelled the NU's new executive chairman, the mercurial Abdurrahman Wahid (Gus Dur), into the role of key critic of the regime.[28] Erudite and fluent in Arabic and English, Abdurrahman Wahid's profile is hardly that of a conventional religious scholar. Educated in the *pesantren* milieu and at schools in Jakarta during his father Wahid Hasyim's stints in government, Gus Dur did not attend Islamic universities, but went to Cairo and Baghdad to study Arabic literature, although he never graduated. Upon his return, he quickly moved up the ranks in the NU, culminating in his 1984 election as chairman of the executive board. From then on, he used this platform to evolve into the role of *de facto* opposition leader against Suharto.[29]

Leaving aside the regime's imposition of the Pancasila Doctrine and the NU's decision to avert (and subvert) this as much as possible by refocussing on its original mission, it was the government's own religious policy towards the Muslim population that accelerated the Islamisation process in the second half of the 1980s – leading to what is called the *penghijauan* or 'greening' of Indonesian society. The name is symbolic in a double sense, as the word does not only refer to green as the symbolic colour of Islam, but also to the military.

The combined effects of the initiatives of the DDII, Nurcholish Madjid's Renewal Movement, and the changes introduced under Mukti made Indonesia look much more 'Islamic' than twenty-five years earlier. Much of this was driven by a growing middle class of educated, upwardly mobile, urban Muslims. Living and working in major cities, with their immediate material needs increasingly met, they also formed a market for the 'commodification' of religion.[30] This was not only exemplified commercially – by an expanding halal food and Islamic fashion industry – but also manifested itself intellectually and spiritually, in the appearance of NGOs and 'think tank'-like organisations catering to the immaterial needs of this new Muslim bourgeoisie. Former student activists such as Nurcholish Madjid set up research institutes and foundations, which not only offered educational courses and programmes on religion, spiritual well-being and self-improvement to urban Muslim professionals, but also provided employment opportunities for graduates from the IAINs. Some entrepreneurial individuals were able to combine the commercial and the spiritual, such as the singer Rhoma Irama (b. 1949) and the TV preacher Abdullah Gymnastiar (b. 1962), also known as Aa Gym.

This Islamisation trend also began to affect the political elites, until it even reached the very top – with President Suharto and his family performing hajj in 1991. In the course of the 1980s, Suharto had been reducing his reliance on generals from Christian backgrounds and, with his trust diminishing in other senior officers with their own political ambitions, the president had been putting out feelers to the Muslim camp. Aside from the symbolic step of presenting himself as a practising Muslim, which in turn motivated other top government and military officials to emphasise their own Islamic credentials, Suharto approved the formation of a platform for bringing together the country's Muslim intelligentsia as a new political power base. Both observers of political and religious developments in contemporary Indonesia and some of the actors who were involved in these events have provided different accounts of the establishment of what became known as the Ikatan Cendekiawan Muslim se-Indonesia (ICMI, All-Indonesian Association of Muslim Intellectuals). It is generally agreed that what had started out as an impromptu plan of five Muslim student leaders for a symposium was quickly turned into a grander scheme when the former DDII campus activist Imaduddin Abdulrahim and Muhammadiyah intellectual Dawam Rahardjo suggested turning the one-off campus event into a more sustained effort to bring various groups of Muslim intellectuals together. In order to get the necessary official support, they approached Suharto's confidant, Minister of Technology B. J. Habibie. Realising the political possibilities of this initiative, Suharto gave his consent and instructed Habibie to personally take charge of what was now becoming a government-led plan for a formal discussion forum bringing together Muslim government officials, technocrats, academics, activists and – last but certainly not least – the leaders of Indonesia's Muslim mass organisations.

From the outset, ICMI's main vulnerability was the refusal of NU leader Abdurrahman Wahid to sign up to the project. Instead, he founded an alternative, more inclusivist and critical body of intellectuals called Forum Demokrasi. Optimism regarding ICMI's potential as a new political power base soon evaporated when participants and observers began presenting different and diverging interpretations of its role, ranging from protecting the economic interests of the Muslim middle class to the cultural and symbolic significance that such a new Islamic organisation could harness. ICMI's initial success as a regime-friendly umbrella organisation bringing together a broad spectrum of intellectuals of varying Muslim backgrounds was thus undermined by its own internal ideological diversity and the inevitably resulting differences of opinion on how to relate and be loyal to the regime. Its demise was only hastened when key figures became disenchanted, either departing of their own volition or being unceremoniously expelled from the organisation. Even though ICMI's founding had initially been perceived as a 'watershed of the state's politics of accommodation towards Islam', its importance was outweighed by the continuing structural significance of Muslim mass organisations such as the Muhammadiyah and NU, as well as state- and regime-related institutions like New Order's government party Golkar, MUI and the state bureaucracy in general (Effendy 2004: 196).

Regime change and reformation: taking Indonesian Islam into the twenty-first century

Although 1995 started with celebrations to commemorate fifty years of independence, the half-centenary mark also saw an upsurge of politically motivated religious violence which would mar the final years of Suharto's rule, as he and his government tried to come to terms with a rapidly changing globalising world. As the Internet began making inroads into Indonesia's mediascape, state sovereignty and nationalist protectionism felt under siege from a worldwide surge of (neo-)liberalism. Trying to demonstrate its democratic credentials and respect for human rights, the regime ordered the release of the last former ministers from the Sukarno era still remaining in detention.

The unforeseen effect of this decision was a campaign by young Muslims demanding a similar amnesty for imprisoned Islamic activists, while the detractors of ICMI responded by establishing alternative platforms and organisations for safeguarding national unity by expressing their unwavering support for the Pancasila Doctrine. Another of the government's major concerns was the establishment of an alliance of political opponents of Suharto, uniting the Partai Demokrasi Indonesia (PDI, Indonesian Democratic Party) led by the daughter of the late President Sukarno, Megawati Sukarnoputri, Abdurrahman Wahid's NU, and what the government called *Organisasi Tanpa Bentuk* (OTB, Organisations Without Form).

The Muslim opposition and the end of Suharto's reign

In a desperate attempt to fend off imminent challenges to his authority, Suharto attacked the PDI–NU tandem by orchestrating Megawati's ousting from her position as party leader and a failed bid to depose Abdurrahman Wahid from his top seat in the NU. Suharto's last full year in power turned into a veritable *annus horribilis*, as Indonesia felt the full impact of the 1997 international currency crisis and was put at the mercy of the IMF. Despite the governing party Golkar's victory in the national elections, the regime was unable to quell a rebellion in ICMI against Suharto's intention to seek a seventh term in office as president. More than a thousand Muslim intellectuals proposed Muhammadiyah leader Amien Rais as an alternative candidate, while the Islamic periodical *Ummat* added to the pressure by naming him its 'man of the year'. The regime retaliated by expelling Rais from ICMI, thus further eroding its envisaged role as a rainbow coalition of Muslim New Order loyalists. The only ones left in the Muslim camp propping up Suharto's presidency were government bureaucrats and – as an ultimate irony – representatives of the DDII and the Komité Indonesia untuk Solidaritas dengan Dunia Islam (KISDI, Indonesian Committee for Solidarity with the Muslim World), which operated under the patronage of

Suharto's then son-in-law, Lieutenant General Prabowo Subianto and his coterie of so-called Green Generals.

By early 1998, thousands of students began taking to the streets in order to protest against Suharto's re-election. In the ensuing riots, 1,200 lost their lives; not least due to Prabowo and KISDI's involvement in sowing dissent within the Muslim camp by sending in thugs associated with self-proclaimed Islamist vigilante organisations. With student opposition coordinated by the Kesatuan Aksi Mahasiswa Muslim Indonesia (KAMMI, United Front of Indonesian Muslim University Students), it was now manifestly clear that the Muslim bloc was the new political lynchpin of manoeuvres that were under way within the regime for an internal handing-over of power. While Amien Rais was posturing as the main face of the opposition and NU leader Abdurrahman Wahid left everybody guessing where his ultimate loyalty lay, Suharto sought the advice of nine influential Muslim intellectuals led by Nurcholish Madjid. On 21 May 1998, they managed to convince the ageing president to hand over the reins to Vice-President Habibie. Although greeted with enthusiasm by the middle classes, the new measures would prove too little and too late to save New Order. The newly opened political space was quickly filled by a proliferation of new political parties; no fewer than 130 had registered before the year was out, but there were only five serious contenders and most of these were led by familiar faces from the political arena.

Vying for power were a reunified PDI–Perjuangan (struggle) of Megawati Sukarnoputri; the government party Golkar now led by former Muslim student activist and HMI chairman Akbar Tanjung; and three major Muslim parties: (1) a revamped New Order-era PPP under NU stalwart Hamzah Haz, (2) Amien Rais's Partai Amanat Nasional (PAN, National Mandate Party) and (3) the NU's Partai Kebangkitan Bangsa (PKB, National Awakening Party). DDII activists and its highly effective youth wing were quick to establish more openly Islamist competitors, such as the Partai Bulang Bintang (PBB, Crescent Star Party), Sarekat Islam, Masyumi and the Partai Keadilan Sejahtera (PKS, Justice and Prosperity Party). However, they were dwarfed in size when compared with NU- and Muhammadiyah-affiliated parties. Although results for all Islamic parties in the first free and fair elections since 1955 were very disappointing, some individual Muslim politicians performed very well: in 1999, NU leader Abdurrahman Wahid became the first democratically elected president since the declaration of independence almost fifty-five years earlier, and Muhammadiyah chairman Amin Rais took the position of Speaker of the People's Consultative Assembly (Majelis Permusyawaratan Rakyat, MPR)

Reformation or restoration?

After decades of authoritarianism and with the leaders of the country's largest Muslim mass organisations now holding the two highest political offices in the land, Indonesia's transition period was inaugurated under the name *Reformasi* – 'Reformation'. This democratisation process came with its own set of challenges.

Due to the breakdown of law and order in the wake of the 1998–9 regime change, and as the military struggled to redefine its role in a drastically changed political environment, political violence erupted once again. During the final years of New Order, there had already been clashes between indigenous Dayaks and Madurese migrants in West Kalimantan and new fermentations in the notoriously rebellious northern Sumatran province of Aceh, while Muslim gangs elsewhere turned to burning churches and assaulting Indonesia's ethnic Chinese community. At the turn of the century, this violence took on a distinctly religious garb: not only did Muslim vigilantes, youth gangs and self-defence militias (*PAM Swakarsa*) clash along Islamic and Christian lines, but there were also intra-Muslim attacks on – for example – traditionalist *dukuns* and *bomohs* accused of practising black magic. John Sidel describes this change in character as a shift from 'riots' to 'pogroms'. Amidst the chaos, it was very difficult to determine who held political responsibility for this escalation.

President Abdurrahman Wahid's term in office was brief and unsuccessful. An unorthodox and mercurial figure both as a religious leader and head of state, he also lacked the administrative aptitude to bring the necessary structure to democratic governance. In 2001, this led to his impeachment and replacement by Megawati Sukarnoputri. Aside from having to shepherd through important changes to the political culture and government system, she also had to contend with the occurrence of acts of terrorism on Bali and in the capital Jakarta, perpetrated by radicalised Islamists with links to Al-Qaeda and its alleged proxy in Southeast Asia, Jemaah Islamiyah (JI). These incidents turned Indonesia into the US's key Southeast Asian ally in the 'War on Terror'. However, Megawati was unable to hold onto office in the elections of 2004 due to the actions of the *Poros Tengah* or 'Central Axis' – an alliance of moderate Muslims who objected to a female head of state. Forged by PAN leader Amien Rais, it had already succeeded in denying Megawati the presidency after her PDI-P won the 2001 elections. This opened the way for retired General Susilo Bambang Yudhoyono, usually referred to as 'SBY'. His decade in office can be considered as a comeback of sorts for New Order; an observation corroborated by the narrow loss of the 2014 presidential elections by Prabowo Subianto, Suharto's erstwhile son-in-law and a former special forces officer, against Djoko Widoyo, the candidate endorsed by Megawati Sukarnoputri. The continuing presence of such figures from both the Old and New Order era evince the resilience and sustained political relevance of what I have called elsewhere Indonesia's 'eternal political elites' (Kersten 2015: 33).

On the other hand, it cannot be denied that *Reformasi* has also led to an unprecedented opening-up of the public sphere. It has had mixed effects on Indonesia's Islamisation process at the beginning of the twenty-first century. Islamic political parties have not performed well in the four elections that have been held since 1999. With their collective share hovering around a quarter of the total cast votes, it seems that the Muslim electorate prefers secular parties like the PDI-P and Golkar. Political openness has also resulted in a polarisation between what I refer to as 'reactionary' and 'progressive' Muslims. While the former consist not only of supporters of Islamist parties, but also include vigilante organisations such as the Front Pembela Islam (FPI, Islamic Defenders Front), the latter are mainly found among activists working for NGOs, think tanks and advocacy groups or academics associated with the IAINs. These Muslim intellectuals come from both NU and Muhammadiyah backgrounds. The ideological stand-off between the two camps revolves around a number of issues.

Islamic statehood and the role of Islamic law in society continue to be debated. While the election results of Islamist parties, such as PBB and PKS, lack the critical mass to make these viable issues in the political process, they have adjusted their strategies and tactics to achieve maximum results.[31] When it became clear that an introduction of the Jakarta Charter in the new constitution proved again not feasible, the PKS took the lead in trading it for another Islamic concept: proposing the *Mithaq Madina* or the 'Madina Charter' of the Prophet Muhammad, which had brought together Muslims, Jews and Christians in seventh-century Arabia, as a model for Indonesia's multi-ethnic and multi-religious society. Similarly, they took advantage of the political decentralisation during *Reformasi,* using the devolution of power and delegation of administrative responsibilities from the central government to provincial and local authorities to introduce and implement aspects of Islamic law through regional by-laws called *Peraturan Daerat Syariat* or *Perda Syariat* for short.

Tensions between reactionary and progressive Muslims rose in 2005–6, which constitutes yet another watershed year in the Islamisation of postcolonial Indonesia. This coincided with the seven- or eight-year mark in a democratisation process, which experts consider a litmus test for its success as it moves from the transition to the consolidation phase. In July 2005, the Majelis Ulama Indonesia (MUI, Indonesian Ulama Council) issued a number of controversial *fatwas,* the most significant one being 'Fatwa 7', in which the notions of secularism, pluralism and liberalism are condemned as 'un-Islamic'. Reactionary Muslim intellectuals and Islamist politicians regard this ruling as a vindication of their criticism of progressive Muslims, whom they have accused of encouraging *ghazwul fikri*; allowing an 'intellectual invasion' of Western ideas regarding minority rights and gender relations to take root in Indonesia. Islamic vigilante organisations considered the *fatwa* as a licence to persecute 'deviant' Muslims, including Indonesia's tiny Shi'a minority and the Ahmadiyyah movement. A year later, on the occasion of Pancasila Day 2006, the progressive bloc responded with a 'Declaration of Indonesianess' (*Maklumat Keindonesiaan*), in which they countered that the MUI *fatwa* violated the underpinnings of the Indonesian state, especially because the notion of pluralism represented the same principles enshrined in the Pancasila.

The situation was not helped by the indecisiveness of the SBY administration and the hesitation of law enforcement agencies to protect religious minorities. Nor did a 'conservative turn' in the top leadership of the Muhammadiyah and – to some extent – also in the NU, during the national congresses of these two mass organisations in 2005, do any good to the causes of progressive Muslims. Until that year, outgoing chairman Ahmad Syafii Maarif had been supportive of the accommodation of a 'cultural Islam' attuned to the situation in Indonesia and offered patronage to a group of junior cadres, united in the Jaringan Intelektual Muhammadiyah Muda (JIMM, Network of Young Muhammadiyah Intellectuals), which was founded in 2004. The latter formed the modernist counterparts of the Anak Muda NU, or young NU cadres, who had been formulating a comparable progressive discourse since 2001, which they presented under the name Islamic Post-Traditionalism. Two years earlier, another young NU intellectual, Ulil Abshar-Abdalla, had taken an even bolder step by founding the Jaringan Islam Liberal (JIL, Liberal Islam Network), which had worked like a lightning rod for Islamist intellectuals on the reactionary side of the spectrum. These progressive NU cadres were protégés of Said Aqil Siraj, who – in 2010 – succeeded PPP politician and former Vice-President Hamzah Haz as executive chairman of the NU, but who also had to contend with more conservative *ulama* in the NU's Consultative Council, in particular Maarif Amin. As head of MUI's Fatwa Drafting Committee, Amin had not only been the man behind the controversial Fatwa 7, but had also managed to become the president's closest adviser on religious affairs. In 2015, he was able to consolidate his standing by his appointment as chairman of MUI and election as general president of the NU.

Concluding remarks

The decade that has passed since the issue of Fatwa 7 has given rise to grave concerns regarding the prospects of religious plurality, the rights of minorities, freedom of thought, and the manoeuvring space for progressive Muslim intellectuals and activists in the face of challenges from the reactionary Islamic camp. However, in the summer of 2015, two publications were released at the national congresses of the NU and the Muhammadiyah. Entitled *Islam Nusantara* ('Southeast Asian Islam') and *Islam Kebinekaan* (a pun on Indonesia's national slogan *Bhinneka Tunggal Ika* – 'Unity in Diversity'), these books make a case for a distinctly Indonesian Islam, offering a counter-narrative to the internationalist Islamist discourse of the reactionary Muslims, whose tendencies toward Arabisation can considered just as much an instance of *ghazwul fikri* or 'intellectual invasion' as the openness of the progressives to ideas of non-Islamic provenance.

Conclusion

The history of Islam in Indonesia is best understood as an ongoing story. Its beginnings and origins remain uncertain, but we do know that it commenced relatively late on the timeline of the emergence and expansion of Islam, and it did not reach Indonesia as part of the early Arab conquests. Also it can be safely said that the arrival of Islam was not the result of an instantaneous big bang. Affecting a sprawling archipelago with an amazing ethno-linguistic and cultural-religious diversity to begin with, the arrival and introduction of Islam is best conceived as having multiple starting points, different modalities and involving a variety of mediators. In regards to the latter, and in order to come to a correct interpretation and accurate understanding, it is imperative to acknowledge the roles of both external and internal actors in encounters that set in motion a process of adhesion, conversion and adaptation that has been going on for more than 700 years.

This is why this book's narrative has presented this Islamisation process as a dynamic interplay of centrifugal and centripetal forces which has produced a distinct variant of what Marshall Hodgson called the Islamicate cultures of which the globalised Muslim civilisation is composed. The result of the absorption of influences from other parts of the Muslim world mediated by Arabised versions of regional languages, filtered through older cultural deposits and adapted to local circumstances, Islam in what is now the unitary Republic of Indonesia forms part of a wider geographical zone on the eastern periphery of the Indian Ocean. The notion of a network offers a suitable trope for capturing this interactive dynamism.

Within this Southeast Asian island world, the Islamisation process has evolved into different manifestations. It transformed coastal and riparian Malay petty states into new political entities, sometimes with imperial aspirations. Its Muslim population used cultural references to heroic figures and merged into political institutions that had been carried across the Indian Ocean from the Mediterranean, and West and South Asia. With conditions in Java's interior more favourable to the development of intensive rice cultures similar to those in the mainland river plains and deltas of Burma, Thailand and Cambodia, Islamic religious influences were creatively absorbed into an intensively Indianised Javanese cultural environment, producing a 'mystic synthesis' which continues to exist until today alongside other manifestations of Islam.

   While the Islamisation of Southeast Asia was pushed in particular directions by increasingly intensive European colonisation and the region's eventual territorial occupation during the age of high imperialism, this development must not be isolated as a distinct sequential stage, but rather as part of a continuum of overlapping phases involving repetitive introductions, extending and intensifying into increasingly intricate patterns of networking, and responses and adaptations to ever new challenges. As parts of maritime Southeast Asia were integrated into a new political entity known as the Netherlands East Indies, its Muslim population began developing a sense of self-awareness in line with this imperialist construct and aided by new means of communication. This led to a new self-identification as Muslims from the Indies and the formulation of different forms of solidarity shaped by exposure to Islamic reformism, notions of modernity and nationalist ideologies. This bred a degree of assertiveness that motivated Muslims to explore different avenues of emancipation and political activism.

   The subsequent decolonisation was a confusing experience for the Muslims of what had now become the independent Republic of Indonesia. Aspirations for an Islamic state competed and clashed with the formation of what was initially conceived as a federal, but quickly evolved into a unitary, nation-state, coextensive with the territory of the former colony. This led to ideological tensions, political power games, and even regional opposition against the allegedly imperialist designs of what many in the outer islands regarded as a Java-centric polity rather than an egalitarian multi-ethnic and multi-religious state. Out of this political turmoil evolved a conceptualisation of an Indonesian Islam which gradually took shape through a process informed by pragmatism and compromise, but also circumscribed by political constraints. As the infant republic moved from an aborted experiment with parliamentary democracy to a presidential system of Guided Democracy, interrupted by a military coup and followed by more than three decades of autocratic rule, it arrived at the eve of the new millennium to face the challenge of another democratisation process. During these seventy years as an independent country, the majority of its citizens continue to explore, but also wrestle with, their identity as both Indonesians and Muslims.

Notes

Chapter 1

1. *Nusantara* is mentioned in a fourteenth-century Javanese text (Vlekke 1943). The other designations became current with increased interaction with the Muslim world and during the age of European exploration and expansion (see Laffan 2009; Clifford [1904] 1990; Reid 1988, 1993).

2. The term came into circulation after World War II, during which there had been a 'Southeast Asian theatre' of military operations that was put under the command of the British naval officer Lord Mountbatten (Heryanto 2007: 76).

3. The evidence for this is not only linguistic, but also material and cultural in terms of shipbuilding techniques, utensils, musical instruments, artistic patterns and practices such as headhunting (Taylor 1976: 26).

4. It also has been referred to as 'Hinduisation' (Cœdès 1948). The editor and translator of the English version of this seminal work have corrected this less accurate designation (Cœdès 1968).

5. For the influence of the mandala model in Indonesia, see Lombard (1990: III).

6. As discussed in works like Lombard (1990) and Guillot et al. (1998).

7. The name seems to indicate an awareness of the styles used by the Mamluk rulers of Egypt (Feener and Laffan 2005: 194 n. 34).

8. Pires ended his days in China, but there is no certainty as to the exact date of his death, which has been given as either 1524 or 1540.

9. Pointing at a similar style used in Ayyubid Yemen (Laffan 2009: 38).

10. On Java itself, a comparable transliteration of Javanese into Arabic script became known as *pegon*. Something similar also happened on Sulawesi (Celebes), where a Bugi-Arabic script called *serang* was used (Ali 2016: 24).

11. See Levtzion (1979); Nock (1933).

12. A dated, but still insightful, study of these aspects of Southeast Asian Islam is found in Skeat (1900).

13. From the Arabic *hikāya* meaning 'story'.

14. The continuing relevance of geography is also illustrated in Hefner (1985, 1990).

15. These include the first vice-president of Indonesia, Mohammad Hatta; two early prime ministers, Sutan Sjahrir and Mohammad Natsir; the leader of Masyumi, Indonesia's main postcolonial Islamic party – again Natsir; the linguist, philosopher and literary figure, Sutan Takdir Alisjahbana; and Indonesia's leading Muslim man of letters in the twentieth century, Hamka – an acronym of Haji Abdul Malik Karim Amrullah.

16. See Chapter 2. Cham–Javanese connections are also discussed in Kersten (2006).

17. For recent examinations of Tamil influences on Muslims in maritime Southeast Asia, see Tschacher (2001).

18. The arrival of Europeans during the 'Age of Discovery' may not have been one of the incentives for initial acceptance of Islam, but – as will be discussed in later chapters – it

did provide a politico-religious rallying point for Muslim solidarity in resisting the ensuing incursions of European colonialism.

19. Van Bruinessen has recorded the names and deaths from Abd al-Qadir al-Jilani in 1166 to ᶜAbdullah al-Shattar in 1429 CE (Bruinessen 1994b: 2).

20. See Julian Baldick's entry on the subject in the *Encyclopaedia of Islam* (Baldick 2016).

21. See Goitein's seminal multivolume publication of the documents found in the Geniza (1967–2000). Of particular relevance for the present account is his so-called *India Book*, which was still unfinished at the time of his death (Goitein and Friedman 2007).

22. See Alatas (1997: 32–3).

23. Also spelled as Hamza al-Fansuri or even al-Pansuri.

24. He also used to make a case for Persian domination of the Muslim Indian Ocean and China trade (Attas 1967: 51).

25. Only a limited number of texts were signed and the attribution of others is often contested. Further complications are that none of these texts are in manuscripts that can be attributed to Fansuri personally; the addition of interpellations and other 'updates' when copying manuscripts was a common and widespread practice acknowledged by most scholars (Guillot and Kalus 2000: 10–12).

26. A similar argument can be made in regards to Masᶜud al-Jawi of Uwaja.

27. Vladimir Braginsky has written a riposte in which he makes some valid reservations regarding the reliability of the epitaph text, but for the rest mainly rehashes the arguments informed by his own philological focus (Braginsky 2001).

Chapter 2

1. More appropriately transcribed as 'al-Mukammal'.

2. The characterisation 'gunpowder empire' for the realms of the Ottoman Turks, the Shiᶜa Safavid dynasty in Persia and the Moghuls of India, is taken from the final volume of Marshall Hodgson's *Venture of Islam* (Hodgson 1974).

3. For a detailed study of this episode from Ottoman history, see Casale (2010).

4. Important evidence of the latter is the century-long presence of a large gun known as *lada sa-ckupak*, which was later taken by the Dutch and dispatched to the Netherlands (Reid 1969: 397).

5. For an additional perspective, featuring the involvement of Portuguese and Luso-Asian traders with both Jewish and New Christian backgrounds, see Alves (2015).

6. Also known as *Kyahi Gundil*, Anta Kusuma has since become a *pusaka* or heirloom with magical powers, under the name *Kotang Antakusuma*. It is said to have been made from goatskin (see Moertono 2009: 75). It was passed on to Sunan Kalijaga's heir Ngadi Langu, who then bestowed it on Panembahan Senapati, the founding father of the House of Mataram.

7. Jaᶜfar al-Sadiq (d. 765) was the fifth and last imam to be recognised by all Shiᶜa Muslims before they split off into the Sevener (Ismaᶜili) and Twelver (Imami) branches. Retrospectively, he is also the founder of the Jaᶜfari School of Law, and his scholarship in both *fiqh* and *hadith* studies is even acknowledged by Sunni Muslims.

8. A corruption of the Arabic word *shaykh*.

9. All principalities and fiefdoms of the Pasisir had family ties to Demak through descent or marriage.

10. Accounts of this eastward expansion of Islamic influences are found in *Oud and Nieuw Oost-Indiën*, an encyclopaedic work written in the early eighteenth century by a VOC minister (Valentijn 1724); see also Hägerdal (2001).

11. The shrine of Tembayat holds central stage in the Islamisation of Java's interior and also has a connection with Sunan Kalijaga (Rinkes 1996: 69–121).

12. There was another 'international incident' in 1688, when the VOC arrested, on suspicion of inciting trouble, one Sharif Habib Allah, a wandering scholar from Surat in India, who was en route to Palembang. This led to remonstrations by the Muslim governors of Surat, who claimed this individual was under the protection of the Mughal Emperor Aurangzeb (1658–1707). Wanting to avoid a diplomatic scandal, the VOC set the holy man free (Ricklefs 2006: 75).

13. Al-Attas's writings on *shaᶜir* formed part of a polemics he had with Andries Teeuw, Professor of Malay Literature at Leiden University, whose statement that 'in Malay literature copyists were always potential rewriters' sounded too negative to al-Attas – reading connotations of fraud into it (Teeuw 1966: 440; Attas 1968: 8, 12–15).

14. See Ibn Rushd's *Definitive Statement* (Colville 1999: 76–110).

15. The characterisation is from Anthony Reid (1969: 397).

16. A detailed study of al-Burhanpuri's book, also in relation to its Southeast Asian context, is found in Johns (1965).

17. Michael Feener, personal communication, 18 October 2006.

18. For detailed studies of Al-Raniri's wujudiyya, see Attas (1966).

19. John Bousfeld has drawn parallels with 'Monist' philosophies, including later thinking such as that of Spinoza (Bousfeld 1983: 104–8).

20. A notion that has been critically interrogated by O'Fahey and Radtke (1993).

21. For a detailed discussion of this episode, see Rinkes (1996: 15–46).

22. See also Michael Feener's study of the influence of probably the most famous mystic in the history of Sufism, al-Hallaj (Feener 1998).

23. According to some sources, he was actually related to Hamzah Fansuri in one way or another (Azra 2004: 71).

24. For the significance of the Yemen connection, see also Feener and Laffan (2005).

25. This is based on a saying attributed to the Prophet Muhammad that, after his death, every century a scholar will rise up to reinvigorate the Islamic faith.

26. It has been suggested that this text, entitled *Ithaf al-Dhaki*, was written at the personal request of al-Singkili (Azra 2004: 75; Riddell 2001: 127–8).

27. On ᶜAbd al-Muhyi, see Rinkes (1996: 1–14). Both lineages featured prominently in the politico-religious unrest and wars affecting Sumatra and Java in the first half of the nineteenth century.

28. On the influence of Sufi orders in Banten in the wake of al-Maqassari's stay, see van Bruinessen (1995: 180–3).

29. Al-Palimbani's year of birth is given as 1704 by Azyumardi Azra (2004: 113) and as 1719 by Michael Laffan (2011: 29).

30. A Khalwatiyya-Sammaniyya branch also sprang up in South Sulawesi, where it functions alongside and – to some extent – in rivalry with the Khalwatiyya-Yusuf order. However, this branch is not traceable to Abd al-Samad al-Palimbani; instead, its introduction is attributed to another Indonesian student of al-Samman, Yusuf of Bogor, who was a judge at the court of the Bugi ruler of Bone (Bruinessen 1991: 259–60).

31. Azyumardi Azra's claim that this was the first instance of a Southeast Asian scholar being included in such sources (2004: 113) is now called into question by Feener and Laffan's article on Masᶜud al-Jawi (2005).

32. As early as 1715, Ratu Pakubuwono had already commissioned the writing of the *Serat Menak*, a lengthy collection of romantic tales featuring the Prophet Muhammad's Uncle Hamza, which are still popular among South and Southeast Asian Muslims. The

Serat Menak is a Javanese recast of the Malay rendition of these stories (Ricklefs 2006: 86).

33. Other *Garebeg* ceremonies were held on the occasion of the end of Ramadan (*Eid al-Fitr*) and the final day of the pilgrimage to Mecca (*Eid al-Adha*); see Carey (2014: 16). An excellent account of the survival of such practices until the present day is found in Woodward (2011).

34. Hamengkubuwono I of Yogyakarta; Susuhunan of Surakarta Pakubuwono III (1749–88); and Prince Mangkunegoro I of the other, competing, court in Surakarta.

35. The term *santri* received much wider circulation as a result of Clifford Geertz's *The Religion of Java* (1960) and *Islam Observed* (1968). It has become a referent for pious urban Muslims as opposed to the nominally Muslim peasantry of Java, known as *abangan*.

36. Even today, leading scholars who have also made the pilgrimage are designated 'K.H.' – *Kyai Haji*.

37. Technically, *pondok* refers to the accommodation part of what is in fact a *pesantren* 'complex', providing the students with board and lodging.

Chapter 3

1. After much speculation, it is now assumed that the name 'padri' is a corruption of the term 'padre' – used in early eighteenth-century English records for rebellious religious figures in the Bengkulu area (Kathirithamby-Wells 1986).

2. They never managed to attain the same level of supremacy on the Malacca Straits (Dobbin 1983: 65).

3. First presented in a fragmented version as part of a Malay language textbook (Hollander 1857).

4. For a detailed study of the historical and historiographical significance of Imam Bondjol for Minangkabau identity and Indonesia nationalism, see Hadler (2008).

5. The Dutch believed that Jalal al-Din was actually Tuanku Nan Tua's son (Laffan 2011: 92).

6. See also the descriptions of an equivalent phenomenon and practice found among Sufis in Banten, known as *debus* (Bruinessen 1995: 187–9).

7. I follow Hadler's practice of using the spelling Bonjol for the village and Bondjol to refer to the person of Peto Syarif (Hadler 2008: 972).

8. Since 2001, his face features on the 5,000 Rupiah banknote (Hadler 2008: 973, 2009: 18).

9. Fort van der Cappellen was named after Godert van der Cappellen (1778–1848), who served as governor-general from 1815 until 1825, and Fort de Kock after Hendrik Merkus de Kock (1779–1845), the lieutenant-governor-general (1825–30) commanding Dutch forces during the Java War.

10. Indicative of the political destabilisation, Hamengkubuwono II held the office of Sultan three times: 1792–1810, 1811–12 and 1826–8, not only twice trading places with his own son (Hamengkubuwono III), but also with a great-grandson (Hamengkubuwono V).

11. Diponegoro was considered ineligible to the throne on account of being Raden Mas Surojo's son by an unofficial consort.

12. Only one prince can bear one particular titled name. His father considered his appointment as the third sultan an auspicious moment to bestow the long-vacant title on his oldest son (Carey 2014: 148).

13. Such 'lending' of children is very common in Javanese society (Geertz 1960: 36–41). Prominent contemporary examples include Presidents Suharto and B. J. Habibie.

14. For example, Louw and de Klerck (1893–1909); Nypels (1895).

15. Alternatively, they can also be translated as 'new' and 'old faction', respectively (Saleh 2001: 85).
16. To be distinguished from Ahmad Khatib al-Minankabawi (1860–1915/16), who will be discussed in Chapter 4.
17. Sayyid Uthman ibn Abdullah ibn Aqil and Christiaan Snouck Hurgronje would henceforth stimulate and reinforce each other's careers. For a detailed biography of Sayyid Uthman, see Kaptein (2014).
18. For contemporary manifestations, see Daniels (2009) and Woodward (2011), as well as the many publications on contemporary religion in Indonesia from the hand of Julia Day Howell.
19. A student of Snouck Hurgronje, Gobée had served as consul in Jeddah (1917–21), before becoming deputy adviser of native affairs (1922–4) and eventually again returning to Batavia as adviser of native affairs (1926–37); see Hering [2002] (2013).
20. For a detailed study of this formative period, see Laffan (2011: 162–70).
21. For a critique of this representation, see Ismail Hakki Kadi's examination of documents and accounts of Southeast Asian Muslims from the pre-Hamidian period which challenge this 'Eurocentric/colonial perception' (Kadi 2015: 150).
22. While there appears to be agreement as to the start date of the war – the invasion by a Dutch expeditionary force in 1873 – in the absence of a peace agreement, the suggested end dates range from 1904 to 1927.
23. Mansur Shah became de facto ruler of Aceh in 1838, but was only formally acknowledged as sultan in 1857.
24. For a detailed discussion of the Acehnese embassy to Istanbul of 1849–52, see Kadi et al. (2011).
25. Teuku Umar, also known as Johan Pahlawan, was a dubious character; repeatedly changing sides in the course of the war, he collaborated with the Dutch in 1894 and 1866 (Göksoy 2015: 194).

Chapter 4

1. For a detailed discussion, see Latif (2008: 57–66).
2. His name is also spelled 'Achmad Chatib'.
3. For more details on Snouck Hurgronje's key informant in the Hijaz, see Laffan (1999).
4. Both Laffan and Latif record very similar 'roll calls' of leading Muslim intellectuals and activists of the first half of the twentieth century, including the Minangkabau reformists Muhammad Tahir Jalal al-Din, M. Djamil Djambek, Abdullah Ahmad, Abdul Karim Amrullah, M. Thaib Umar and Haji Agus Salim; the Javanese founder of the modernist Islamic mass organisation Muhammadiyah, K.H. Ahmad Dahlan, and his successor K.H. Ibrahim; and the traditionalists K.H. Hasyim Asyᶜari (founder of the Nahdlatul Ulama), Shaykh Sulaiman al-Rasuli, Khatib Ali and Djamil Djaho.
5. For more on these individuals consult: Keddie (1972, 1983); Kedouri (1997); Kerr (1966).
6. For a more detailed discussion of these early modernisations in Egypt, see Hourani (1983: 67–102).
7. Claims that Abdullah Ahmad was even appointed as an adviser to the Office of Native Affairs in 1924 have so far remained unsubstantiated (Laffan 2003: 174).
8. Haji Rasul expanded his activities to *daᶜwa* campaigns in British Malaya and Java. He established relations with Islamic organisations such as the Sarekat Islam and Muhammadiyah, becoming the latter's chief propagandist in west Sumatra (Latif 2008: 81).
9. On the continuity-change dynamics in the modern Muslim world, see Voll (1994).

10. The earliest identifiable newspapers ever printed in Southeast Asia using *jawi* script were *Jawi Peranakan* (Straits Settlements, 1876) and *Wazir Indië* (Batavia, 1878); see Laffan (2003: 145).

11. See also Othman and Haris (2015).

12. He was the model for the character of 'Minke', the protagonist in Pramoedya Ananta Toer's (1925–2006) magisterial *Buru* tetralogy (Latif 2008: 97–8).

13. On the growing importance of Surbaya in the Netherlands East Indies, including its role as a centre of Muslim activism, see Formichi (2012: 19–25).

14. Also Masyhudulhak – from the Arabic Mashhud al-Haqq.

15. Yudi Latif has recorded the anecdote that detractors of the *Ethici* around Governor-General Alexander Idenburg (1861–1935, in office 1909–16) referred to the SI as *Salah Idenburg* – 'Idenburg's error' (Latif 2008: 427).

16. A spin-off from Jong Java, the JIB may not be a mass organisation in its own right, but was nevertheless very important for the intellectual formation of future Muslim leaders, including Mohammad Natsir, Mohammad Roem and Kartosuwirjo (Latif 2008: 203–11; Formichi 2012: 28).

17. For a detailed discussion of Budi Utomo (Boedi Oetomo in the old spelling), see Ricklefs (2006: 175–213).

18. In the run-up to the Muhammadiyah's centenary in 2012, there was a flurry of new publications about the organisation and its founder. Among them is a recent biography of Ahmad Dahlan by one of the Muhammadiyah's foremost intellectuals and a former member of its Central Board (2005–10); see Mulkhan (2010).

19. Fauzan Saleh makes a similar point (Saleh 2001: 155–6).

20. Originally it was called *Perkumpulan Musyawaratul Ulama* or 'Association of the Deliberation of the Ulama' (Saleh 2001: 108).

21. The Ahmadiyyah was introduced by Indonesian students returning from Panjab, who were accompanied by a representative from India, Rahmat Ali. Initially, the organisation's activities were restricted to Sumatra, in particular the Minangkabau region, but they soon spread also to Java (Federspiel 2001: 61–2). The most detailed study in English of the Ahmadiyyah in Indonesia is Burhani (2013).

22. For its continuing relevance, see Zuly Qodir, quoted in Kersten (2015: 58).

23. Based on an interview with Abdul Munir Mulkhan, Kota Gede (Indonesia), 23 October 2012.

24. Surkati's background is discussed in Abu Shouk (2002).

25. For a discussion of this conflict, see Mobini-Kesheh (1999: 91–107).

26. For details on the history of this schooling system and its curriculum, see Mobini-Kesheh (1999: 71–90).

27. Among the graduates of its education system was Muhammad Rasjidi (1915–2001), a Javanese *abangan*-turned-*santri*, who later became state minister for religious affairs, a diplomat and leading academic figure (Azra 1994: 89; Mobini-Kesheh 1999: 77).

28. The name is still used for a journal published by an NU-affiliated NGO (Kersten 2015: 47, 65–6).

29. Although one of the leaders of its youth wing, Ansor, was an Acehnese nobleman, Zainul Arifin (1909–63).

30. See Sura 3: 103.

31. Citing Clifford Geertz, Fauzan Saleh notes that a particular form of self-defensive martial arts known as *pencak silat* forms part of the *pesantren* curriculum (Saleh 2001: 88).

32. I have retained the original spelling, to distinguish Dr Soetomo from another independence fighter, Sutomo or Bung Tomo (1920–81).

33. According to Boland, Kartosuwiryo only became General Secretary in 1931 (Boland 1971: 56).
34. This would change in Mohammad Natsir's post-war political career.
35. For a detailed study of Sukarno's views on Mustafa Kemal and Turkey, see Formichi (2013).
36. Boland has a different opinion, claiming that neither the NU nor Muhammadiyah joined the MIAI (1971: 11).

Chapter 5

1. Quite exceptional for an NU leader, who tend to come from Java and Madura, Zainul Arifin was Acehnese and a descendant of the sultans of Barus.
2. He had replaced Mas Mansur in 1944. After the Japanese surrender, Mas Mansur was arrested on collaboration charges. Briefly imprisoned, his health suffered and he died in 1946 (Madinier 2015: 57).
3. For a detailed discussion of these proceedings, see Boland (1971: 24–34).
4. Based in Minangkabau, Perti's support base also extended to Kalimantan and Sulawesi.
5. For a more detailed discussion of the 1955 elections, see Madinier (2015: 202–18). The most extensive and authoritative study of this crucial episode in Indonesian political history is still Feith (1957).
6. Quoting an article written by Natsir in 1958.
7. For a detailed discussion, see Kahin (2012: 114–38).
8. For a discussion of the Masyumi prison years, see Kahin (2012: 139–53).
9. The name is taken from the Arabic term *suffa*, which refers to a part of the Prophet's mosque in Medina which functioned as makeshift accommodation for travelling converts. Ahl al-Suffa or 'People of the Bench' has also been offered as an explanation for the origins of the word Sufi, although this is contentious.
10. Not to be confused with the Muhammadiyah intellectual Abdul Kahir Muzakir.
11. For detailed discussions, see Boland (1971); Jabali and Jamhari (2002); Saeed (1999).
12. This section draws on the discussions on Islamic law found in my previous book on Islam in Indonesia (Kersten 2015: 182–8) and is informed by the seminal work conducted by Michael Feener (2002, 2007) and Yudian Wahyudi (2006, 2007).
13. Hazairin was the first and only Indonesian legal scholar during the colonial period to receive a local doctorate in law with a thesis on the legal system of the Rejang people of his native Bengkulu in Sumatra; see Hazairin (1936).
14. For a detailed discussion of *ahl al-hall wa'l-'aqd*, see Zaman (2016).
15. Also known as Banser – an abbreviation of Barisan Ansor Serba Guna or 'Ansor All-Purpose Forces' (Ricklefs 2012: 68).
16. One of the earliest and most thorough attempts is the so-called 'Cornell Paper', named after the American university where the academics who have conducted the underlying research are based. Their report created much furore and its findings were contested by the new Indonesian regime, with one of the main contributors, the late Ben Anderson, being declared persona non grata in Indonesia until the end of the New Order Regime in 1998; see Anderson and McVey (1971). A more recent study is Kammen and McGregor (2012).
17. For more detailed discussions, see Boland (1971: 149–56); Kahin (2012: 154–62); Madinier (2015: 426–33).
18. The most detailed study of the relation between NU and the military is Feillard (1995).
19. See Kersten (2017).

20. For detailed discussions, see Kahin (2012: 196–203); Ricklefs (2012: 180–5). The most elaborate study of JI is Barton (2004).
21. For a detailed discussion of the early life and career of Nurcholish Madjid, see Kersten (2011: 45–68).
22. After cutting short his diplomatic career, Mohammed Rasjidi went to study at the Sorbonne under the supervision of the famous French Orientalist and Sufi expert, Louis Massignon, obtaining a doctorate with a study of Javanese religion, which was only published in 1977 as *Documents pour server à l'histoire de l'Islam à Java*. Both Ricklefs and Steenbrink have criticised Rasjidi's thesis for ridiculing NU *ulama* and its lack of academic rigour, respectively (Ricklefs 2012: 45; personal communication from Karel Steenbrink, 14 March 2007).
23. For biographical sketches, see Muzani (1994); Munhanif (1996).
24. This *pesantren* was modelled after the Western schooling system and – together with Hasyim Asy'ari's *Pesantren Tebuireng* – it is regarded as being at the top of Indonesia's *pesantren* hierarchy (Steenbrink 1996: 156).
25. Between 1953 and 1964, the number of Catholics on Java almost doubled, while Protestantism grew by about 20 per cent annually (Hefner 2000: 107).
26. Serving from 1971–8, Mukti Ali was the first minister of religion not to represent either Masyumi or the NU.
27. In 1987, published in Indonesian with the provocative title *Muhammad Abduh dan Teologi Rasional Mu'tazila*.
28. For a detailed study of the NU during the 1980s and 1990s, see Barton and Fealy (1996).
29. The literature on the life and personality of Abdurrahman Wahid in Indonesian is vast; the most detailed biography in English has been written by Greg Barton (2002).
30. This phenomenon is discussed in various contributions to Fealy and White (2008).
31. Detailed discussions are provided in Hilmy (2010) and Platzdasch (2009).

Bibliography

Abu Shouk, Ahmed Ibrahim (2002), 'An Arabic Manuscript on the Life and Career of Ahmad Muhammad Sorkati and his Irshadi Disciples in Java', in Huub de Jong and Nico Kaptein (eds), *Transcending Borders: Arabs, Politics, Trade and Islam in Southeast Asia*, Leiden: KITLV Press, pp. 203–18.

Alatas, Syed Farid (1985), 'Notes on Various Theories Regarding the Islamization of the Malay Archipelago', *The Muslim World*, 75 (3–4): 162–75.

— (1997), 'Hadhramaut and the Hadhrami Diaspora: Problems in Theoretical History', in Ulrike Freitag and William Clarence-Smith (eds), *Hadhrami Traders, Scholars, and Statesmen in the Indian Ocean, 1750s–1960s*, Leiden, New York and Cologne: Brill, pp. 19–34.

Albin, Michael (2009), 'The Islamic Book', in Eliot Simon and Jonathan Rose (eds), *The Companion to the History of the Book*, Malden, MA and Oxford: Wiley-Blackwell, pp. 165–77.

Ali, Muhamad (2016), *Islam and Colonialism: Becoming Modern in Indonesia and Malaya*, Edinburgh: Edinburgh University Press.

Alves, Jorge Santos (2015), 'From Istanbul with Love: Rumours, Conspiracies and Commercial Competition in Aceh–Ottoman Relations: 1550s to 1570s', in A. C. S. Peacock and Annabel Teh Gallop (eds), *From Anatolia to Aceh: Ottomans, Turks and Southeast Asia*, London: Oxford University Press for the British Academy, pp. 47–62.

Anderson, Benedict and Ruth McVey (1971), *A Preliminary Analysis of the October 1, 1965, Coup in Indonesia*, Ithaca: Cornell Modern Indonesia Project.

Aspinall, Edward (2009), *Islam and Nation: Separatist Rebellion in Aceh, Indonesia*, Singapore: NUS Press.

Attas, Syed Naguib al- (1966), *Raniri and the Wujudiyyah in 17th-century Aceh*, Singapore: Malayan Branch of the Royal Asiatic Society.

— (1967), 'New Light on the Life of Hanzah Fansuri', *Journal of the Malayan Branch of the Royal Asiatic Society*, 40 (1): 42–51.

— (1968), *The Origin of the Malay Sha'ir*, Kuala Lumpur: Dewan Bahasa dan Pustaka.

— (1969), *Preliminary Statement on a General Theory of the Islamization of the Malay-Indonesian World*, Kuala Lumpur: Dewan Bahasa dan Pustaka.

— (1970), *The Mysticism of Hamzah Fansuri*, Kuala Lumpur: University of Malaya Press.

Azra, Azyumardi (1992), 'The Transmission of Islamic Reformism to Indonesia: Networks of Middle Eastern and Malay-Indonesian "Ulama" in the Seventeenth and Eighteenth Centuries', unpublished PhD thesis, New York: Columbia University.

—(1994) 'Guarding the Faith of the Ummah: The Religio-Intellectual Journey of Mohammad Rasjidi', *Studia Islamika*, 1 (2): 87–119.

—(2004) *The Origins of Islamic Reformism in Southeast Asia: Networks of Malay-Indonesian and Middle Eastern 'Ualama' in the Seventeenth and Eighteenth Centuries*, Crows Nest, NSW: Allen & Unwin and Honolulu: University of Hawai'i Press.

—(2006), 'The Transmission of Al-Manar's Reformism to the Malay-Indonesian World: The Case of Al-Imam and Al-Munir', in Stéphane A. Dudoignon, Komatsu Hisao and Kosugi Yasushi (eds), *Intellectuals in the Modern Islam World: Transmission, Transformation and Communication*, London and New York: Routledge, pp. 143–58.

Baldick, Julian (2016), 'Uwaysiyya', in P. Bearman, Th. Bianquis, C. E. Bosworth, E. van Donzel and W. P. Heinrichs (eds), *Encyclopaedia of Islam, Second Edition*, Brill Online, <http://referenceworks.brillonline.com/entries/encyclopaedia-of-islam-2/uwaysiyya-SIM_7782> (last accessed 10 April 2016).

Barton, Greg (1995), 'Neo-Modernism: A Vital Synthesis of Traditionalist and Modernist Islamic Thought in Indonesia', *Studia Islamika*, 2 (3): 1–75.

—(2002), *Abdurrahman Wahid, Muslim Democrat, Indonesian President: A View from the Inside*, Honolulu: University of Hawai'i Press.

—(2004), *Indonesia's Struggle: Jemaah Islamiyah and the Soul of Islam*, Sydney: University of New South Wales Press.

Barton, Greg and Greg Fealy (1996), *Nahdlatul Ulama, Traditional Islam and Modernity in Indonesia*, Clayton, VIC: Monash Asia Institute.

Boland, B. J. (1971), *The Struggle of Islam in Modern Indonesia*, The Hague: Martinus Nijhoff.

Bousfeld, John (1983), 'Islamic Philosophy in South-East Asia', in M. B. Hooker (ed.), *Islam in South-East Asia*, Leiden: Brill, pp. 92–129.

Braginsky, Vladimir (1996), 'On the Qasida and Cognate Poetic Forms in the Malay-Indonesian World', in Stefan Sperl and Christopher Shackle (eds), *Qasīda Poetry in Islamic Asia and Africa. Volume One: Classical Traditions and Modern Meanings*, Leiden, New York and Cologne: Brill, pp. 371–88.

—(1999), 'Towards the Biography of Hamzah Fansuri. When Did Hamzah Live? Data from his Poems and Early European Accounts', *Archipel*, 57: 135–75.

—(2001), 'On the Copy of Hamzah Fansuri's Epitaph Published by C. Guillot & L. Kalus', *Archipel*, 62: 21–33.

Brakel, L. F. van (1969), 'The Birth Place of Hamza Pansuri', *Journal of the Malayan Branch of the Royal Asiatic Society*, 42 (2): 206–12.

Bruinessen, Martin van (1990), 'Kitab Kuning: Books in Arabic Script Used in the Pesantren Milieu', *Bijdragen tot de Taal-, Land en Volkenkunde*, 146 (2/3): 226–69.

—(1991), 'The Tariqa Khalwatiyya in South Celebes', in Harry A. Poeze and Pim Schoorl (eds), *Excursies in Celebes: Een bundel bijdragen bij het afscheid van J. Noorduijn als directeur-secretaris van het KITLV*, Leiden: KITLV Uitgeverij, pp. 251–69.

—(1994a), 'Najmuddin al-Kubra, Jumadil Kubra and Jamaluddin al-Akbar: Traces of Kubrawiyya Influence in Early Indonesian Islam', *Bijdragen tot Taal-, Land- en Volkenkunde*, 150 (2): 305–29.

—(1994b), 'The Origins and Development of Sufi Orders (tarekat) in Southeast Asia', *Studia Islamika: Indonesian Journal for Islamic Studies*, 1 (1): 1–23.

—(1995), 'Shari'a Court, Tarekat and Pesantren: Religious Institutions in the Banten Sultanate', *Archipel*, 50: 165–99.

—(1997), 'A Note on Source Materials for the Biographies of Southeast Asian Ulama', *La transmission du savoir dans le monde musulman périphérique*, 17: 57–66.

—(1998a), 'Studies of Sufism and the Sufi Orders in Indonesia', *Die Welt des Islams*, 38 (2): 192–219.

—(1998b), 'Kurdish Ulama and their Indonesian Disciples (revised version of "The Impact of Kurdish Ulama on Indonesian Islam")', *Annales de l'autre Islam*, 9: 1–25.

—(2000), 'Shaykh 'Abd al-Qadir al-Jilani and the Qadiriyya in Indonesia', *Journal of the History of Sufism*, 1 (2): 261–395.

—(2015), 'Muslims of the Dutch East Indies and the Caliphate Question', in Carool Kersten (ed.), *The Caliphate and Islamic Statehood: Volume III, Modern and Contemporary Interpretations*, Berlin: Gerlach Press, pp. 100–17.

—(2016), 'Gunung Jati, Sunan', in Kate Fleet, Gudrun Krämer, Denis Matringe, John Nawas and Everett Rowson (eds), *Encyclopaedia of Islam, THREE*, Brill Online, <http://referenceworks.brillonline.com/entries/encyclopaedia-of-islam-3/gunung-jati-sunan-COM_27552> (last accessed 10 April 2016).

Burhani, Ahmad Najib (2012), 'Al-Tawassuṭ wa-l I'tidāl: The NU and Moderatism in Indonesian Islam', *Asian Journal of Social Sciences*, 40: 564–81.

—(2013), 'When Muslims Are Not Muslims: The Ahmadiyya Community and the Discourse on Heresy in Indonesia', unpublished PhD dissertation, Santa Barbara: University of California Santa Barbara.

Burke, Peter (1991), *The French Historical Revolution: The Annales School, 1929–89*, Stanford: Stanford University Press.

Carey, Peter (2014), *Destiny: The Life of Prince Diponegoro, 1785–1855*, London: Peter Lang.

Casale, Giancarlo (2010), *The Ottoman Age of Exploration*, London: Oxford University Press.

Clifford, Hugh [1904] (1990), *Further India: Being the Story of Exploration from the Earliest Times in Burma, Malaya, Siam and Indo-China*, Bangkok: White Lotus.

Cœdès, Georges (1948), *Les états hindouisés d'Indochine et d'Indonésie*, Paris: De Boccard.

—(1968), *The Indianized States of Southeast Asia*, ed. Walter F. Vella, trans. Susan Brown Cowing, Canberra: Australian National University Press.

Colville, James (trans.) (1999), *Two Andalusian Philosophers: Hayy Ibn Yaqzan and The Definitive Statement*, London: Kegan Paul International.

Daniels, Timothy (2009), *Islamic Spectrum in Java*, Farnham and Burlington: Ashgate.

Day, A. (1983), 'Islam and Literature in South-East Asia: Some Pre-modern, Mainly

Javanese Perspectvies', in M. B. Hooker (ed.), *Islam in South East Asia*, Leiden: Brill, pp. 130–59.

Dhofier, Zamakhsyari (1999), *The Pesantren Tradition: The Role of the Kyai in the Maintenance of Traditional Islam in Java*, Tempe: Program for Southeast Asian Studies, Arizona State University.

Dijk, C. van (2002), 'Colonial Fears, 1890–1918: Pan-Islamism and the Germano-Indian Plot', in Huub de Jonge and Nico Kaptein (eds), *Transcending Borders: Arabs, Politics, Trade and Islam in Southeast Asia*, Leiden: KITLV Press, pp. 53–89.

Dobbin, Christine (1983), *Islamic Revivalism in a Changing Peasant Economy: Central Sumatra, 1784–1847*, London and Malmo: Curzon Press.

Drewes, G. W. J. (1954), *Een Javaanse Primbon uit de zestiende eeuw*, Leiden: Brill.

—(1968), 'New Light on the Coming of Islam to Indonesia', *Bijdragen Koninklijk Instituut voor Taal-, Land- en Volkenkunde*, 124 (4): 433–59.

—(1969), *The Admonitions of Seh Bari*, The Hague: Martinus Nijhoff.

—(1978), *An Early Javanese Code of Muslim Ethics*, The Hague: Martinus Nijhoff.

—[1985] (2013), 'Snouck Hurgronje, Christiaan (1857–1936)', in *Biografisch Woordenboek van Nederland*, <http://resources.huygens.knaw.nl/adviezensnouckhurgronje/BWN/lemmata/bwn2/snouckc> (last accessed 10 April 2016).

Effendy, Bahtiar (2004), *Islam and the State in Indonesia*, Athens, OH: Ohio University Press and Singapore: ISEAS.

Fealy, Greg (1996), 'Wahab Chasbullah, Traditionalism and the Political Development of Nahdlatul Ulama', in Greg Fealey and Greg Barton (eds), *Nahdlatul Ulama, Traditional Islam and Modernity in Indonesia*, Clayton VIC: Monash Asia Institute, pp. 1–41.

Fealy, Greg and Sally White (2008), *Expressing Islam: Religious Life and Politics in Indonesia*, Singapore: ISEAS.

Federspiel, Howard M. (2001), *Islam and Ideology in the Emerging Indonesian State: The Persatuan Islam (Persis), 1923–1957*, Leiden: Brill.

Feener, R. Michael (1998), 'A Re-examination of the Place of al-Hallaj in the Development of Southeast Asian Islam', *Bijdragen Koninklijk Instituut voor Taal-, Land-en Volkenkunde*, 154 (4): 271–92.

—(1998/9), 'Shaykh Yusuf and the Appreciation of Muslim "Saints" in Modern Indonesia', *Journal of Islamic Studies*, 18–19: 112–31.

—(2002), 'Indonesian Movements for the Creation of a "National Madhhab"', *Islamic Law and Society*, 9 (1): 83–115.

—(2007), *Muslim Legal Thought in Modern Indonesia*, Cambridge and New York: Cambridge University Press.

Feener, R. Michael and Michael F. Laffan (2005), 'Sufi Scents Across the Indian Ocean: Yemeni Hagiography and the Earliest History of Southeast Asian Islam', *Archipel*, 70: 185–208.

Feillard, Andrée (1995), *Islam et armée dans l'Indonésie contemporaine. Les pionniers de la tradition*, Paris: L'Harmattan.

—(2011), 'The Constrained Place of Local Tradition: The Discourse of Indonesian Traditionalist Ulama in the 1930s', in Michel Picard and Rémy Madinier (eds), *The Politics of Religion in Indonesia: Syncretism, Orthodoxy, and Religious Contention in Java and Bali*, London and New York: Routledge, pp. 48–70.

Feith, Herbert (1957), *The Indonesian Elections of 1955*, Ithaca: Modern Indonesia Project, Southeast Asia Program, Department of Far Eastern Studies, Cornell University.

Formichi, Chiara (2012), *Islam and the Making of the Nation: Kartosuwiryo and Political Islam in 20th Century Indonesia*, Leiden: KITLV Press

—(2013), 'Mustafa Kemal's Abrogation of the Ottoman Caliphate and its Impact on the Indonesian Nationalist Movement', in Madawi al-Rasheed, Carool Kersten and Marat Shterin (eds), *Demystifying the Caliphate: Historical Memory and Contemporary Contexts*, London: Hurst Publishers and New York: Columbia University Press, pp. 95–115.

—(2015), 'Indonesian Readings of Turkish History, 1890s–1940s', in A. C. S. Peacock and Annabel Teh Gallop (eds), *From Anatolia to Aceh: Ottomans, Turks and Southeast Asia*, Oxford: Oxford University Press for the British Academy, pp. 241–59.

Geertz, Clifford (1960), *The Religion of Java*, Glencoe, IL: Free Press.

—(1968), *Islam Observed: Religious Development in Morocco and Indonesia*, Chicago: University of Chicago Press.

Goitein, Shelomo Dov and Mordechai Akiva Friedman (2007), *India Traders of the Middle Ages: Documents from the Cairo Geniza*, Leiden: Brill.

Göksoy, Ismail Hakki (2015), 'Acehnese Appeals for Ottoman Protection in the Late Nineteenth Century', in A. C. S. Peacock and Annabel Teh Gallop (eds), *From Aceh to Anatolia: Ottomans, Turks and Southeast Asia*, Oxford: Oxford University Press for the British Academy, pp. 175–98.

Graaf, H. J. de and Th. G. Th. Pigeaud (1974), *De Eerste Vorstendommen op Java: Studien over de Staatkundige Geschiedenis van de 15e en 16e Eeuw*, 's-Gravenhage: Martinus Nijhoff.

Guillot, Claude and Ludvik Kalus (2000), 'La stèle funéraire de Hamzah Fansuri', *Archipel*, 60: 3–24.

Guillot, Claude, Denys Lombard and Roderick Ptak (1998), *From the Mediterranean to the China Sea*, Wiesbaden: Harassowitz Verlag.

Hadi, Amirul (2011), 'Exploring Acehnese Understanding of Jihad: A Study of the Hikayat prang sabi', in R. Michael Feener, Patrick Daly and Anthony Reid (eds), *Mapping the Acehnese Past*, Leiden: KITLV Press, pp. 182–97.

Hadler, Jeffrey (2008), 'A Historiography of Violence and the Secular State in Indonesia: Tuanku Imam Bondjol and the Uses of History', *Journal of Asian Studies*, 67 (3): 970–1010.

—(2009), *Muslims and Matriarchs: Cultural Resilience on Minangkabau through Jihad and Colonialism*, Singapore: NUS Press.

Hägerdal, Hans (2001), *Hindu Rulers, Muslim Subjects: Lombok and Bali in the Seventeenth and Eighteenth Centuries*, Bangkok: White Lotus.

Hassan, Muhammad (1980), *Muslim Intellectual Responses to 'New Order' in Indonesia*, Kuala Lumpur: Dewan Bahasa dan Pustaka.

Hazairin (1936), *The Redjang. De volksordening, het verwantschaps-, huwelijks- en erfrecht*, Bandoeng: A. C. Nix.

Hefner, Robert W. (1985), *Hindu Javanese: Tengger Tradition and Islam*, Princeton: Princeton University Press.

——(1990), *The Political Economy of Mountain Java: An Interpretive History*, Berkeley: University of California Press

——(2000), *Civil Islam: Muslims and Democratization in Indonesia*, Princeton: Princeton University Press.

——(2011), 'Where Have All the Abangan Gone? Religionization and the Decline of Non-Standard Islam in Contemporary Indonesia', in Michel Picard and Rémy Madinier (eds), *The Politics of Religion in Indonesia: Syncreticism, Orthodoxy, and Religious Contention in Java and Bali*, London and New York: Routledge, pp. 71–91.

Hering, B. B. [2002] (2013), 'Gobée, Emile (1881–1954)', in *Biografisch Woordenboek van Nederland*, <http://resources.huygens.knaw.nl/bwn1880-2000/lemmata/bwn5/gobee> (last accessed 10 April 2016).

Heryanto, Ariel (2007), 'Can There Be Southeast Asians in Southeast Asian Studies?', in Laurie J. Sears (ed.), *Knowing Southeast Asian Subjects*, Seattle: University of Washington Press, pp. 75–108.

Hilmy, Masadar (2010), *Islamism and Democracy in Indonesia: Piety and Pragmatism*, Singapore: ISEAS.

Hodgson, Marshall G. S. (1974), *The Venture of Islam: Conscience and History in a World Civilization*, 3 vols, Chicago: University of Chicago Press.

——(2016), 'Djaʿfar al-Ṣādiḳ', in P. Bearman, Th. Bianquis, C. E. Bosworth, E. van Donzel and W. P. Heinrichs (eds), *Encyclopaedia of Islam, Second Edition*, Brill Online, <http://referenceworks.brillonline.com/entries/encyclopaedia-of-islam-2/djafar-al-sadik-SIM_1922> (last accessed 10 April 2016).

Hollander, J. J. de (1857), *Handleiding bij de Beoefening der Maleische Taal en Letterkunde*, Breda: Royal Military Academy.

Hourani, Albert (1983), *Arabic Thought in the Liberal Age 1798–1939*, Cambridge: Cambridge University Press.

Ihza, Yusril (1995), 'Combining Activism and Intellectualism: The Biography of Mohammad Natsir (1908–1993)', *Studia Islamika*, 2 (1): 111–47.

Jabali, Fuad and Jamhari (2002), *IAIN & Modernisasi Islam di Indonesia*, Ciputat: Logos Wacana Ilmu.

Johns, A. H. (1961), 'The Role of Sufism in the Spread of Islam to Malaya and Indonesia', *Journal of the Pakistan Historical Society*, 9: 143–61.

——(1963), 'Muslims, Mystics and Historical Writing', in D. G. E. Hall (ed.), *Historians of Southeast Asia*, Oxford: Oxford University Press, pp. 37–49.

——(1965), *The Gift Addressed to the Spirit of the Prophet*, Canberra: Australian National University Press.

—(1975), 'Islam in Southeast Asia: Reflections and New Directions', *Indonesia*, 19: 33–55.

—(1976), 'Islam in Southeast Asia: Problems of Perspective', in C. D. Cowan and O. W. Wolters (eds), *Southeast Asian History and Historiography: Essays Presented to D. G. E. Hall*, Ithaca and London: Cornell University Press, pp. 304–20.

—(1980), 'From Coastal Settlement to Islamic School and City: Islamization in Sumatra, the Malay Peninsula and Java', in James Fox (ed.), *Indonesia: Australian Perspectives*, Canberra: ANUU, Research School of Pacific Studies, pp. 163–82.

—(1984), 'Islam in the Malay World: An Exploratory Survey and Some Reference to Quranic Exegesis', in R. Israeli and A. H. Johns (eds), *Islam in Asia. Volume II: Southeast and East Asia*, Boulder, CO: Westview Press, pp. 115–61.

—(1993), 'Islamization in Southeast Asia: Reflections and Reconsiderations with Special Reference to the Role of Sufism', *Southeast Asian Studies*, 31 (1): 43–61.

—(1995), 'Sufism in Southeast Asia: Reflections and Reconsiderations', *Journal of Southeast Asian Studies*, 26 (1): 169–83.

Kadi, Ismail Hakki (2015), 'The Ottomans and Southeast Asia Prior to the Hamidian Era: A Critique of Colonial Perceptions of the Ottoman–Southeast Asian Interaction', in A. C. S. Peacock and Annabel Teh Gallop (eds), *From Anatolia to Aceh: Ottomans, Turks and Southeast Asia*, Oxford: Oxford University Press for the British Academy, pp. 149–74.

Kadi, Ismail Hakki, A. C. S. Peacock and Annabel Teh Gallop (2011), 'Writing History: The Acehnese Embassy to Istanbul, 1849–1852', in R. Michael Feener, Patrick Daly and Anthony Reid (eds), *Mapping the Acehnese Past*, Leiden: KITLV Press, pp. 163–81.

Kahin, Audrey R. (2012), *Islam, Nationalism and Democracy: A Political Biography of Mohammad Natsir*, Singapore: NUS Press.

Kammen, Douglas and Katherine McGregor (2012), *The Contours of Mass Violence in Indonesia, 1965–68*, Singapore: NUS Press and Copenhagen: NIAs Press.

Kaptein, Nico (2014), *Islam, Colonialism and the Modern Age in the Netherlands East Indies: A Biography of Sayyid 'Uthman (1822–1914)*, Leiden: Brill.

Kathirithamby-Wells, Jeyamalar (1986), 'The Origin of the Term Padri: Some Historical Evidence', *Indonesia Circle*, 41: 3–9.

—(2015), 'Hadhramis and Ottoman Influence in Southeast Asia', in A. C. S. Peacock and Annabel Teh Gallop (eds), *From Anatolia to Aceh: Ottomans, Turks and Southeast Asia*, Oxford: Oxford University Press, pp. 89–119.

Keddie, Nikki (1972), *Jamāl al-Dīn al-Afghānī: A Political Biography*, Berkeley: University of California Press.

—(1983), *An Islamic Response to Imperialism: Political and Religious Writings of Sayyid Jamāl al-Dīn al-Afghānī*, Berkeley and London: University of California Press.

Kedouri, Elie (1997), *Afghānī and 'Abduh: An Essay on Religious Unbelief and Political Activism in Modern Islam*, London: Frank Cass.

Kerr, Malcolm (1966), *Islamic Reform: The Political and Legal Theories of Muhammad 'Abduh and Rashid Rida*, Berkeley: University of California Press.

Kersten, Carool (2006), 'Cambodia's Muslim King: Khmer and Dutch Sources on the Conversion of King Reameathipadei I, 1642–1658', *Journal of Southeast Asian Studies*, 37 (1): 1–22.

—(2011), *Cosmopolitans and Heretics: New Muslim Intellectuals and the Study of Islam*, London: Hurst Publishers and New York: Columbia University Press.

—(2014), 'Urbanization, Civil Society and Religious Pluralism in Indonesia and Turkey', in Chiara Formichi (ed.), *Religious Pluralism, State and Society in Asia*, London and New York: Routledge, pp. 13–34.

—(2015), *Islam in Indonesia: The Contest for Society, Ideas and Values*, London: Hurst Publishers and New York: Oxford University Press.

—(2017), 'Renewal, Reactualization and Reformation: The Trajectory of Muslim Youth Activism in Indonesia', in Tahir Abbas and Sadek Hamid (eds), *Political Muslims*, Syracuse: Syracuse University Press.

Kraus, Werner (1984), *Zwischen Reform und Rebellion: Uber die Entwicklung des Islams in Minangkabau (Westsumatra) zwischen den beiden Reformbewegungen der Padri (1837) und der Modernisten (1908)*, Wiesbaden: Franz Steiner Verlag.

Laffan, Michael Francis (1999), 'Raden Aboe Bakar: An Introductory Note Concerning Snouck Hurgronje's Informant in Jeddah (1884–1912)', *Bijdragen Koninklijk Instituut voor Taal-, Land- en Volkenkunde*, 155 (4): 517–42.

—(2003), *Islamic Nationhood and Colonial Indonesia: The Umma Below the Winds*, London and New York: Routledge.

—(2009), 'Finding Java: Muslim Nomenclature of Insular Southeast Asia from Srivijaya to Snouck Hurgronje', in Eric Tagliacozzo (ed.), *Southeast Asia and the Middle East: Islam, Movement, and the Longue Durée*, Stanford: Stanford University Press, pp. 17–64.

—(2011), *The Makings of Indonesian Islam: Orientalism and the Narration of a Sufi Past*, Princeton: Princeton University Press.

Lambourn, Elizabeth (2003), 'From Cambay to Samudera-Pasai and Gresik – The Export of Gujarati Grave Memorials to Sumatra and Java in the Fifteenth Century C.E.', *Indonesia and the Malay World*, 31 (90): 221–84.

—(2004), 'The Formation of the Batu Aceh Tradition in Fifteenth-century Samudera-Pasai', *Indonesia and the Muslim World*, 32 (93): 211–48.

Larsson, Goran (2011), *Muslims and the New Media: Historical and Contemporary Debates*, Farnham and Burlington: Ashgate.

Latif, Yudi (2008), *Indonesian Muslim Intelligentsia*, Singapore: ISEAS.

Leur, J. C. van (1967), *Indonesian Trade and Society: Essays in Asian Social and Economic History*, The Hague: W. van Hoeve Publishing.

Levtzion, Nehemia (1979), *Conversion to Islam*, New York: Holmes & Meier.

Lombard, Denys (1967), *Le Sultanat d'Atjéh au temps d'Iskandar Muda 1607–1636*, Paris: École Française d'Extrême Orient.

—(1990), *Le carrefour javanais: essai d'histoire globale*, 3 vols, Paris: Éditions de l'École des Hautes Études en Sciences Sociales.

Louw, P. J. F. and E. S. de Klerck (1893–1909), *De Java Oorlog van 1825 tot 1830*, Batavia: Landsdrukkerij and The Hague: Nijhoff.

Maarif, A. Syafii, Haedar Nashir and Muhadjir Efendy (2010), *Menggugat Modernitas Muhammadiyah: Refleksi Satu Abad Perjalanan Muhammadiyah*, Jakarta: Penerbit Best Media & Pusat Study Islam dan Filsafat (PSIF) UMM.

Madinier, Rémy (2015), *Islam and Politics in Indonesia: The Masyumi Party between Democracy and Integralism*, trans. Jeremy Desmond, Singapore: NUS Press.

Mandal, Sumit (1994), 'Finding their Place: A History of Arabs in Java under Dutch Rule, 1800–1924', unpublished PhD thesis, New York: Columbia University.

Mietzner, Marcus (2009), *Military Politics, Islam, and the State in Indonesia: From Turbulent Transition to Democratic Consolidation*, Singapore: ISEAS.

Milner, A. C. (1983), 'Islam and the Muslim State', in M. B. Hooker (ed.), *Islam in South East Asia*, Leiden: Brill, pp. 23–49.

Mitrasing, Ingrid Saroda (2011), 'The Age of Aceh and the Evolution of Kingship 1599–1641', PhD thesis, Leiden: University of Leiden.

Mobini-Kesheh, Natalia (1999), *The Hadrami Awakening: Community and Identity in the Netherlands East Indies, 1900–1942*, Ithaca: Southeast Asia Program Publications at Cornell University.

Moertono, Soemarsaid (2009), *State and Statecraft in Old Java: A Study of the Later Mataram Period, 16th to 19th Century*, Singapore: Equinox Publishing (Asia).

Mulkhan, Abdul Munir (2010), *Kiai Ahmad Dahlan: Jejak Pembaruan Sosial dan Kemanusiaan*, Jakarta: Kompas.

Munhanif, Ali (1996), 'Islam and the Struggle for Religious Pluralism in Indonesia: A Political Reading of the Religious Thought of Mukti Ali', *Studia Islamika*, 3 (1): 79–126.

Muzani, Saiful (1994), 'Mu'tazilah Theology and the Modernization of the Indonesian Muslim Community: An Intellectual Portrait of Harun Nasution', *Studia Islamika*, 1 (1): 91–131.

Nock, Arthur Darby (1933), *Conversion: The Old and the New in Religion from Alexander the Great to Augustine of Hippo*, Oxford: Clarendon Press.

Nypels, George (1895), *De Oorlog in Midden-Java van 1825 tot 1830*, Breda: Koninklijke Militaire Academie.

O'Fahey, R. S. and Bernd Radtke (1993), 'Neo-Sufism Re-considered, with Special Reference to Ahmad ibn Idris', *Der Islam*, 70: 52–87.

Othman, Mohammad Rezuan Othman and Abu Hanifah Haris (2015), 'The Role of Egyptian Influences on the Religious Dynamics and the Idea of Progress of Malaya's *Kaum Muda* (Young Faction) before the Second War', *British Journal of Middle Eastern Studies*, 42 (4): 465–80.

Perret, Daniel (2007), 'Some Reflections on the Ancient Islamic Tombstones Known as Batu Aceh in the Malay World', *Indonesia and the Malay World*, 35 (103): 313–40.

Platzdasch, Bernhard (2009), *Islamism in Indonesia: Politics in the Emerging Democracy*, Singapore: ISEAS.

Proudfoot, Ian (1993), *Early Malay Printed Books: A Provisional Account of Materials Published in the Singapore-Malaysia Area up to 1920, Noting Holdings in Major Public Collections*, Kuala Lumpur: Academy of Malay Studies and the Library, University of Malaya.

Qodir, Zuly (2007), *Islam Liberal: Paradigma Baru Wacana dan Aksi Islam Indonesia*, Yogyakarta: Pustaka Pelajar.

Reid, Anthony (1969), 'Sixteenth Century Turkish Influence in Western Indonesia', *Journal of Southeast Asian History*, 10 (3): 395–414.

—(1988), *Southeast Asia in the Age of Commerce 1450–1680. Volume One: The Lands Below the Wind*, New Haven, CT: Yale University Press.

—(1993), *Southeast Asia in the Age of Commerce 1450–1680. Volume Two: Expansion and Crisis*, New Haven, CT and London: Yale University Press.

—(2015), 'Rum and Jawa: The Vicissitudes of Documenting a Long-distance Relationship', in A. C. S. Peacock and Annabel Teh Gallop (eds), *From Anatolia to Aceh: Ottomans, Turks and Southeast Asia*, Oxford: Oxford University Press for the British Academy, pp. 25–44.

Ricklefs, M. C. (1974), 'Dipanagara's Early Inspirational Experience', *Bijdragen tot de Taal-, Land en Volkenkunde*, 130 (2/3): 227–58.

—(2006), *Mystic Synthesis in Java: A History of Islamization from the Fourteenth to the Early Nineteenth Centuries*, Norwalk, CT: East Bridge Signature Books.

—(2007), *Polarizing Javanese Society: Islamic and Other Visions (c. 1830–1930)*, Honolulu: University of Hawai'i Press.

—(2009), 'The Middle East Connection and Reform and Revival Movements among the Putihan in 19th-century Java', in Eric Tagliacozzo (ed.), *Southeast Asia and the Middle East: Islam, Movement, and the Longue Durée*, Stanford: Stanford University Press, pp. 111–34.

—(2012), *Islamisation and its Opponents in Java: c. 1930 to the Present*, Singapore: National University of Singapore Press.

Riddell, Peter G. (1990), *Transferring the Tradition: 'Abd al-Ra'uf al-Singkili's Rendering into Malay of the Jalalayn Commentary*, Berkeley: Centers for South and Southeast Asian Studies, University of California.

—(2001), *Islam and the Malay-Indonesian World: Transmission and Responses*, Honolulu: University of Hawai'i Press.

Rinkes, D. A. (1996), *Nine Saints of Java*, Kuala Lumpur: Malaysian Sociological Research Institute.

Saeed, Abdullah (1999), 'Towards Religious Tolerance through Reform and Islamic Education: The Case of the State Institute of Islamic Studies in Indonesia', *Indonesia and the Malay World*, 27 (79): 177–91.

Saleh, Fauzan (2001), *Modern Trends in Islamic Theological Discourse of 20th Century Indonesia: A Critical Survey*, Leiden, Boston and Cologne: Brill.

Samson, Alan A. (1978), 'Conceptions of Power, Politics, and Ideology in Contemporary Indonesian Islam', in Karl D. Jackson and Lucian W. Pye (eds), *Political Power and Communication in Indonesia*, Berkeley: University of California Press, pp. 198–226.

Schrieke, B. (1957), *Indonesian Sociological Studies*, The Hague: W. van Hoeve.

Scott, James C. (1990), *Domination and the Arts of Resistance: Hidden Transcripts*, New Haven, CT and London: Yale University Press.

—(2009), *The Art of Not Being Governed: An Anarchist History of Upland Southeast Asia*, New Haven, CT and London: Yale University Press.

Siegel, James T. (2000), *The Rope of God*, Ann Arbor: University of Michigan Press.

Skeat, Walter W. (1900), *Malay Magic: Being an Introduction to the Folklore and Popular Religion of the Malay Peninsula*, London: Macmillan.

Smail, John R. W. (1993), 'On the Possibility of an Autonomous History of Modern Southeast Asia', in Laurie J. Sears (ed.), *Autonomous Histories, Particular Truths: Essays in Honor of John Smail*, Madison: University of Wisconsin Centre for Southeast Asian Studies, pp. 39–70.

Steenbrink, K. A. (1974), *Pesantren, Madrasah, Sekolah: Recente ontwikkelingen in Indonesisch Islamonderricht*, Meppel: Krips Repo.

—(1996), 'Recapturing the Past: Historical Studies by IAIN Staff', in Mark Woodward (ed.), *Toward a New Paradigm: Recent Developments in Indonesian Islamic Thought*, Tempe: Program for Southeast Asian Studies, Arizona State University, pp. 155–92.

—(1999), 'The Pancasila Ideology and an Indonesian Muslim Theology of Religions', in Jacques Waardenburg (ed.), *Muslim Perceptions of Other Religions: A Historical Survey*, Oxford: Oxford University Press, pp. 180–96.

Steinberg, David Joel (ed.) (1985), *In Search of Southeast Asia: A Modern History*, Oxford and New York: Oxford University Press.

Subrahmanyam, Sanjay (1998), 'Notes on Circulation and Assymmetry in Two Mediterraneans', in Claude Guillot, Denys Lombard and Roderick Ptak (eds), *From the Mediterranean to the China Sea*, Wiesbaden: Harassowitz Verlag, pp. 21–44.

Tagliacozzo, Eric (2005), *Secret Trades, Porous Borders: Smuggling and States along a Southeast Asian Frontier, 1865–1915*, New Haven, CT and London: Yale University Press.

—(ed.) (2009), *Southeast Asia and the Middle East: Islam, Movement, and the Longue Durée*, Stanford: Stanford University Press.

Taylor, Keith (1976), 'Madagascar in the Ancient Malayo-Polynesian Myths', in Kenneth R. and John K. Whitmore Hall (eds), *Explorations in Early Southeast Asian History: The Origins of Southeast Asian Statecraft*, Ann Arbor: Center for South and Southeast Asian Studies, University of Michigan, pp. 25–60.

Teeuw, Andries (1966), 'The Malay Sha'ir: Problems of Origin and Tradition', *Bijdragen Koninklijk Instituut voor Taal-, Land- en Volkenkunde (BKI)*, 122 (4): 429–46.

Tschacher, Torsten (2001), *Islam in Tamil Nadu: Varia*, Halle (Saale): Institut für Indologie und Südasienwissenschaften der Martin-Luther-Universität Halle-Wittenberg.

Valentijn, François (1724), *Oud en Nieuw Oost-Indiën*, Dordrecht: Van Braam and Amsterdam: onder de Linden [2003 facsimile publication, Franeker: Van Wijnen]

Vlekke, Bernard H. M. (1943), *Nusantara: History of the East Indian Archipelago*, Cambridge, MA: Harvard University Press.

Voll, John O. (1994), *Islam: Continuity and Change in the Modern World*, 2nd edn, Syracuse: Syracuse University Press.

Wahyudi, Yudian (2006), *Ushul Fiqh versus Hermeneutika: Membaca Islam dari Kanada dan Amerika*, Yogyakarta: Nawesea Press.

—(2007), *Hasbi's Theory of Ijtihad in the Context of Indonesian Fiqh*, Yogyakara: Nawesea Press.

Woelders, M. O. (1975), *Het Sultanaat Palembang 1811–1825*, The Hague: Martinus Nijhoff.

Wolters, Oliver W. (1967), *Early Indonesian Commerce: A Study of the Origins of Srivijaya*, Ithaca: Cornell University Press.

—(1982), *History, Culture and Religion in Southeast Asian Perspectives*, Ithaca: Southeast Asia Program Publications at Cornell University.

Woodward, Mark (2011), *Java, Indonesia and Islam*, Dordrecht: Springer.

Young, Ken (1994), *Islamic Peasants and the State: The 1908 Anti-tax Rebellion in West Sumatra*, New Haven, CT: Yale Center for International and Area Studies.

Zaman, Muhammad Qasim (2016), 'Ahl al-ḥall wa-l-ᶜaqd', in Kate Fleet, Gudrun Krämer, Denis Matringe, John Nawas and Everett Rowson (eds), *Encyclopaedia of Islam, THREE*, Brill Online, <http://referenceworks.brillonline.com/entries/encyclopaedia-of-islam-3/ahl-al-hall-wa-l-aqd-COM_0027> (last accessed 10 April 2016).

Index

abangan, 86–7, 156
Abbasid Caliphate, 17, 26
Abd al-Hamid II, Sultan, 88, 90, 103
Abd al-Mutallib, Isma'il, 83, 99
Abduh, Muhammad, 96, 98, 99, 113
Abdul Kadir, Sultan, 27, 34
Abdulrahim, Imaduddin, 157, 158, 163
Abshar-Abdalla, Ulil, 168
accommodationism, 156
Aceh, 2, 11, 14, 26, 27
    and insurgence, 147, 148
    and learning, 41–3
    and Ottoman Empire, 27–8
    and PUSA, 122–3
Aceh War, 88–90
Adat, Raja, 14, 62
Adipati Natakusuma, Raden, 49–50
al-Afghani, Jamal al-Din, 88, 97, 98
Ageng, Sultan (Tirtayasa), 37, 46
agriculture, 13, 80–1, 85
Agung of Mataram, Sultan, 27, 36–7, 48–9, 50, 69–70, 74
Agus Salim, Haji, 107–8, 109, 120, 126, 127, 128
    and independence, 136
Ahmad, Abdullah, 99, 100, 101, 104
Ahmad Khatib, 95–7, 99, 100, 102–3, 108, 110, 113, 120
Ahmadiyyah Movement, 114, 117, 167
Akbar, Emperor, 27
Alam, Raja, 14, 62, 64
Alam Bagagar Syah, Sultan, 64, 79
Alauddin Ri'ayat Shah, 21, 27
alcohol, 49, 60
Alexander the Great, 18, 47
Ali Mubarak Pasha, 97–8
Ali Ri'ayat III, 21
Alwi, Sayyid, 50
Amangkurat I, 37
Amangkurat II, 37
Amin, Maarif, 168
Ampel, Sunan, 30, 34, 35, 36, 37, 69, 122
Annales School, 7, 8, 10

Anom of Kudus, Ketib, 47
al-Ansari, Shaykh Abdullah, 71
Anshari, Endang Saefudin, 157, 159
Anshary, Isa, 140, 147
Ansor, 154, 155
Arab Association for Reform and Guidance, 115
Arabia, 3, 15
Arabic language, 39, 40
Arabs, 11, 115
architecture, 32
al-Arifin, Ahmad Abd, 13, 30, 31
Arifin, Zainul, 133
Arnold, T. W., 15
Ash Shiddieqy, Muhammad Hasbi, 105, 151–2, 153
ashrams, 52–3
Asyᶜari, Kyai Hasyim, 119, 120, 133, 136, 137
Atatürk, Mustafa Kemal, 119, 125, 130
Austronesians, 8
al-Azhar University, 42, 53, 94, 98–9, 150, 160

Baᶜasyir, Abu Bakar, 158
Babad Diponegoro, 69
Babad Tanah Jawi, 18
Badr al-Din, Sultan Mahmud, 47
banditry, 60
Bandung, 116–18, 126, 127, 141, 146
al-Banjari, Muhammad Arshad, 46, 47, 51, 52, 53, 81, 101
al-Banna, Hasan, 118
Banten, 31, 25, 26, 32–4, 45–6, 53, 83, 95–6
Barisan Sabilillah, 136
Barus, 21, 22–3, 44, 79, 89
Batavia *see* Jakarta
al-Batini, Nawawi, 95, 96, 97
bendaharas (dignitaries), 14
Bengal, 15, 18, 58
benzoin, 13, 14
Beureu'eh, Teungku Daud, 147, 148
Bin Aqil bin Yahya, Sayyid Muhammad, 102
Bodi Caniago, 57, 62

Bonang, Sunan, 30, 34, 35, 68
Borneo, 25, 31, 35, 45–7, 82, 88, 146–7
Britain *see* Great Britain
Brunei, 1
Buchari, Achmad, 147–8
Buddhism, 8–9, 12
al-Bugisi, Abd al-Wahhab, 52
al-Bunduqari, Baybars, 19
al-Burhanpuri, Muhammad Fadl Allah, 41,
    44, 47, 50, 53, 59, 72
Burhanuddin, 45, 59
Burma, 7, 8

Cairo, 94–5, 97–9, 104, 150
Caliphate Question, 119–20, 125
Cambodia, 7, 8, 15
camphor, 13, 14, 21
Capita Selecta (Natsir), 105
Carita Sultan Iskandar, 47, 51
Carita Yusuf, 47, 51
cassia, 58, 60
Celebes *see* Sulawesi
Chalil, Munawar, 113
Champa, 15, 29
Chasbullah, Wahab, 120–1, 130, 139, 142,
    148, 155
China, 9, 10, 11, 15, 16, 27
Christianity, 3, 87, 110–11, 156, 160
Cik di Tiro, Teungku, 90
Cilegon massacre, 83
Cirebon, 31, 32–3, 34, 35, 36
cock fighting, 49, 60
coffee, 58, 60, 62, 73, 76
Cokroaminoto, H. O. S., 104, 107, 109, 115,
    126, 127–8
colonialism, 1, 2, 3, 47–8, 93
    and Java, 64, 66–8
    and Minangkabau, 13, 76
    see also imperialism
Committee of 62, 133
communications, 92
communism, 1, 107, 137, 142, 154
Concert of Europe, 65
Crawfurd, John, 66, 67
criminal code, 145–6
Crusades, the, 19
Cucuf, 35
Cultivation System, 79–80, 85, 93

Daendels, Herman, 55, 65, 66, 67
Dahlan, Ahmad bin Zaini, 81, 95, 96
Dahlan, K. H. Ahmad, 109–10, 111, 112,
    121, 124
Dalem, Sunan, 35

Dan Fodio, Usman, 45
Dar al-Islam, 1, 9, 23, 46
Darsono, Raden, 107
DDII (Indonesian Islamic Propagation
    Council), 157, 158, 162, 163, 164,
    165
De Kock, Gen. Hendrik, 76
Dekker, Eduard Douwes, 93
Demak, 13, 30–3, 34, 35, 36, 129
Desawarnana (*Nagarakrtagama*) (poem), 12
DI (Darul Islam), 126, 137, 143–8
Diponegoro, Prince, 63, 64, 65–6, 67–72,
    73–6
Djajadiningrat, Aboe Bakar, 96, 133
Djajadiningrat, Hoesein, 133
Djambek, Djamil, 136
dress codes, 61, 76
Dutch East India Company, 28, 34, 37, 46,
    50, 57–8

East India Company *see* Dutch East India
    Company; English East India Company
Egypt, 15, 42, 43, 55, 125; *see also* Cairo
'Eight Tigers', 61–2
English East India Company, 58
Ethical Policy, 93, 105

Fadjar Asia (newspaper), 126, 127
Fansuri, Hamzah, 20–3, 37–8, 39–40, 41–2,
    44
Al-Fatwa (newspaper), 118
fatwas, 112, 136–7, 139, 167–8
Faysal of Saudi Arabia, King, 157
financial crisis, 164
FPI (Islamic Defenders Front), 167
France, 55
Fu'ad of Egypt, King, 125

gambir, 13, 14, 58
gambling, 49, 60
al-Ghazali, Abu Hamid, 26, 40, 46, 53, 105,
    122, 128
Giri, Sunan, 35, 36, 74, 122
gold, 14, 57, 58
Golkar, 154, 155, 163, 164, 165, 167
GPII (Movement of Young Indonesian
    Muslims), 136, 147–8
Great Britain, 55, 58, 66, 67
Gresik, 12, 29, 30, 31, 32, 34–7, 69
guerrilla forces, 146
Guided Democracy, 131, 132, 140–1, 142,
    148
Gujurat, 12, 15, 28, 42, 45
Gunung Jati, Sunan, 30, 32–3, 34

guru ordinance, 83
Gymnastiar, Abdullah, 162

Habibie, B. J., 163, 165
Hadhramaut, 3, 20, 42, 50, 90
Hadhrami, 3, 20, 37, 42, 84, 87, 90, 94, 96,
    102, 106, 115, 149
al-Hadhrami, Isma‘il, 19
al-Hadi, Ahmad, 102
Hadikusomo, Jarnawi, 113, 154
Hadikusomo, Ki Bagus, 134, 136
Hadiths, 113, 152
hajj pilgrimage, 27, 44, 84–5
Hajji Mataram, Kyai, 50
Hamengkubuwono I, Sultan, 50, 75
Hamengkubuwono II, Sultan, 66, 67
Hamengkubuwono III, Sultan, 69, 70
Hamengkubuwono IV, Sultan, 67, 72
Hamka, 105, 111, 114, 124, 139, 143, 158
Harahap, Burhanuddin, 141, 143
Hasanuddin, 33
Hasjmy, Dr Ali, 148
Hassan, Ahmad, 116, 117, 118–19, 127, 129,
    130, 146
Hasyim, Wahid, 133, 134, 136, 139, 150, 162
Hatta, Mohammad, 124, 125, 127, 129, 135,
    138, 154
  and Masyumi, 141, 142, 143
  and Natsir, 146, 150
Haz, Hamzah, 165, 168
Hazairin, 151, 152–3
Hijaz Committee, 120
Hikayat Jalal al-Din, 58
Hikayat Raja-Raja Pasai, 12, 18
Himpunan Putusan Tarjih, 114
Hinduism, 9, 12, 83
Hizbullah, 133, 136
HMI (Association of Muslim Students), 159,
    165
Husayn of Mecca, Sharif, 119–20, 125

IAIN (State Institutes for Islamic Studies),
    150–1, 153, 160
Ibadat, Raja, 14, 62
Ibn Abd al-Wahhab, Muhammad, 51, 55, 61
Ibn al-‘Arabi, Muhyi al-Din 19, 20, 27, 40,
    41, 42–3, 46–7
Ibn Battuta, 11, 12, 15
Ibn Rushd, 40
Ibn Saud, Abd al-Aziz, 120, 125
Ibnu Hadjar, Kyai, 147
ICMI (All-Indonesian Association of Muslim
    Intellectuals), 163, 164
Al-Imam (newspaper), 102–3, 113

Imam Bondjol *see* Syarif, Peto
imperialism, 56, 65, 79–80
India, 8, 9, 15
Indian Ocean, 6, 8, 9, 10, 11, 29
indigenous people, 2, 12, 14–15, 26, 57, 93
Indonesia, 1–2, 7–8, 170–1
  and 'greening', 162–3
  and independence, 94, 133–8
  and Reformation, 165–7
  see also Aceh; Java; Sumatra
Indonesian army (TNI), 133, 145, 148,
    153–4
Ingalaga, Senapati, 36
insan kamil ('perfect man'), 26–7, 41
Internet, 164
Irama, Rhoma, 162
iron, 14
Al-Irshad, 115
Iskandar II, 28
Iskandar Muda, 21, 27, 28, 41–2, 123
Islam, 2, 3, 18, 170–1
  and Aceh, 89
  and Arabia, 15–16
  and Diponegoro, 69–72, 73–5
  and education, 52–4, 80–1, 99–100
  and 'greening', 162–3
  and independence, 133–4
  and Java, 29–31, 85–7
  and Kartosuwiryo, 144–5
  and law, 25–6, 27, 45, 151–3
  and literature, 37–40
  and mass organisations, 94, 105–23
  and Mataram, 36–7
  and Minangkabau, 14, 59, 60–2, 76–7, 78
  and modernism, 97–8, 159–61
  and Natsir, 156–7
  and networking, 43–4
  and politics, 88, 124–30, 167
  and Southeast Asia, 9–13
  and worship, 123–4
  see also Ministry of Religion; Pan-Islamism;
    Sufism; Wahhabism
Al-Islam (newspaper), 104
Al-Islam Conferences, 125, 128
Islamic Defence Committees, 117
Islamic Education Association, 117
Al-Ittihad (newspaper), 104

Ja‘far al-Sadiq, 30, 31–2
Jahangir, Emperor, 27
Jakarta, 33, 34, 135, 142–3, 150–1, 160, 162,
    166
Jakarta Charter, 134–5, 142, 149, 150, 151,
    167

Jalal al-Din Ahmad, 58, 60, 61, 82
Jamaat-e-Islami, 118
Jambi/Melayu, 10
Jamʿiyat al-Khayr, 115, 116
Jangkung, Seh, 31
Japan, 27, 130, 131, 132–3
Japara, 32, 36
Java, 9, 10, 81
    and Diponegoro, 69–71
    and Islam, 11–12, 85–7
    and literature, 38–9, 40, 48–9
    and religious practice, 49–51
    and state-building, 28–30
    and Sufism, 82–3
    see also Banten
Java War, 64–7, 68, 75–6
al-Jawi, Masʿud, 19, 20, 22, 37
Jeddah, 84
Jerusalem, 32
JI (Jemaah Islamiyah), 158, 166
jihad, 47, 144, 145
JIL (Liberal Islam Network), 168
al-Jilani, Abd al-Qadir, 19
al-Jili, Abd al-Karim ibn Ibrahim, 27, 40,
    41
JIMM (Network of Young Muhammadiyah
    Intellectuals), 168
Joedah, Molana, 33–4
Joseph, 47
jungle produce, 13, 14
al-Junusi, Zainuddin Labai, 100, 101

Kajoran, Raden, 37
Kali Nyamat, Ratu, 32
Kali Raja, 79
Kalijaga, Sunan, 30, 31, 33, 36, 43, 69, 70,
    122
Kamil, Mustafa, 115
KAMMI (United Front of Indonesian Muslim
    University Students), 165
Kartawidjaja, 82–3, 87
Kartosuwiryo, Sekarmaji Marjan, 126, 127,
    128, 143–6, 147–8
KGCC (Union of South Sulawesi Guerrillas),
    146
kingship, 26–7
KISDI (Indonesian Committee for Solidarity
    with the Muslim World), 164–5
kitab kuning, 104, 155
Kitab Usulbiyah, 47
KNIP (Central Indonesian National
    Committee), 135, 144
Komando Jihad, 158
Kota Piliang, 57, 62

Kudus, Sunan, 30, 31–2
al-Kurani, Ibrahim, 44, 45, 47

Lampung, 33
language, 2, 10, 39
League of Indonesian Muslims, 139
Lemah Abang, Seh, 31
Al-Lisan (newspaper), 118
literature, 37–40, 47–8, 104–5
Logan, James, 1
Lombok, 83
Lubis, Col Zulkifli, 142

Maarif, Ahmad Syafii, 168
McGill University, 159–60, 161
Madina Charter, 167
Madiun Affair, 137, 139
Madjid, Nurcholish, 159, 162
madrasas (schools), 99–100
al-Mahdi, Muhammad Ahmad, 45
Mahdi Uprising, 83
Majapahit dynasty, 10, 13, 28, 30–1
Majlis Tarjih, 112, 113, 114
Malabar Coast, 15
Malacca, 10, 11, 13, 14
Malay states, 1, 7, 12, 25, 26–8
    and Islam, 16, 18
    and law, 26
    and literature, 39–40
Al-Manar (newspaper), 102, 104
'mandalas', 8, 9
Mangkubumi, Prince, 50, 60, 69
Mangkunegoro I, Prince, 50, 69, 75, 78
Mangkunegoro IV, Prince, 85–6
Mangkusasmito, Prawoto, 141, 142, 143
Manipol, 142
Mansur, Mas, 105, 121, 126–7, 133
Mansur Shah, Sultan, 89
Mantri Muhamad Ngarip, Raden, 71
al-Manufi, Muhammad, 43
Maolana, Seh, 31
al-Maqassari, Yusuf, 45–6
Maret, Sebelas, 158
Mas Rahmat, 82
Mas Surojo, Raden, 66, 67
Mas Suryadi, Raden, 50
Masyumi (Consultative Council of Indonesian
    Muslims), 131, 133, 134, 135–40, 141–3,
    165
    and DI, 147–8
    and New Order Regime, 154
Mataram dynasty, 32, 34, 35–7
matrilineal kinship, 13–14
Maududi, Syed Abul A'la, 118, 158

Max Havelaar (Dekker), 93
Mecca, 18, 27, 44, 81
  and hajj, 84–5
  and occupation, 55, 56
  and Reformism, 94–5
  and Saudi Arabia, 119–20
Medina, 44, 55, 56
Megawati Sukarnoputri, 164, 165, 166
MIAI (Supreme Council of Indonesian
    Muslims), 128, 130, 133
Minangkabau, 13–14, 56–64, 76–9, 81–2
al-Minankabawi, Isma'il, 99
Ministry of Religion, 149–51
Mintaredja, Muhammad Syafa'at, 154
'mirrors of princes' genre, 26, 43
Miskin, Haji, 61, 63, 64
missionaries, 3, 18
Moestapa, Hasan, 94
Mojo, Kyai, 71–2, 74–5
monarchy, 26–7
Mongols, 17, 19
mosques, 30, 31, 32
Mughals, 27
Muhammad Iskandar Shah, 12
Muhammadiyah, 109–15, 123–4
muhaqqiqun, 43, 45, 47
al-Muhyi, Shaykh Abd, 45
MUI (Indonesian Ulama Council), 167–8
Mukti Ali, Abdul, 159–60, 161
al-Mulk, Nizam, 26
Al-Munir (newspaper), 103–4, 113
Murmo Wijoyo, Kyai, 68
Muslim Brotherhood, 118, 150
Muslim World League (MWL), 157
Muslims *see* Islam
Mutamkin, Kyai Haji Ahmad, 47
Muzakir, Abdul Kahar, 133, 150
Muzakkar, Kahar, 146, 148
mystic synthesis, 48, 64, 69, 76, 85, 86, 170
mysticism, 82–3, 85–6

Napoleon Bonaparte, 55
Naqshbandiyya, 41, 46, 59–60, 62, 81–2, 83,
    88, 96, 99–101
Naro, Djaelani (John), 154
NASAKOM, 142
Naskah Tuanku Imam Bondjol, 58, 77
Nasser, Gamal Abdel, 141, 143
Nasution, Harun, 159, 160–1
nationalism, 78, 92, 129–30, 133–4
Natsir, Mohammad, 105, 115–16, 117, 150
  and DI, 146, 147
  and independence, 136, 138
  and Islam, 156–7, 158, 159

and politics, 126, 127, 129–30
  and Sukarno, 141, 143
Nehru, Jawaharlal, 141
Neo-Sufism, 42, 44–5
Netherlands Indies Civil Administration
    (NICA), 135
Netherlands, the, 1, 3, 55–6, 63–4, 93
  and Aceh, 88–90
  and Java, 64, 65, 66, 67–8
  and the law, 112
  and Minangkabau, 76–9
  and segregation, 87–8
  and Sufism, 83
  see also Dutch East India Company
New Order Regime (*Orde Baru*), 132, 153–5,
    156, 160
newspapers, 102–4
NII (Islamic State of Indonesia), 137, 145
NU (Nahdlatul Ulama), 119–22, 123–4,
    138–40, 155, 161–2
Nusantara, 1, 7, 168

opium, 49, 60, 87
Ormas (mass organisations), 105–23
Ottoman Empire, 44, 55, 88, 89–90

Padri Wars, 56, 58, 61–3, 64, 77–9
Pajajaran, 33–4
PAKAM (Observation of People's Belief
    Streams), 156
Pakualam I, 67, 75
Pakubuwono II, 49–50
Pakubuwono IV, 51
Pakubuwono, Ratu, 47, 49, 50, 51
Palembang, 8, 9, 10, 46, 47
al-Palimbani, Abd al-Samad, 46–8, 51, 52, 53,
    81, 101, 116
Pamuncak, 79
PAN (National Mandate Party), 165
Pan-Islamism, 88, 94, 103, 109, 127
Pancasila Doctrine, 134–5, 161, 168
Pangaran Tranggana, 13
Pangeran Ratu, 33
Parameswara, 12
Pasisir, 11, 13, 18, 29, 31, 36, 65–6, 86
Patah, Raden, 30
pawang (spirit doctor), 12, 57
PBB (Crescent Star Party), 165, 167
PDI (Indonesian Democratic Party), 164
PDRI (Emergency Government of Indonesia),
    138
Pembela Islam (newspaper), 117–18
Penang, 58
pengajian (schools), 53–4

pepper, 14, 28, 57
Persia, 9, 11, 26, 39
Persis, 115–19, 129
pesantren (schools), 52–3, 72, 80, 160
Philippines, the, 1, 7
PII (Islamic Party of Indonesia), 128
Pijnappel, 15
Pires, Tomé, 11, 15, 35
PKB (National Awakening Party), 165
PKI (Indonesian Communist Party), 106, 107, 137
PKS (Justice and Prosperity Party), 165, 167
PMI (Parmusi), 154
PNI (Indonesian National Party), 126, 127, 128, 138, 139–40
Polo, Marco, 11, 15
pondok (school), 53, 53, 59, 80, 81
Portugal, 13, 16, 28
PPP (United Development Party), 154, 155, 165
PPPKI (Agreement of the Indonesia's People's Political Associations), 126–7, 128
Prapañca, 12
Prapen, Sunan, 35
Prawata, Susuhunan, 31
Prawiranegara, Sjafruddin, 136, 138, 141, 143
print media, 101–5, 117–18
prostitution, 60
PRRI (Revolutionary Government of the Republic of Indonesia), 141, 142, 143
PSI (Partai Sarekat Islam), 125–6
PSII (Partai Sarekat Islam Indonesia), 126–7, 128–9, 144
PUSA, 122–3
putihan, 86–7, 92

Qadiriyya, 20, 44, 46, 59, 83, 96
Al-Qaeda, 166
al-Qarani, Uways, 19
Qur'an, the, 53, 112, 113, 152
al-Qushashi, Ahmad, 44, 45
Qutb, Sayyid, 150, 158

Raffles, Thomas Stamford, 66, 67
Rahardjo, Dawam, 163
Rahmanudin, Kyai, 74
Rahmat, Raden, 29–30
Rahmatullah, 30
Rais, Amien, 164, 165
Raja di Buo, 79
Raja Pandita, 29
rajas (rulers), 12, 18, 26

al-Raniri, Nur al-Din, 42, 43, 44, 45, 47, 101, 123
Rasjidi, Mohammad, 149–50, 159, 161
Rasul, Haji, 99–100, 101, 124
religion, 2, 12, 156, 166, 167, 168; *see also* Buddhism; Christianity; Hinduism; Islam
rice, 7–8, 13, 18, 28
Rida, Rashid, 97, 99, 102, 104
Ridhwan, Afandi, 147–8
Roem, Mohammad, 133, 138, 143
Ronggo Prawirodirjo III, Raden, 65–6
royalty, 12, 14
rural life, 52, 59

Sahid, Raden *see* Kalijaga, Sunan
Sailendra dynasty, 9
Salafism, 56, 98
al-Salih, Sultan al-Malik, 12, 19
Samanhudi, Haji, 106, 107
al-Samman, Muhammad ibn Abd al-Karim, 46
Sammaniyya, 46, 53, 61
santri, 51, 71–2, 75, 86, 92
al-Sanusi, Muhammad ibn Yusuf, 43, 53
Sarekat Dagang Islamiah (SDI), 106–7
Al Saud dynasty, 120
Saudi Arabia, 76–7, 101, 157
Sayf al-Rijal, 42
seafaring, 7, 8
Sejarah Banten, 18, 33, 34
Sejarah Melayu, 12, 18
Semaun, 107
Sentot, 78–9
Serat Cabolek, 47
Serat Centhini, 85
Shah Jahan, 27
Shaltut, Shaykh Mahmud, 151–2, 153
Shamil, Imam, 45
Shams al-Din al-Sumatrani (Shamsuddin), 22, 41–2, 44, 47
al-Shaᶜrani, 47
al-Sharji, Shihab al-Din Ahmad, 19
Shattariyya, 44–5, 48, 51, 53, 59, 60, 61–2, 82
Shiᶜa community, 167
SI (Sarekat Islam), 104, 106–8, 109, 125, 165
Siddiq, Achmad, 162
Singapore, 64, 82, 90, 99, 102, 116, 129
Singasari dynasty, 10
al-Singkili, Abd al-Raᶜuf, 43, 44, 45, 53, 59
Siraj, Said Aqil, 168
Sjadzali, Munawir, 161
Sjahrir, Sutan, 124, 127, 129, 149

Snouck Hurgronje, Christiaan, 3, 4, 15, 47, 93–4
  and Aceh, 88, 90
  and Agus Salim, 108
  and Mecca, 85
socialism, 107
Soetomo, Dr, 124, 127, 129
South Africa, 46
South China Sea, 10, 11, 29
Southeast Asia 24
  and geography, 7, 9
  and immigration, 87–8
  and intellectual tradition, 37–8
  and Islam, 9–13, 15–18, 23, 170–1
Spice Islands, 25
Srivijaya, 8–10
state-building, 25–6
STI (Higher Islam School), 150
student riots, 165
Subianto, Lt Gen. Prabowo, 165, 166
Suez Canal, 84, 87, 92
Sufism, 16–19, 20–1, 22–3, 44, 81–3
  and Java, 51
  and Minangkabau, 59
  and Sammaniyya, 46
  and 'Unity of Being', 41, 42–3
  see also Neo-Sufism
Suharto, Gen., 132, 153, 154, 156, 164
  and Islam, 162–3
  and resignation, 165
Sukarno, 117, 121, 124, 125, 126, 127–8
  and Aceh, 147
  and coup, 132, 154
  and economics, 160
  and Guided Democracy, 140–1, 142–3, 148
  and nationalism, 129, 130
  and Pancasila, 134, 135
  and presidency, 131, 138, 139
Sulawesi, 25, 45, 46, 146
Sulayman the Magnificent, 27
Suluk Garwa Kancana, 49
Sumatra, 10, 46, 81
  and Islam, 11–12, 13, 21, 22
  and kaum muda, 99–101
  see also Malay states; Minangkabau
Sunda Straits, 10
Sungkar, Abdullah, 158
Sunni Islam, 53
Surabaya, 29, 30, 31, 32, 34–5
Surakarta, 50, 51, 65–7, 71–2, 74, 78, 86, 100, 106, 146, 151, 158
surau (school), 59, 60

Surkati, Ahmad Muhammad, 115, 121, 149
al-Suyuti, 47
Syarif, Peto, 58, 63, 64, 77–8

Tahir Jalaluddin, 96, 99, 102
al-Tahtawi, Rifa'a Badawi Raf'i, 97
Taj al-Din, Sultan Ahmad, 47
Tanaka, Kakuei, 158
Tanjung, Akbar, 165
Taptojani, Kyai, 71
Al-Taqwa (newspaper), 118
Tarjuman al-mustafid (al-Singkili), 45, 53
Tasauf Moderen (Hamka), 105
Tax Revolt (1908), 78, 81
taxation, 67, 68, 76
technology, 84, 92
Tegalrejo, 70–1
Tembayat, 36
terrorism, 166
Teuku Umar, 63
Thailand, 1, 7, 8, 12–13
al-Thani, Iskandar, 27
TII (Indonesian Islamic Army), 144, 145
Tirto adhi Suryo, Raden Mas, 106–7
TNI see Indonesian Army
tobacco, 60, 76
tombstones, 11, 12, 15, 35
trade, 7–8, 9, 16, 20
  and Minangkabau, 57, 60
  see also Dutch East India Company
Trunajaya, 37
Tuanku Lintau, 62, 64, 77
Tuanku Mensiangan, 61
Tuanku Nan Rinceh, 61, 63, 64, 77, 95
Tuanku Nan Salih, 61–2, 64
Tuanku Nan Tua, 60, 61, 63, 64
Tuban, 32, 34
al-Tuhfa al-mursala ila ruh al-nabi (al-Burhanpuri), 41, 53
Turkey, 125, 130, 134, 149

UII (Universitas Islam Indonesia), 150
Umar, Teuku, 90
United States of America, 58, 142, 166
'Unity in Diversity', 2
'Unity of Being', 27, 40, 41–2
USDEK, 142
Uthman, Sayyid, 94, 96, 101

Van den Bosch, Johannes, 76, 78
Van der Cappellen, Godert, 68, 72–3
Vietnam, 7, 15
violence, 61, 62, 165, 166

VOC *see* Dutch East India Company

Wahhabism, 51, 55, 56, 101
Wahid, Abdurrahman, 160, 162, 163, 165, 166
Wali Songo ('Nine Saints'), 20, 22, 29–32, 34, 38, 43, 68–9, 74, 118, 122
West New Guinea, 141
Westphalia, Treaty of (1648), 2
Wibisono, Jusuf, 142
Widoyo, Djoko, 166
Willem I of the Netherlands, King, 55–6, 63, 68, 73
Wiryosanjoyo, Sukiman, 136, 146
women, 111

World Muslim Congress, 157
writing culture, 20, 22

al-Yafiᶜi, ᶜAbdallah ibn Asᶜad, 19–20
Yemen, 19
Yogyakarta, 50–1, 64, 69–74, 78, 110, 135, 138, 150
   and Java War, 65, 66, 67, 68
youth activism, 155–6, 157–8
Yudhoyono, Susilo Bambang, 166
Yusuf of Makassar, Shaykh, 37
Yusup (Yusuf), 33–4

al-Zahir, Sultan al-Malik, 11
al-Zawawi, Abdallah, 104, 120